SELF EXPRESSIONS

SELF EXPRESSIONS

MIND, MORALS, AND
THE MEANING OF LIFE

Owen Flanagan

New York   Oxford
OXFORD UNIVERSITY PRESS
1996

Oxford University Press

Oxford   New York
Athens   Auckland   Bangkok   Bombay
Calcutta   Cape Town   Dar es Salaam   Delhi
Florence   Hong Kong   Istanbul   Karachi
Kuala Lumpur   Madras   Madrid   Melbourne
Mexico City   Nairobi   Paris   Singapore
Taipei   Tokyo   Toronto

and associated companies in
Berlin   Ibadan

Copyright © 1996 by Oxford University Press, Inc.

Published by Oxford University Press, Inc.
198 Madison Avenue, New York, New York 10016

Oxford is a registered trademark of Oxford University Press

Library of Congress Cataloging-in-Publication Data
Flanagan, Owen J.
Self expressions : mind, morals, and the meaning of life / Owen Flanagan
p. cm.
Includes bibliographical references and index.
ISBN 0-19-509696-7
1. Self.   2. Identity (Psychology)   3. Life.   4. Philosophy of
mind.   5. Psychology and philosophy.   I. Title.
BF697.F575   1996
126—dc20   95-5919

1 3 5 7 9 8 6 4 2

Printed in the United States of America
on acid-free paper

To Ruth Anna Putnam, David H. Sanford, and Kenneth P. Winkler

Prologue

It has gradually dawned on me that the unity of my work, insofar as it has unity, lies in an underlying concern with identity, self, and self-expression. There is a story, of interest only to myself and my loved ones, about why I am so concerned with the problems of the self. But the short version involves my disenchantment with the transcendental—precipitated when I was a teenager, when puberty met conventional Christian morality and theology.

My rejection of the idea of an immaterial soul required making sense of the mind, of my embodied self, really, in naturalistic terms. The idea that "if there is no God, then everything is allowed" worried me at the very same time that the prospect of everything being allowed elated me. But then there was the specter of nihilism. If everything is allowed, and if I am just an animal, and if my existence is just some very temporary cosmic accident, then what makes life worth living? Why does anything matter?

There at once—in a typical adolescent happenstance—I had my three problems: mind, morals, and the meaning of life.

The essays gathered here don't add up to a theory of the self, nor do they do anything like solve the problems of mind, morals, and meaning. Insofar as there is something like a theory presented here, some of its main tenets are these:

The word "self" has many meanings—personality, character, an individual's central character traits, the way(s) one carries oneself in the world, the way one represents oneself to oneself and to others, the dynamic integrated system of thoughts, emotions, lived events, and so on, that make up who one is from the God's eye point of view. All these senses are useful.

The asymmetry between the first-personal question "Who am I?" and the third-personal question "Who is he?" matters greatly to the assessment of the worth of a life.

Whether a life is good, decent, happy, perceptive, self-deceived, and so on, depends in essential ways on the perspective.

Not all perspectives are equal. We need to talk, including to ourselves *sub voce*, about matters of the quality and direction and meaning of life.

We are animals. But we are self-creating in certain respects. How self-creation, self-control, and authorship are possible for animals like *Homo sapiens* can be explained. It is a nonmystery that "mysterians" like to spread magic dust over.

Our selves are complex, and we can change significantly over time but remain the same person.

What matters to identity preservation is that we are involved in making changes in our selves.

Self-control is at least as important as integration. That is, being in charge of your self matters as much, possibly more, than does being integrated or unified or consistent.

Self-knowledge is a good. But it is not necessary, to any high degree, for a good and meaningful life.

Self-knowledge does confer, however, a certain protection. Self-knowledge is a prophylactic that confers the "what-if" advantage, the "counterfactual advantage." It is wiser to wear it than not to.

Life's meaning comes, if it does come, from having chances to express and carry through on projects that matter, that have value and worth, first and third-personally.

Living meaningfully and living morally, as the latter is conventionally understood, can and do conflict.

Since morality is not sovereign, it is not always wrong to let considerations of meaning trump considerations of morality. Doing this, however, is risky.

But so too is letting some considerations of meaning trump other considerations of meaning. It is hard to find one's way. Life is tough. Play hard.

It may be that certain political ideals—equality and justice, for example—have a sovereignty that moral ideals, friendliness, temperance, and modesty, do not. If so, a good and meaningful life will involve making certain political ideals overriding.

The idea that personal, moral, or political progress track time, that is, that these things improve with time is a common, false, and dangerous idea.

Knowing—knowledge of the external world—grows with time at the group level, that is, in the libraries. But goodness, integrity, self-improvement, mental health, and their ilk, defy time—both for individuals and groups.

Self-respect, especially when it is deserved, is considerably more important than self-confidence, with which it is confused, and which is overrated.

A meaningful life often requires risk taking (this is less true of meaningless lives—consult meaning-in-life underachievers). Meaning sometimes requires proceeding unconfidently.

Most of the essays collected here were written after my last two books, *Varieties of Moral Personality* (1991) and *Consciousness Reconsidered* (1992), and they develop themes from those books. The topics range from whether a scientific theory of persons and their minds is possible to whether dreams are noise or forms of self-expression—or possibly both at once—to the question of the relation between normal complex persons (what I call "multiplex" persons) and patients with multiple personality disorder (MPD), and questions of the relation of identity and memory: Can who I am depend upon false but confident remembering? The essays take up the issue of whether persons need to be—or, what is different, ought to be—reflective, as well as the issue of the connections between virtue and knowledge and between meaning and morals. On these last two points, my position is heretical, and I'm convinced it is right. Knowledge does not track goodness in any interesting way, nor does meaning track being moral (and vice versa in both cases).

I think that doing moral philosophy is important. But it is hard for moral philosophers to avoid being moralistic, self-righteous, and overconfident. I have some things to say about how to do naturalistic ethics—how to employ empirical findings in doing normative ethics—about how to think about living in a way that pays attention to our natures as animals, but as socially constructed ones. Like everyone else, I'm an amateur about living and about thinking about it.

What unifies these essays, if I am right that they have unity, is that they concern problems of the self and how to mesh commitment to the scientific image of humans with the view of ourselves as meaning-makers. How could what physics, chemistry, and neuroscience say there is—how could what they say makes up the world—particles and that sort of stuff—make up a *truly* human life? How could my emergence from matter add up to anything of *real* significance? How am I to understand being an animal and caring about value and worth, especially value and worth that seems different in kind from what matters to nature's other children?

I have taught three graduate courses over the last three terms (1993–1994), one on moral relativism, one on problems of self and identity, and one on philosophical psychology. Duke University is a very interdisciplinary place and I am grateful to the faculty and students from anthropology, art, computer science, divinity, English, modern languages, literature, neurobiology, philosophy, psychology, and religion for attending my seminars and colloquia, and for teaching me many things. Students and friends from the University of North Carolina—Chapel Hill also provided inspiration.

I have had opportunities to present this work and to receive immensely helpful responses from various audiences of philosophers, psychologists, neuroscientists, and anthropologists. I thank audiences at the Universities of Arizona, and Alabama–Birmingham; Carnegie-Mellon, Clemson, Cornell, Delaware, Duke, and East Carolina Universities; Guilford College and St. John Fisher College; Stanford and Syracuse Universities; the University of Missouri–St. Louis; Washington and Wake Forest Universities and LaTrobe and Monash Universities in Melbourne, Australia. I am grateful as well for invitations to speak at meetings of the Society for Neuroscience in Anaheim, California; the Society for Philosophy and Psychology in Vancouver, British Columbia, and Memphis, Tennessee; the American Philosophical Association in New York, Chicago, and Los Angeles; at the Triangle Ethics Group, at the Wilson Center of the Smithsonian in Washington, D.C., and the International Institute for Advanced Study in Kyoto, Japan.

Friends, family, colleagues, and students: They help one see one's way and provide various kinds of inspiration. I thank them all.

This book is dedicated to three friends who have taught me more than I can express about myself, about friendship, and about philosophy. Coming up against the limits of language is what happens when I try to think or say what these three have meant to me and my life: Ruth Anna Putnam, David Sanford, and Ken Winkler.

Acknowledgments

Thomas Polger, my student, friend, and research assistant, helped enormously in the final preparation of this book, as did Xinia Arrington and Fran Finney. I also thank Robert Miller and Grace Suh from Oxford University Press for their unfailing interest and help, and I thank anonymous reviewers for extremely helpful advice. Maura High was a manuscript editor from Heaven. Chapters 1, 4, 12, and 13 appear for the first time. Several of the essays are revisions, sometimes—as in the cases of chapters 2, 3, and 6—very significant revisions of previously published work. In many cases the titles have been changed to indicate changes of content and/or focus. I am grateful to the original publishers for permission to use material from the following essays: "Prospects for a Unified Theory of Consciousness," in *Scientific Approaches to the Study of Consciousness*, ed. J. Cohen and J. Schooler (Hillsdale, N.J.: Erlbaum, 1995); "Deconstructing Dreams: The Spandrels of Sleep," *Journal of Philosophy* (1995): 5–27; "Other Minds, Obligation, and Honesty," *Cognitive and Social Factors in Early Development*, ed. S. Ceci, M. Leichtman, and M. Putnik (Hillsdale, N.J.: Erlbaum, 1992) "Ethics Naturalized: Ethics as Human Ecology," in *Mind and Morals*, ed. L. May, M. Friedman, and A. Clark (Cambridge: MIT press 1995); "Multiple Personality, Character Transformation, and Self-Reclamation," in *Philosophical Psychopathology*, ed. G. Graham and L. Stephens, (Cambridge: MIT press 1995); "Memory Playing False: Repression and the Critique of Psychoanalysis," *Times Literary Supplement* October 29, 1993; "Admirable Immorality and Admirable Imperfection," *Journal of Philosophy* (1986): 41–60; "Identity and Strong and Weak Evaluation," in *Identity, Character, and Morality*, ed. O. Flanagan and A. O. Rorty, (Cambridge: MIT Press, 1990); "Virtue and Ignorance," *Journal of Philosophy* (1990): 420–28.

Durham, North Carolina   O. F.
January 1995

Contents

SELF EXPRESSIONS

1

Introduction: What Makes Life Worth Living?

Identity and Self-Expression

The question "What makes life worth living?" assumes that life is or can be worth living. Perhaps this is an unwarranted assumption. The question "Is life worth living?" comes first. The question is not "Is life lived?" or even "Do people seek to live out their lives?" Nor is it "Do people care about going on—possibly for as long as possible—sometimes even longer than is sensible?" These are easy questions.

We live our lives in the sense that we spend time *not* dead. And by and large people try to go on, to survive. But this proves nothing about worth. Mosquitoes spend time not dead, and they too will do what it takes to live as long as they can. Is it worth anything to live out a mosquito's life? Objectively, the answer is probably yes. It contributes ecologically to the planet that mosquitoes live lives. Does it matter to the individual mosquito? Does it matter subjectively? This is not a question that should worry us since mosquitoes don't worry about it. They can't. But we have minds, and we can ask the question "Is life worth living?" and if it is, "What, or what sorts of things make it so?" And the answers matter to us.

For us, the objective fact that we live out our lives—and even the fact that we have passion to do so (perhaps the result of biological imperatives)—proves nothing. One can do worthless things. I do them all the time. One can even have passion for worthless things. Perhaps a life is one extended worthless thing.

Why entertain this depressing thought? The answer is that it forces reflection on the question "Is life worth living, and if it is, what makes it

3

so?" Why is reflection on this question worthwhile? I'm not sure how to answer. It may well be that a life can be worth living even for an unreflective agent, unreflective generally, or unreflective enough to be befuddled by this two-part question. Asking the question may even move a life that is worth living to fear and trembling, to sickness unto death, to the edge of despair; and not because the life is not worth living. It may be that the person to whom the question is addressed can't see her way to the answer that her life in fact reveals. She cannot articulate value or worth and wrongly thinks value and worth are not there.

On the other side, the question may move us to consider what matters, how it matters, and why it matters. Mattering might, if we are lucky, add up to value, to worth.

The question "Is life worth living and if it is, what makes it so?" is hard enough. It is connected to a more basic and equally bewildering question. "What does it mean to *live* a life?" Again, there is a trivial sense in which we know the answer: To live a life is to spend time *not* dead. Some people choose death quite deliberately while they are alive. Their suicide is partly constitutive of their life. Perhaps the question, intended as it is existentially, can be put this way: Do we *live* our lives? Do we in any sense make ourselves and control our characters and destinies, or are we just puppets, live puppets—whose lives are lived, but not lived or directed by us—the organisms who live these very lives by being, as it were, alive? The question is about living in some stronger sense than simply being alive, and it involves issues of self and agency.

Some philosophers distinguish between things that have some property—for example, value—intrinsically and things that have the property derivatively. Money is worthless until we make it worth something. Happiness is said to have worth in and of itself. Suppose this is true. Would it follow that a life with many happy times in it was worth living? Not necessarily. Properties of parts do not confer the property on the whole. My parts are small, I am large. Happy times, even many of them, might not constitute a worthwhile life. But I am skeptical in any case that a life's meaning could be intrinsic—could come from just being alive or from something that has value, no matter what. Life's meaning must derive from things other than just being alive. Happiness is probably one of the things that confers worth, but it is not enough. After all, one might perversely find happiness in evil things. Perhaps happiness is not necessary even. One might live a life largely devoid of happiness but still live a good and worthwhile life—even as seen from the subjective point of view.

Suppose, however, that happiness is normally a desired component of a life worth living, what else is needed? Having an identity and expressing it. This is the answer that strikes me as most promising: self and self-expression. The idea is romantic, Western, Nietzschean even. But it is also non-romantic, non-Western, Buddhist even. To make myself a "not-self," to work at creating in myself a mode to transcend caring about mundane things is a form of self-expression, as is suicide. But normally in the West and in the East, having a self and expressing it is not a matter of doing things alone, or doing them only your way, or of being Zarathustra-like. Many, probably most, worthwhile forms of self-expression, require others in crucial ways. Even the decision of the cloistered Christian monk or nun or the ascetic Buddhist *arahant* to remove himself or herself from certain dependencies on other people requires that there be social practices in place—certain economies of desire, for example—that are thought to be worth transcending. Sometimes stopping caring about money, fame, and sex are thought to be worthwhile because these things take time and energy away from more worthwhile human things: love, friendship, peace of mind, for example. Other times, the attempt to shift one's orientation from mundane desire is not motivated by the desire to connect with other, more worthwhile, human goods, but with the transcendental—God, or something of that sort.

Wherever one looks, or so I claim, humans seek, and sometimes find worth in possessing an identity and expressing it. This is why I think having a self and expressing it reign when it comes to answering the question of what makes life worth living. Of course, self and self-expression are not sufficient for living well, but they are necessary. If something—if anything, that is—is necessary for a life worth living, it is this: that I develop an identity and that I express it. The idea awaits refinement since, of course, not any identity or form of expressing it will do. But you get the drift.

It is important that I not be understood as promoting a particular conception of self or identity, especially not some controversial individualistic one. Philosophers from Aristotle to the present, as well as anthropologists, have taught us that in every culture, becoming a self capable of expressing anything of worth requires a community, as does self-expression. Furthermore, what an individual is like and what he or she seeks to express may be things of largely communal *or* largely personal value. This will be a matter of great contingency, as will the degree to which a particular individual develops powers of self-authorship and occupies a world in which she can use these powers in creative ways (luck matters—indeed, it matters far too much). What will *not* be contingent, I am claiming, is that there will be individual selves and that if they find meaning and worth, it will be through self-expression. This, I claim, is true of Nietzscheans, Libertarians, Buddhists, and Benedictines. It is as true of Mother Teresa as it is of Madonna.[1]

The Death of the Subject

I'll be alone when I die. Or better: Dying is something I will do alone. Or better: My passing from being alive to being dead is something that will happen to me alone. This is true even if loved ones are there for the event. When I die, I'll be nothing. But for the time being, I am something rather than nothing.[2]

One thing that would undermine the idea that *this* subject of experience will die, as well as the ideas about the importance of self and self-expression would be if there were no subjects, no agents. If there were no subjects there would be no selves, and if my self was nothing it could hardly die, and self-expression would be illusory. The very thought I just had, "that for the time being I am something rather than nothing," might be considered to be some sort of mistake. Indeed, there is talk in the air of the "death of the subject." Why think there are no subjects? There are three standard sorts of arguments that one sees in the postmodern literature.

First, there is a metaphysical argument that promotes the idea that I am merely a location at which and through which, like all other locations, certain things happen. The universe just is a complex causal network and what is "me" is just a location, one among an uncountable number of other locations—locations that *sub specie aeternitatis* just nudge each other from place to place.

Second, there is a sociological argument according to which I am just a bunch of roles melded together in the here and now, as differentiated and complex and situation-specific as the various social niches that I occupy require me to be. *Homo sapiens* learns how to be a "self," but a self is no more than a name like "the university," which names nothing in particular, but only a disparate collection that seems to possess, but invariably lacks, any more than nominal unity.

Third, there are developmental, life span sorts of arguments according to which "I" am a series of self-stages. There is no I, no ego, no self, that is *me* over time. "I"—now in raised-eyebrow quotes to indicate that grammar is causing trouble—have a name. It stays the same. But my body changes, my beliefs, my desires, my projects, and commitments, my interpersonal relations change radically over the course of life. Owen Flanagan is the name, but changing is my game. The illusion of identity or sameness is just that: an illusion. Its cause is that all these changes happen incrementally. But just as it does not follow from the fact that 2 is not far from 1, nor 23 from 22, nor 6,000,000 from 5,900,000, that 6,000,000 is not far from 1, so too it does not follow that Owen Flanagan at 45 is remotely close to Owen Flanagan at 1 or even at 20.

Strategically, and ever so briefly, here is how I recommend dealing with all three arguments. First, concede the last argument. There are subjects, they change, some more than others, across a variety of dimensions over the course of a life. The argument proves nothing about the death of the subject, only that subjects are not identical over time. But those philosophers are right who have taught us that self-sameness is not what matters. Continuity and connectedness matter, not strict identity. Second, there is something to the social-role argument. Before and after we gain powers of self-authorship we express ourselves in ways particular situations call upon us to be. But even supposing that I am nothing more than some package of socially responsive roles, I am still something rather than nothing. So the argument hardly establishes the death of the subject; it simply makes the subject a social construction all the way down. But houses are completely constructed, and they exist. Being constructed hardly makes something into nothing. Usually it is the other way round.

Third, regarding the metaphysical argument: It is based upon two tricks at once: one, it evokes the specter of determinism to undermine the idea that there are metaphysically free subjects; two, it paints a picture in which "I" am caused by things, but never cause anything. Even if there are no metaphysically autonomous agents, there still might be agents. A finch may not be metaphysically free, but it expresses its needs and satisfies them when it finds and eats from my bird feeder. Furthermore, even under the deterministic picture, each thing that is an effect is in turn a cause, a something-that-makes-other-things-happen. So the existence of agents, in the sense of systems with beliefs and desires and complex motivational economies, who do things is hardly undermined by the argument. Furthermore, even if nothing matters *sub specie aeternitatis,* the fact remains that evolution has resulted in the existence of organisms that have temporally extended lives and are self-organizing and self-moving in certain well-understood ways.

Death-of-subject arguments, even if interpreted generously, do not show that there are no subjects of experience nor that there are no agents. Depending on the type of argument, they deflate our conception(s) of subjects and agents, but they hardly destroy these conceptions—indeed they presuppose invariably that subjects and agents exist.

The arguments just rehearsed are heard among poststructuralists and postmodernists who are enchanted with human contingency and disenchanted with the idea that a person might be essentially constituted by an immutable soul or transcendental ego. I share the enchantment and disenchantment, respectively, but resist the conclusion. There is another quarter from which worries about self and meaning and worth continue to be heard—the ferment here is caused by the attempt to mix the scientific image of the cosmos and of biological evolution with more traditional pictures of persons. I'll explain a bit.

Why Me?

Why is there something rather than nothing? Why is there anything at all? And why in particular am *I* among the things that there are? Here are two answers:

1. An omniscient, omnipotent, all-good, and all-loving God decided in his infinite wisdom that the universe and its creatures should exist. He created humans in his own image. He endows us with immortal souls, souls that will join him and all the other saved persons if we use our free will to follow the right path, to worship him, and follow his moral commandments.
2. It is an inexplicable and irrational feature of things that there is something rather than nothing, that there is anything at all, and that there are particular individuals. But once there was something purely natural up and running, the aftermath of the Big Bang perhaps, then we can give some sketchy accounts of how life emerged on earth, and how natural selection worked to produce *Homo sapiens,* a new kind of animal.

One feature the stories have in common is that they both start by positing an originary force that seems to answer, but does not answer the original question. They both say that there just always was something rather than nothing. To which the original question can then be posed: Why anything at all? And why this, a God who always was, in the first instance, or some set of physical facts, a "singularity" from which the Big Bang emerged, in the second? Both stories stop further questioning and are found satisfying by different groups of people. But this cannot be due to their satisfactoriness as answers. Their appeal must lie elsewhere.

Transcendent Meaning

One reasonable suspect for where the appeal of the first story lies is in the fact that it provides the possibility that life has transcendent meaning—an omniscient God shows the way, I follow, and I achieve personal immortality. His plan must be the right one; it must make sense and ground a good and meaningful life. He is God, after all.

The second story generates a host of worries. If there is no God, if I am just an animal subject to the same finite fate—becoming nothing when I die as I was before my birth—then of what significance am I? And what basis could there be for thinking that one way of living is better than another? And if my time is limited, why should anything else matter than that I get pleasure, as much and as quickly as I can get it? And why, as I push the thought of my utter contingency to the limit, why think that I am in fact anything at all, rather than some sort of chimera or ephemera, at most a location from which self-expressive and self-generative forces seemingly emerge, but which in fact is simply, like all else, a place where certain things come together in a manner that creates the illusion that I am an agent, a self.

The second image, the scientific image, is thought by many to be deflationary and nihilistic, destroying at once the very idea that *I* am an agent as I conceive of myself, that my life matters, and that being ethical matters in this scheme where nothing matters. There is Dostoevsky's worry that if there is no God then everything is permitted. How could anything be better than anything else if there is no transcendent ground for meaning? But then there is Nietzsche's question: Why should the fact that a certain plan is God's plan assure its meaningfulness? Even if it does assure that the plan is meaningful for God, what makes it meaningful for me? And what assures that the plan is good, or that it grounds meaning, just because it is God's plan. If God always was and always shall be, isn't it the case that he just came with this plan. How could something (two things: God and his plan) so inexplicable, reassure me that the meaning of my life is secure, that it is in good hands, that it is not simply a derivative surd—an offshoot of the originary surd, a God who always was and just had this plan. How is this different from the second picture according to which I am nature's surd?

If it seems like the originary force of all things including this life lies in something personal and spiritual rather than material, then the next philosophical move is to motivate skepticism that God's creation, and God himself are good. I am to be reassured because I was made in *his* image. Why?

William James quotes this poem by James Thomson in his essay "Is Life Worth Living?" The poem makes the worry vivid:[3]

> Who is most wretched in this dolorous place?
> I think myself; yet I would rather be
> My miserable self than He, than He
> Who formed such creatures to his own disgrace.
>
> The vilest thing must be less vile than Thou
> From whom it had its being, God and Lord!
> Creator of all woe and sin! abhorred,
> Malignant and implacable! I vow
>
> That not for all Thy power furled and unfurled,
> For all the temples to Thy glory built,
> Would I assume the ignominious guilt
> Of having made such men in such a world.

My Way

It is hard to see why or how either story, the theological one or the naturalistic one, could ground meaning and worth in something instrinsic, timeless, and itself comprehensible. The scientific image seems no worse off at any rate than the theological one.

Perhaps looking for the ground of meaning and worth in origins is the wrong place to be looking. Still, the theological story contains an interesting suggestion. It claims that God needs us as much as we need him for the plan to work. This leads Robert Nozick to ask, "[I]f it were possible for man and God to shore up each other's meaningfulness in this fashion, why could not two people do this for each other as well?"[4]

Or, to put the point more generally: If meaning and worth come with relations of certain sorts, perhaps in the first instance to other selves, but possibly also to nature, to work, to oneself, then perhaps we are wisest to look for grounds of meaning and worth in this life—in relations we can have during this life. Does science say that this life doesn't exist, or that it doesn't matter? I don't see how, any more than I see that "death-of-the subject" arguments in the humanities succeed.

The claim is that it matters a lot that I do what *I* want to do. And it matters at least as much that what I do is something worth doing, something of value. These things of value need not be momentously important—ordinary things matter, eating a tasty meal, throwing a stick for the dog to fetch, shooting a basketball. These are things worth doing. If life was comprised only of such ordinary short-term goods, we might feel that something was missing. Why? Because we think that a person ought to have some long-term projects and plans and these ought to be about things that matter, things that are worth caring about, worth a bit more than the things just mentioned. Love and friendship and work, creative work, are among these things.

What I do and think reflect on me, on who I am. What I think and do also help constitute who I am. Expressing myself, making and modifying myself, and respecting myself all matter, and they are interconnected. Questions of meaning only arise because I am a thinking thing and, in particular, because I am a conscious thinking thing. My conscious thinking abilities stretch to knowing such things as that I will someday be dead. Being dead means once again being nothing at all. For creatures who thrive on self-expression, no longer being able first-personally to express anything thwarts a basic desire. Here is where leaving parts of ourselves in the world, by having changed that world in directions that matter, that are positive, lessens the threat of my demise. This is a kind of naturalistic transcendence, a way each of us, if we are lucky, can leave good-making traces beyond the time between our birth and death. To believe this sort of transcendence is possible is, I guess, to have a kind of religion. It involves believing that there are selves, that we can in self-expression make a difference, and if we use our truth detectors and good detectors well, that difference might be positive, a contribution to the cosmos.

Notes

1. In this passage, Richard Rorty expresses the sort of picture I want to endorse: "[E]very human life is the working out of a sophisticated idiosyncratic fantasy, and a reminder that no such working out gets completed before death interrupts. It cannot get completed because there is nothing to complete, there is only a web of relations to be rewoven, a web which time lengthens every day.

But if we avoid Nietzsche's inverted Platonism—his suggestion that a life of self-creation can be as complete and as autonomous as Plato thought a life of contemplation might be—then we shall be content to think of any human life as the always incomplete, yet sometimes heroic, reweaving of such a web. We shall see the conscious need of the strong poet to *demonstrate* that he is not a copy or replica as merely a special form of an unconscious need everyone has: the need to come to terms with the blind impress which chance has given him, to make a self for himself by redescribing that impress in terms which are, if only marginally, his own" (Richard Rorty, *Contingency, Irony, and Solidarity* [Cambridge: Cambridge University Press, 1989], 42–43).

2. Robert Nozick, like me, has a relational rather than intrinsic view of how life's meaning must accrue, and he captures nicely the deep psychological urge to avoid becoming totally nothing. "Death wipes you out. Dead, you are no longer around—around *here* at any rate—and if there is nowhere else where you'll be (heaven, hell, with the white light) then all that will be left of you is your effects, leavings, traces. People do seem to think it important to continue to be around somehow. The root notion seems to be this one: it shouldn't *ever* be as if you had never existed at all. A significant life leaves its mark on the world. A significant life is, in some sense, permanent; it makes a permanent difference to the world—it leaves traces" (*Philosophical Explanations* [Cambridge: Harvard University Press], 1979, 582).

3. William James, "Is Life Worth Living?" In *The Will to Believe and Other Essays in Popular Philosophy* (1897; reprint, New York: Dover, 1956).

4. Nozick, *Philosophical Explanations,* 589.

2

Is a Science of the Conscious Mind Possible?

My Incorporeal Soul

What are the prospects for a unified scientific theory of consciousness? Traditionally, mind, consciousness, and self have all named roughly the same thing, whatever it is that makes some individual a person. My conscious self is who I am. Can science explain the conscious self? That is the question. It is one that needs to be addressed if we are to deal honestly with the conflict between the scientific image of persons and our ordinary conception. Whether there can be a science of our conscious minds, of persons, of selves depends on two things: our smarts, and whether we are fully natural beings—animals, as it were.

Whether we are smart enough to do the science is unclear, although I am an optimist about our prospects. I am even more confident that we are animals, and that our minds, our consciousness, our selves are governed by natural laws.

Descartes thought that all mental events were conscious and that an autonomous conscious mind is both distinct from all things bodily and, at the same time, is the thing that makes humans distinctively human, that makes a person, a self. We spend time in the natural world, but our essence transcends this world. Indeed, our conscious minds transcend the natural world in two senses: Our conscious mind is not itself a natural phenomenon—it is not physical, and it is not governed by natural law; furthermore, it exists for all eternity after our bodily death. If Descartes is right, a science of the conscious mind is impossible. I'll give the case for the other side.

The scientific image of persons is not something that need spook us. It is not incompatible with the view of ourselves as agents with certain special features: capacities for knowing what is true and good, for shaping our lives in accordance with what we know to be true and good, and for finding deep meaning in understanding the nature of things, for having relations of love and friendship with others, and for making a positive difference to the world.

My aim in this essay is, first, to exemplify and defend the method I proposed in *Consciousness Reconsidered* (1992) for tackling the problem of consciousness, what I call "the natural method," and, second, to respond to three different objections to the very idea that there could be a scientific theory, especially a unified theory of consciousness. These objections are "the hodgepodge objection," "the heterogeneity objection," and "the superficiality objection." Dreams are used throughout as illustrative of distinctive scientific and philosophical concerns and as a good example of one of the multifarious types of conscious experience.

The objections come from within the naturalistic tradition, not from the nonnaturalistic Cartesian tradition. But in trying to show that a scientific theory of the conscious mind is possible and that it need not be reductive or dehumanizing, I try to ease the anxiety that occurs when we try to think about persons as agents and subjects, on the one hand, and as objects of scientific explanation, on the other. Many of the chapters that follow try to allay the underlying anxieties further.

No Hodgepodges Allowed

Let me begin with three claims:

1. *Consciousness exists.* I mean this claim to be as innocent as possible, so it is probably better to put it this way: There exist conscious mental states, events, and processes; or, if you like, there are states, events, and processes that have the property of being conscious.
2. *Consciousness has depth, hidden structure, hidden and possibly multiple functions, and hidden natural and cultural history.* Consciousness has a first-personal phenomenal surface structure. But from a naturalistic point of view, the subjective aspects of consciousness do not exhaust the properties of consciousness. Part of the hidden structure of conscious mental states involves their neural realization. Conscious mental states supervene on brain states. These brain states are essential aspects or constituents of the conscious states, as are the phenomenal aspects of these states. But of course nothing about neural realization

is revealed at the phenomenal surface, not even that there is such realization. The phenomenal surface often hints at or self-intimates the causal role of conscious states, indeed it often seems as if we place certain conscious intentions onto the motivational circuits in order to live as we wish. But the phenomenology leaves us clueless as to how these conscious intentions actually get the system doing what it does; and of course, experience intimates nothing about the causal origins and evolutionary function, if there are any, for the different kinds of consciousness.

3. *Conscious mental states, processes, events—possibly conscious supervisory faculties, if there are any—are heterogeneous in phenomenal kind.* Again I mean this claim to be innocent and uncontroversial. "Consciousness" is a superordinate term meant to cover all mental states, events, and processes that are *experienced*—all the states that there is *something it is like for the subject to be in them*. So, for example, sensory experience is a kind in the domain of consciousness that branches out into the types of experience familiar in the five sensory modalities. Each of these branches further, so that, for example, visual experience branches off from sensory experience and color experiences branch off from visual. My experience of red, like yours, is a token color experience—a token of the type red-sensation. So sensory experience divides into five kinds and then branches and branches again and again as our taxonomic needs require. But of course consciousness covers far more than sensory experience. There is, in the human case, linguistic consciousness, and there is conscious propositional attitude thought that *seems* heavily linguistic but may or may not be; there are sensory memories, episodic memories, various types of self-consciousness, moods, emotions, dreams, and much else besides.

The first two claims, that consciousness exists *and* that it has depth and hidden structure, suggest the need for a theory. We should have theories for what exists, for what is real, and this is especially so when what interests us is ubiquitous and has a heretofore hidden structure, a hidden function, and a mysterious natural (and cultural) history.

But the third claim—*the heterogeneity claim*—has led many to express skepticism about the prospects for a theory, certainly for a *unified* theory of consciousness. But heterogeneity *in itself* is not a good basis for skepticism.

Consider elementary particle physics. Here, heterogeneity of particle types reigns to a degree that surpasses normal capacities to count types. But elementary particle physics flourishes; heterogeneity of particle types does not thwart it.[1] Or, to take a different example, the periodic table just is a table of the heterogeneous element types—one hundred and two, the last time I looked—that constitute chemistry. So elementary particle physics and chemistry exist and provide theoretical cohesion to heterogeneous kinds in their domain of inquiry. These examples are sufficient, I think, to show that heterogeneity of the phenomena in the domain to be explained has *in itself* no bearing on whether theory can be developed for that domain. The inference from the premise that there are zillions of different kinds of elementary particles, heterogeneous in structure and function, to the conclusion that there can be no elementary particle physics is false because the implicit premise about heterogeneity thwarting theory development is false. The point is that the heterogeneity of forms of consciousness in itself should not worry us as we proceed to try to develop a theory of consciousness.

Some naturalists are skeptical about the prospects for a theory of consciousness not simply because of heterogeneity but because of the *kind* of heterogeneous array that the superordinate term "consciousness" names—it names a heterogeneous hodgepodge.[2] A "hodgepodge," according to the dictionary on my desk, is a "heterogeneous mixture of incongruous and ill-suited elements." Patricia Churchland compares "consciousness" to the kind "dirt" or the kind "things-that-go-bump-in-the-night."[3] Kathleen Wilkes thinks that "conscious phenomena" is more like the arbitrary set consisting of "all the words with 'g' as the fourth letter" than it is like a superordinate category such as "metal," "mammal," "fish" or like a subcategory of such a superordinate category, "gold," "whale," "flounder."[4]

The problem is not with heterogeneity as such but with the hodgepodginess of the heterogeneous array. Perhaps one can develop a scientific theory for a heterogeneous set of phenomena, especially if the phenomena constitute a natural kind, but one cannot develop a scientific theory for a hodgepodge.

Wilkes's argument turns on the conviction that in order for a superordinate category to be nonarbitrary it must display a certain coherence, but that "conscious phenomena" fail to display the required coherence. "What sort of coherence? Well, even though most of the interesting laws may concern only the subclasses, there might be some laws that are interestingly—non-trivially—true of all the subclasses; or even if this is not so, the laws that concern the subclasses may have significant structural analogy or isomorphism."[5]

We can put Wilkes's concern in terms of the two examples I have used so far. The heterogeneous types of elementary particle physics and chemistry have shown themselves to have a certain theoretical unity, as evidenced by certain cross-kind similarities. For example, the kinds on the periodic table are typed according to atomic number, atomic weight, specific gravity, melting point, and boiling point—in some cases, these are not yet known; and in the case of elementary particle physics, typing is based on characteristic mass and quantum properties such as charge and spin. Furthermore, the phenomena in question adhere to a set of coherent laws— the laws of quantum physics in one case; the periodic law in the other case.[6] Chemistry and elementary particle physics are in reasonably good shape because they unify heterogeneous phenomena that are interestingly embedded in connected layers of laws of nature—this making them non-hodgepodgy. We do not think celestial mechanics is suspect because of the heterogeneity of the composition, size, and gravitational force of bodies in our solar system. Nor do we think that the astronomical variety of sub-atomic particles, within the three main classes, forecloses the possibility of quantum theory. A theory of consciousness will in the end be part of a unified theory of the mind. This is compatible with the theory's making generalizations suited to whatever deep local idiosyncrasies exist. Physics tells us that bodies at extremely far distances from each other traveling close to the speed of light are subject to regularities very different from objects moving around our little sphere-like home. It would be no more surprising and no more damaging to the success of the science of the mind if it tells us that visual consciousness obeys very different laws from, and is subserved by different neural mechanisms than, conscious reflection on one's love life. In fact, this is exactly what we expect. One thing worth noticing is that if this correctly characterizes the criterion of being non-hodgepodgy, then there is no requirement that a theory must be unified at the most general or highest level, since neither chemistry nor physics are at present, and possibly not even in principle, unified at that level. The important question for us is whether the category and the subcategories that constitute the kind "consciousness" show signs, taken together or individually, of being a hodgepodge.

In her book *Real People*, Wilkes writes, "Scientific research, it would seem, can manage best if it ignores the notion of consciousness. . . . '[C]onsciousness' . . . is a term that groups a thoroughly heterogeneous bunch of psychological phenomena [and] is unsuited *per se* for scientific or theoretical purposes."[7]

But Wilkes can't mean that heterogeneity dashes hopes for a theory of consciousness; she must be thinking that consciousness is a hodgepodge. According to Wilkes some set of phenomena is a hodgepodge if it lacks a certain kind of coherence. In particular, the demarcation criterion distinguishing phenomena suited for respectable theory and those not so suited rests on this idea, that "even though most of the interesting laws may concern only the subclasses, there might be some laws at least that are interestingly—non-trivially—true of all the subclasses; or even if this is not so, the laws that concern the subclasses may have significant structural analogy or isomorphism."[8]

I'm not positive what the standard here is, especially the last part. What exactly counts as "significant structural analogy or isomorphism"? Imagine, contrary to the truth, that all learning was governed by the laws of classical conditioning and the laws of operant conditioning. If this were so, we should want to say that a theory of learning exists. But the grounds wouldn't be that all the types of learning were governed by some *single* high-level principle. It would be that there are laws governing each subclass, which taken together explain all learning. One might cite the additional fact that the relevant laws display a certain structural analogy or isomorphism, for example, they are stimulus-response laws. But analogies are a dime a dozen, and any imaginative mind can see them most anywhere. What would make the imagined account of learning a theory of learning, and a complete one at that, would revolve around the fact that our taxonomy of a nonarbitrary domain of inquiry was exhaustive *and* our two sets of laws explain everything in need of explanation. I find it hard to imagine anyone worrying about a lack of structural analogy or isomorphism between two sets of explanatory laws *if* the relevant explanatory work got done.

As for the first part of Wilkes's criterion, that a set of phenomena is suited for a theory if, in addition to special laws governing the subclasses, there are laws that unify some, possibly all, the subclasses—it is worth noticing that there is no unified field theory in physics *and* no certainty whatsoever that one exists. To me this suggests that the proposal is too stringent for certain well-developed scientific theories.[9]

How to Naturalize Consciousness

If we hold more reasonable standards of unity and of lawlikeness,[10] I see no basis in the current state of consciousness studies for thinking the skeptical hodgepodgists right. There will undoubtedly be revision of the typologies with which we begin as scientific inquiry proceeds, but the evidence—both phenomenological and nonphenomenological—suggests, even at this very early stage, that conscious phenomena display coherence.

In *Consciousness Reconsidered* (1992), I ask what method consciousness is to be studied by. I propose that we try the most natural strategy—what I call *the natural method*. Start by treating three different lines of analysis with respect. Give *phenomenology* its due. Listen carefully to what individuals have to say about how things seem.[11] Also, let the psychologists and cognitive scientists have their say. Listen carefully to their descriptions about how mental life works, and what jobs if any consciousness has in its overall economy. When I say let the psychologists and cognitive scientists have their say I mean also to include amateurs—let folk wisdom be put out on the table along with everything else. Finally, listen carefully to what neuroscientists say about how conscious mental events of different sorts are realized, and examine the fit between their stories and the phenomenological and psychological stories.

The object of the natural method is to see whether and to what extent the three stories can be rendered coherent, meshed, and brought into reflective equilibrium, into a state where theory and data fit coherently together. The only rule is to treat all three—the phenomenology, the psychology, and the neuroscience—with respect. Any a priori decision about which line of analysis "gets things right" or "has the last word" prejudges the question of whether different analyses might be legitimate for different explanatory purposes and, in fact, compatible with each other, or at least capable of peaceful coexistence. As theory develops, analyses at each level are subject to refinement, revision, or rejection.[12]

I should emphasize here a feature of the natural method that I didn't emphasize in my earlier book: that in the end what counts toward our theory of consciousness is everything we know from every and any source worth paying attention to. Besides the troika of phenomenology, psychology, and neuroscience, evolutionary biology and cultural and psychological anthropology will also be important in the development of a rich and complete theory. The evolution of consciousness in the species is no more well understood than is its emergence in individual brains. There exist at present no good theories about why conscious, experientially sensitive hominids should have been favored over merely informationally sensitive ones. And although it is pretty clear that sensational consciousness—that is, phenomenal awareness in the sensory modalities—comes with the human genome, it is not clear that, for example, moral self-consciousness does. Moral self-consciousness, like the ability to play chess or basketball, are allowed by our genes, but they were hardly selected for.

In any case, one possibility is that in addition to their phenomenological unity (many) conscious event types will be given an adaptationist evolutionary account—even while lacking certain kinds of unity at the psychological and neuroscientific levels. Embedding consciousness into theories of evolution (biological and cultural), thinking about different forms of consciousness in terms of their ecological role, and in terms of the mechanisms of drift, adaptive selection, and free riding will be an important part of understanding what consciousness is, how it works, and what, if anything, it is good for.

How Dreams Are Like Being Awake

The specific example I want to try the natural method on in this chapter is dreams.[13] Dreams are fodder for skeptics about the prospects for a theory of consciousness for a number of reasons. One route to skepticism is simple and straightforward. Common sense says that "conscious" involves, among other things, being awake. But dreaming takes place during sleep, and, thus, by the distinguished deliverances of conceptual analysis, dreams cannot be conscious experiences. But common wisdom also says that dreams are experiences that take place during sleep, so our common-sense taxonomy of "consciousness" is worse than a hodgepodge; it's riddled with inconsistency from the start.

There is a more sophisticated line of attack suggested in different ways and with different degrees of conviction by Norman Malcolm and Daniel Dennett.[14] This line sets aside the unsettling linguistic facts linking "being conscious" with "being awake" and focuses primarily on the received view that dreams are *experiences* that take place during sleep. To be sure, people give reports of experiences they allege to have had during sleep. But surely, if one is in a sufficiently skeptical mood this does not remotely prove that the dream report is in fact about experience that took place during sleep, rather than a combined confabulation-misremembering accompanying waking. Remember, people also insist that they have visited certain places before, or been in certain situations before, only to discover that they are wrong. Déjà vu experiences just are claims to experiences that did not in fact occur. There are, one might say, déjà vu experiences but they are not truly déjà vu—you weren't here before and this didn't happen to you before. It seems that way, it just isn't so.

Dennett calls attention to the possibility (also suggested by Malcolm) that so-called dreams *may* occur while awake or while waking up and not, as most everyone thinks, during sleep at all. Sure this is possible. But why think it more than merely possible? Malcolm's position was verificationist: dreams line up with the verbal reports people sometimes give in the morning, so that's all we can say that dreams are. Dennett (in this case) rejects the verificationist line, and points instead to certain kinds of dreams as support for the skeptical view of dreaming. Dennett reports this dream: "I searched long and far for a neighbor's goat; when at last I found her she bleated *baa-a-a*—and I awoke to find her bleat merging perfectly with the buzz of an electric alarm clock I had not used or heard for months."[15] One way to explain such dreams, but at high cost, as Dennett points out, is to think that powers of *precognition* are operative—the dream narrating mechanism prepares the narrative to fit with the alarm it knows is about to go off!

Even true believers in the theory that dreams are experiences that take place while sleeping think that most every dream report contains either more *or* less than was experienced or *both* more and less than was experienced in the dream state. On most every view, dream reports are poor evidence about *what was experienced* while asleep, even if we accept that they provide reliable evidence that something was experienced while sleeping.

In any case, let's apply the natural method to the case of dreams, and in particular to the question "Are dreams experiences?" to see where it leads. We know that most people, not having read Malcolm or Dennett, will report with confidence that they have dreamt while asleep. They will also say certain things about the content of their dreams. These reports are composed of part phenomenology and part folk wisdom (i.e., the reports are partly provoked by the "wisdom" that people dream while asleep). There are also psychological theories about dreams—the psychoanalytic theory being the best known, if not the best respected.[16] The nice thing about the psychoanalytic view is that it can easily be expressed in terms of the sort of functional flowchartology admired in cognitive science: as sleep ensues, repressor mechanisms loosen their grip on receptacles filled with wishes and strong, socially unacceptable wishes squirm out and find their way to symbolic encoders that work up an "experienced" story that gives the disguised wish some sort of satisfying release, which "experienced" story is then routed (imperfectly) far away from waking memory.

Now, although Freud certainly thought that dreams are experiences, his theory is compatible with the view that dreams are not experiences—at least not ones taking place during sleep. That is, take all the phenomenological reports of dreams, treat them as displaying manifest content that yields in interpretation to latent content and reveals what wish was being fulfilled. All this, as well as the associated view of why dreams are good for you, is compatible with a version of the skeptics' view, namely, a version that says that dreams are disguised wishes we happen to report (or think to ourselves) in the morning. Or to put it another way, dream reports reflect experiences, but not ones that take place while sleeping, rather ones embedded in awake thoughts or reports.

The upshot so far is this: Despite the widespread acceptance of the view that dreams are experiences that take place during sleep, the case is not remotely closed. And one consequence of its not being closed is that we do not have a really decisive reply to the skeptic, and lacking that, we do not know whether dreams actually occur *as* dreams and whether, or in what way, they fall under the concept of "consciousness." And this can be taken as evidence that the very taxonomy of the domain to be explained is ill defined. If we don't even know what falls under the concept of "consciousness," we can hardly be expected to build a coherent theory for it.

This is why the physiological and neuroscientific data are so important. These data both constrain and illuminate the phenomenology and the psychology—and they provide an additional line of evidence against the skeptic. If there is to be a theory of consciousness we will want eventually to know how, or in what ways, conscious mental states are realized.

Several hypotheses has been floated. One of the more widely discussed pertains to synchronous oscillation patterns. It has been suggested that subjective awareness is linked to oscillation patterns in the 40-Hz range in the relevant groups of neurons, that is, neurons involved in a certain decoding task "synchronize their spikes in 40-Hz oscillations."[17] Forty-hertz oscillations have been found in single neurons and neural nets in the retina, olfactory bulb, in the thalamus, and neocortex.

On the basis of this evidence, one logical hypothesis is that if dreams are experiences, then 40-Hz oscillations should appear at the points during the sleep cycle when dreams are alleged to occur. When exactly are dreams alleged to occur? There is much confusion on this point.

Sleep is divided into periods in which the eyes are alive beneath our eyelids (rapid eye movement or REM sleep) and periods during which the eyes are relatively motionless (non-rapid eye movement sleep or NREM sleep). In adults the ratio of NREM sleep (which is itself divided into four distinct phases) to REM sleep is about three to one. It is a myth, one I try to expose at length in the next chapter, that dreaming occurs only during REM sleep. The truth is that a certain bizarre kind of dreaming occurs during REM sleep. Dreaming, however, occurs all night long. But I will defer that argument until the next chapter and focus for now on the easiest way to respond to the skeptic, and that is by focusing on REM sleep since, in most every view, if dreams are experiences that take place during sleep, then surely REM sleep is the best place to try to spot them.

And, as luck would have it, there is now evidence that forty-hertz oscillation patterns similar to the sort detected in awake subjects are found during REM sleep.[18]

These data and hypotheses, in light of other data and theory, increase the credibility of the claim that links REM sleep with vivid experiences. Whether it is really true that dreams are experiences depends, of course, on whether it is true that 40-Hz oscillations turn out to be a marker, a constituent component, or a cause (which one they are is, of course, very important) of vivid conscious experiences. The point is that the neuroscientific data push credible theory in a certain direction. If these data bring us closer to the answer to one question, they open a host of others, suggesting occasional answers—a sure sign of a progressive research program.

For example, one might wonder whether 40-Hz oscillation patterns will turn out to be necessary or sufficient for experience or enable us to differentiate different kinds of experiences. This is a hard question. Forty-hertz oscillation patterns are like dust; there is always some to be found. This suggests the possibility that alive human beings might always be in some experiential state or other, that is, that we are never wholly unconscious—if, that is, 40-Hz patterns are sufficient for experience. If this sounds like an incredible prospect, it is relevant that persons awakened from NREM sleep often report having experiences—albeit experiences lacking the vivacity of post-REM reports. Sleeptalking and sleepwalking are well known to take place during NREM sleep (postural muscles are turned off during REM sleep), and it is obscure whether, or in what precise sense, sleepwalkers and -talkers are experiential blanks.

Allan Hobson's theory, AIM, illuminates many of the puzzles associated with dreaming. AIM is a three component model: A = activation level; I = input-output gating; and M = what excitatory or inhibitory work various neurochemicals are doing. So, forty-Hertz oscillations pertain to activation level (A). Activation level may be the key to why dreams are like being awake in certain respects. The theory also tries to explain the relevant differences between awake states and dream states. Why, for example, despite involving vivid experience, do dreams involve shut downs or dramatic alterations of attentional, motor, and memory systems and insensitivity to disburbance by external stimuli? The answers here involve the closing of certain gates normally open to outside traffic (I), and the modulating or demodulating effects (M) of changes in ratios of various neurochemicals during different stages of sleep.[19]

There is some neurophysiological evidence that auditory stimuli are *slightly discriminated* during REM sleep which would help explain how events in the external world are embedded in dream content, and might take some of the edge off Dennett's alarm clock worry. Some other interesting facts are these: Humans with pontine lesions don't have muscular atonia during dreams and are the same people one reads about who play offensive lineman with their bedroom furniture and endanger their spouses on a nightly basis. These people aren't bad, they are doing what the rest of us would be doing if the relevant brain area wasn't effective at shutting the motor system down.

There are interesting convergences of neuroscientific and phenomenological data in other areas as well. For example, the parts of the brain that reveal robust activity on various types of brain imaging technologies, such as positron emission tomography (PET), magnetic resonance imaging (MRI), magnetoencephalographs (MEG), suggest that "mentation during dreaming operates on the same anatomical substrate as does perception during the waking state."[20]

The Superficiality Objection

So what does the case of dreams show? It shows something I think about the nature of consciousness, or about the nature of one kind of consciousness, or, if you like, about the similarities and differences between two kinds of consciousness. It also shows some of the power of the natural method. Specifically, it shows that phenomenological facts and neurophysiological facts can be brought into reflective equilibrium in certain cases. Phenomenologically, REM dreams and awake consciousness are very different in certain respects. But they also possess phenomenological commonalities, and these together with certain commonalities at the neural level, suggest that they are *two kinds of consciousness*. They are heterogeneous dyad but hardly a hodgepodge, hardly an ill-suited or incongruous dyad.

The case of dreams also carries some weight against the objection that even if consciousness is not a hodgepodge, its only interesting feature is the *superficial* shared phenomenological feature of being experienced. This is not so, since in the case of dreams and awake states, the phenomenological similarities and differences gain some explanation at the neural level. Furthermore, certain psychological facts, for example, why noises in the external world are sometimes incorporated into dream narratives, are also explained by bringing neural facts to bear; in particular, the brain detects, but won't normally wake up for, noises in the external environment during REM sleep.

Nonetheless, one might worry that this case is exceptional. And indeed it might be. We know that there exists an important class of cases where phenomenal similarity is not subserved by similarity at the micro level. For example, the phenomenal property of "wetness" is multiply realized. There is, after all, H_2O, which is wet and heavy water, D_2O, which is also wet. Perhaps consciousness is like this: At the phenomenal level there is the shared property, but this shared property is subserved by all manner of different types of brain processes. I have acknowledged this possibility. I don't see that it harms the prospects for a theory of consciousness as I have been conceiving it. But one might imagine the examples where phenomenal similarity is unsupported by similarities at lower levels being used to press the worry that the shared property of being experienced really is too *superficial* to guide theory or to make us optimists about the prospects for a theory of consciousness.

Patricia Churchland gives an example from the history of science that is designed to feed the superficiality worry.[21] She reminds us how the commonsense concept of "fire" has fared as science has progressed:

'Fire' was used to classify not only burning wood, but also the activity on the sun and various stars (actually fusion), lightning (actually electrically induced incandescence), the Northern lights (actually spectral emission), and fire-flies (actually phosphorescence). As we now understand matters, only some of these things involve oxidation, and some processes which do involve oxidation, namely rusting, tarnishing, and metabolism, are not on the 'Fire' list.

Churchland concludes that "the case of fire illustrates both how the intuitive classification can be re-drawn, and how the new classification can pull together superficially diverse phenomena once the underlying theory is available." This is true and important.

It has been suggested that we imagine a person in an earlier time—a philosophical ancestor of mine, perhaps—saying something like this: "No matter how science goes, we will still be able to talk of a theory of fire." Even if the constituents and causes of the different sorts of fire turn out to be physically very different, the theory of fire can still be constituted by gathering together all the interesting truths "about the class of phenomena that possess the shared property of being fire."[22]

It is possible that Churchland might want to read my position as analogous to this far-seeing fire sage. So I need to be clear that I accept the true and important point that phenomenological similarity, in and of itself—even when it is similarity of *experience itself*, or experience *as such*, and not similarity of *thing experienced*—resolves nothing about the hidden nature and deep structure of the phenomenally similar stuff. Indeed, the very asking of the question—Are dreams experiences?—concedes the possibility that, surprising as it might seem, science could force us to drop dreams from the class of experiences in the way it forced us to drop what goes on in the tails of fireflies from the fire list. One can imagine two extremist views. One view would be that there is verbal behavior associated with waking or being awake that "sounds" to third parties like experiential reports about sleeping mentation, but which are—remember we are at the skeptical extreme—just some narrative noise an awake person produces. To keep skepticism heightened think of *all* parties involved—those producing dream narratives, and those they speak to, including themselves in soliloquy, convinced by the standard theory that the *narrative reports* are of experiences that occurred while sleeping, but that this is false. Another extreme hypothesis would be that dreams are experienced, contentwise, roughly as reported. The dreams that are remembered occur however (very rapidly) while one is awake or as one awakes. Neither view is incoherent

The point is that dreams might have gone off the consciousness list (or changed status on the list) as inquiry proceeded in the same way the lightning bugs were removed from the list of things on fire (if anyone really believes they were once on the list). But the present discussion shows that, in fact, things are going in the other direction—science is helping to secure the place of dreams as experiences, not to make us remove dreams from the class of experiences. It could have worked out the other way (it still might), but it hasn't thus far. So our commonsense concept of consciousness is open to revision, to being "redrawn." How consciousness is conceived depends almost completely on how the science of the mind progresses.[23]

The best evidence against the critics who suspect that "consciousness" names too superficial a phenomenon to play a useful role in scientific explanation or prediction involves deploying the natural method in cases like that of dreams and, in addition, pointing to the existence of predictive and explanatory generalizations that place conscious mental events in important causal roles. For example: there are important functional differences between people with phenomenal awareness in certain domains and those without. Suitably motivated individuals with normal sight naturally carry out voluntary actions toward seen things. When thirsty, we step over to the water fountain we see to our right. However, blindsighted individuals who are identically motivated and who process information about the very same things in the visual field do not naturally or efficiently carry out the suitable actions towards the "seen" things. There are also the differential abilities of amnesiacs to form integrated self-concepts and to create and abide a consistent narratively constructed self-model. And persons incapable of experiencing certain qualia, for example, color-blind people show all sorts of functional differences from non-color-blind people. Check out their wardrobes.[24]

This evidence suggests that there exist true counterfactual generalizations in the domain of consciousness. Some of these generalizations will relate phenomena at the psychological level, for example, persons with qualia of kind q do x in circumstances c but persons without qualia q (but who are otherwise identical) fail to do x in c. Other generalizations will link phenomenological- and psychological-level processes with brain processes; for example, (1) people with damage to the speech centers and, in particular, to the left brain interpreter, will have trouble generating the narratively constructed self; (2) people with certain kinds of frontal lobe damage will have trouble formulating plans and intentions; (3) other kinds of frontal lobe damage will obstruct links between consciously formulated action plans and actually carrying out the plans.

Given that these sorts of generalizations already exist and have been corroborated, it follows that there are laws that conscious mental life answers to. To be sure, the laws are pitched to the heterogeneous multiplicity of events and processes that possess the shared property of being experienced. But taken together, I see no reason to say that they are not part of an emerging theory of consiousness, one basic insight of which is that consciousness is heterogeneous.

Conscious phenomena constitute legitimate explananda, and conscious events play explanatory roles in certain well-grounded generalizations. Broadly speaking, there are two ways one might imagine building a theory of consciousness. Gathering together whatever scientific truths there are about this set of phenomena will constitute one way. Especially in the early stages, building a theory of consciousness might amount to the gathering together of all the interesting truths about the class of phenomena that possess the shared feature of being experienced. If dreams, for example, turned out not to be experiences, they would no longer be taxonomized as conscious, and would fall out of the theory so conceived. But they—no longer dreams but now, "mere dream reports," or alleged dreams, would still require an explanation within our overall theory of mind. A theory of consciousness built in this way, around the shared phenomenological feature would crosscut our theories of perception, memory, and learning. Or, to put it differently, the theory of consciousness, such as it was, would contain generalizations that also show up within these special theories.

A second, related possibility is that we might forego altogether a specially demarcated space for *the* theory of consciousness, allowing instead all the true generalizations about conscious mental life to occur within the special theories.[25] The idea is that the interesting facts and generalizations about consciousness might be gathered under the rubric of the special theories of perception, memory, learning, and so on. Presumably this would happen—and it is a very reasonable prospect—if the most interesting generalizations of the science of the mind weave together conscious and unconscious processes and their neural realizations in accordance with *what, from a functional point of view, the system is doing.* Since perceiving and remembering, and the like, are things we *do*, whereas consciousness may be *a way we are* or *one of the ways* we perceive, remember, and so on, it is easy to imagine embedding most of what needs to be said about consciousness into the special theories. The idea here would be to build a theory of mind, probably domain by domain, competence by competence, and then to embed the generalizations about the conscious, phenomenal aspects in this theory, along with the neural and nonneural generalizations relevant to the competence.

Whichever shape a theory of consciousness takes—either as a theory of consciousness itself or as a theory in which what is true of consciousness gets said, possibly without much ado or fanfare, within all the necessary special theories—it will be part of the larger, more systematic theory of the mind as a whole. *The really important thing is that there can be a science of the mind.* So long as consciousness is given its place within such a theory, it matters little whether it is explained in terms of a theory devoted exclusively to it, or whether it is just explained, period (that is, within the accounts given to domains like memory, problem solving, and so on).[26]

The best strategy is to get on with the hard work of providing the right fine-grained analysis of conscious mental mental life and to see where it leads. It will be our proudest achievement if we can demystify consciousness. Consciousness exists; it would be a mistake to eliminate talk of it because its semantic past is so bound up with fairy tales or because it names such a multiplicity of things. The right attitude is to deliver the concept from its ghostly past and provide it with a credible naturalistic analysis. I have tried to say a bit about how this might be done—indeed about how it is already being done. So dream on about a naturalistic account of consciousness and rest assured that your dream is neither a road to nihilism, nor does it reveal some impure philosophical or scientific wish or fantasy. Being a conscious animal with capacities for friendship and love, for absorbing large portions of the previous history of one's culture, for tracking the good, the beautiful, and the true, and for creating these as well, for engaging in the practices that make self and social improvement possible, is to be a really interesting kind of animal with potentialities that are gripping—exhilirating, anxious-making, frightening, deliciously open-ended and contingent. Being our kind of animal is not for every *Homo sapiens*. Bad luck wins often enough to make a human life not worth living. Sometimes a self doesn't get put together, or it does and social and political forces keep self-expression from being possible. Other times, the self is just situated badly. It would do fine in other places or times, just not here and now. One would be foolish to think that no rational human would choose to be the pig over Socrates in John Stuart Mill's thought experiment. Still, it is important to see that this choice could be made by someone defeated either too often or too soundly by human life, and furthermore, that it would still be a choice between one of two kinds of animal—not between being an animal and something else. That option is not part of the possibility space.

Notes

Acknowledgments—I was fortunate to have received valuable comments on earlier versions of this essay at both the Wake Forest colloquium (May 7–9, 1993) on my book, *Consciousness Reconsidered* (Cambridge: MIT Press, 1992) and the Carnegie-Mellon conference on "Scientific Approaches to the Study of Consciousness" (June

1993). I am especially grateful to David H. Sanford, Allin Cottrell, Bob McCauley, George Graham, Allan Hobson, Marcel Kinsbourne, Ralph Kennedy, David Galin, and Herbert Simon for their helpful comments. Ken Winkler and Robert Brandon also helped on an early draft.

1. Of course, many elementary particle physicists worry about this lack of unity at the highest level.

2. K. V. Wilkes, "———, Yìshì, Duh, Um, and Consciousness," in *Consciousness in Contemporary Science,* ed. A. Marcel and E. Bisiach (Oxford: Oxford University Press, 1988); K. V. Wilkes, *Real People: Personal Identity without Thought Experiments* (Oxford: Oxford University Press, 1988).

3. Patricia S. Churchland, "Consciousness: The Transmutation of a Concept," *Pacific Philosophical Quarterly* 64 (1983): 80–93.

4. Wilkes, *Real People,* 33.

5. Ibid., 33–34.

6. The periodic law says that the physical and chemical properties of the elements depend on atomic structure and thus are, for the most part, periodic functions of their atomic numbers.

7. Wilkes, *Real People,* 192–96.

8. Ibid., 33–34.

9. According to Robert Brandon's account of evolutionary theory in *Adaptation and Environment* (Princeton: Princeton University Press, 1990), it is not unified in Wilkes's strong sense. Evolutionary theory is unified by certain principles of probability theory, but not by any overarching contingently true generalization—this, even though, the principles of natural selection, drift, and so on, instantiate the relevant probability principles.

10. Robert Cummins, *Psychological Explanation* (Cambridge: MIT Press, 1983).

11. At the Wake Forest colloquium on *Consciousness Reconsidered,* there was spirited debate about the status of phenomenology. Bob McCauley argued persuasively that it provides data and that its pronouncements as pronouncements about how things really are must yield to explanation at the other levels. Even claims about how things *seem* can change as our views about how things are changed. The case of dreams is a case in point. If we ever came to have really good theoretical reasons for thinking that dreams are not experiences, they might well seem less like experiences. It is hard to imagine giving up the idea that there are perceptual experiences, since such experiences take place in the specious present (or so it strongly seems); but even dreamers will admit that they are remembering both the alleged experience and the content of the alleged experience. Since we allow false remembering, the intuition that dreams are experiences could yield if theoretical reasons deemed the sense that dream experiences had occurred misbegotten memories, akin to déjà vu experiences.

12. At the Carnegie-Mellon conference, Clark Glymour proposed that theory should be as biologically constrained as possible; he expressed the worry that cognitive information–processing models often fail to attend to biological realism. I quite agree with the normative point. But our present knowledge of the brain is scanty and often hard to interpret. Sometimes it is hard to know what the neuro-

scientific data are or mean and thus hard to know how they should constrain our theories. For example, many effective antidepressants work by affecting nor-epinephrine or serotonin levels, absorption rates, and so on. But in many cases neither the Food and Drug Administration, nor the pharmaceutical companies know exactly how these drugs work. Judgments about what they do at the psycho-logical level, what some of their phenomenological and physiological side effects are, as well as assessments about overall safety and effectiveness are made without anything approaching complete understanding at the level of brain chemistry.

13. Much of what I know about dreams I've learned from Allan Hobson's writings and from conversation with him. For example, J. Allan Hobson, *The Dreaming Brain* (New York: Basic Books, 1988) contains the original statement of the overall theory.

14. Norman Malcolm, *Dreaming* (London: Routledge and Kegan Paul, 1959); D. C. Dennett, "Are Dreams Experiences," in *Brainstorms* (Cambridge: MIT Press, 1978).

15. Ibid., 135.

16. There is also, as I've said, J. Allan Hobson's more credible and brain-based theory of dreams, *The Dreaming Brain.*

17. Francis Crick and Christof Koch, "Towards a Neurobiological Theory of Consciousness," *Seminars in the Neurosciences* 2 (1990): 263–75, p. 272.

18. Rodolfo Llinás and Urs Ribary, "Coherent 40 Hz Oscillation Characterizes Dream State in Humans," *Proceedings of the National Academy of Science* 90 (1993): 2078–81; R. R. Llinás and D. Paré, "Commentary on Dreaming and Wakefulness," *Neuroscience* 44, 3 (1991): 521–35.

19. J. Allan Hobson, *The Dreaming Brain;* and his *The Chemistry of Conscious States: How the Brain Changes Its Mind* (Boston: Little, Brown, & Co., 1994). So being awake and REM sleep both involve 40-Hz oscillations. This might seem neat since both being awake and being in REM sleep are thought to be experiential states, to involve a type of conscious experience. NREM sleep, on the other hand, is often thought to be a state of unconsciousness—a state in which there is nothing it is like to be in it. But as I argue in the next chapter this is wrong. NREM sleep is experientially rich. So 40-Hz oscillations may not turn out to be a marker of experience, or they may be necessary and/or sufficient; it is too early to know. One worry for the 40-Hz necessary condition hypothesis is this: the mentation occur-ring during NREM when measured by EEG doesn't appear to involve the 40-Hz oscillations despite the presence of mentation. So 40-Hz oscillations may be a reliable marker of certain kinds of conscious mentation but not necessary for all mentation (see M. Steriade, D. A. McCormick, and T. J. Sejnowski, "Thalamocorti-cal Oscillations in the Sleeping and Aroused Brain," *Science* 262 (1993): 679–85). On the other hand, when measured with MEG, one does find 40-Hz oscillations in NREM sleep, but much attenuated in amplitude, and we don't pick up much in the way of amplitude modulations. To make matters even more interesting, 40-Hz oscillations are detected in patients under light anesthesia.

20. Llinás and Paré, "Commentary," 524. This helps explain why prosopag-nosiacs don't report dreaming of faces and why people with right parietal lobe

lesions who can't see the left side of the visual field report related deficits in their dream imagery. On the other hand, it tells us something about memory that visual imagery sustains itself better in both the dreams and the awake experiences of people who develop various kinds of blindness in later life.

21. P. S. Churchland, 1983, "Consciousness: The Transmutation of a Concept," 85. It is often and reasonably said that science proceeds best when there are very specific research problems to be addressed. For example, the double helix structure of DNA solved the "copying problem" in genetics. It was well understood by the time Watson and Crick came along that inheritance takes place, but there was no postulated mechanism that was up to the specific task of replication. DNA solved this problem. One problem with the scientific study of consciousness is that there are still open taxonomic questions (e.g., the one about dreams discussed here) about which states are conscious and which are not—even questions about whether there is any shared phenomenological features, as I assume, and thus anything at all that really falls under the concept. But some good questions (about dreams, about automatic behaviors, about deficits of consciousness, about neural underpinnings of various conscious states) are opening up and getting attention.

22. Allin Cottrell, "Tertium Datur? Reflections on Owen Flanagan's *Consciousness Reconsidered*," paper presented at Wake Forest colloquium.

23. Indeed, it would be very surprising if different kinds of consciousness were not realized in different ways. The individuation of conscious events at the neural level will undoubtedly entail tracing complex neural maps originating at different points on the sensory periphery and at different places within the system itself and traversing all sorts of different neural terrain. This will be true even if all the events mapped share a physical property, such as having the same oscillatory frequency. It would also be surprising if the neural underpinnings of certain kinds of conscious states were not also essential components of certain nonconscious states, but not of other kinds of conscious states. For example, it might be that the areas of the brain that light up during ordinary visual awareness, or when we are solving problems in geometry, also light up when we turn over during sleep, but never light up when we are listening to music with our eyes closed. And perhaps there is a deep reason why the relevant area lights up in the conscious and nonconscious cases it lights up in. Imagine that the area is a necessary component of all spatial analysis, so it is activated when one is wide awake and trying to prove the Pythagorean theorem, and when one is sound asleep but computing information about edges and distances in order to keep from falling out of bed. In cases like this our theory of consciousness is interweaved, as it must be, with theories of unconscious processing.

But such results would in no way undermine the idea that conscious phenomena are legitimate explananda for which, and possibly with which, to build theory. It is to be expected that the development of the science of the mind will reveal deep and surprising things about the phenomena with the shared property of being experienced. Such discoveries might include the discovery that there are greater similarities in certain respects between certain phenomena that possess the shared property and those that do not than among all those with the shared phenomenal property. The neural spatial analyzer would be such an example. But this could happen while, at the same time, important generalizations are found to obtain among all or most of the disparate events that possess the shared property.

24. Color-blindness is an interesting example because there is reason to believe that the conscious deficit is caused, as it were, by low-level processing problems in the visual system. Still, it is not implausible to think that it is the deficit at the qualitative level that is the proximate cause of difficulties in color coordination in the color-blind person's wardrobe.

25. Herbert Simon has indicated to me that he favors, as I do, the second approach. It does seem to best represent what is in fact happening in the science of the mind.

26. Not to be frivolous, one might imagine the choice between collecting all and only Mickey Mantle cards versus collecting Yankee cards (even assuming a complete set of the Yankees would yield a complete Mantle set). Mantle is, as a matter of fact, essentially embedded in the history of the Yankees. But the Yankees—a somewhat different version—could have done without number 7. Whether number 7 could have done without the Yankees is more obscure. The point though is a straightforward one about interest relativity. We design baseball and scientific collections within fairly broad constraints, some of which we create and all of which we interpret.

3

Self-Expression in Sleep: Neuroscience and Dreams

Neuroscience and Meaning

Many think that neuroscientific accounts of mental phenomena destroy meaning or significance. There are several different kinds of meaning or significance thought to be at stake, ranging from the meaning or significance of life itself to the meaningfulness of particular kinds of mentation. The basic idea is an old one: the scientific image of humanity is the adversary of the manifest image of human personhood, the image that involves meaning, possibly transcendent meaning—meaning that matters beyond this world, this life, and my particular embodiment.

To be sure, neuroscientific accounts change the way we understand mental phenomena; but there is no way in which the general charge that neuroscience is inherently eliminativist, reductive, or an enemy of meaning can be made to stick. I'll try to show this by way of an example—the case of dreaming—in which I think doing the science does require thinking about the phenomenon (or phenomena) differently; but not so differently that dreams are not still self-expressive, interpretable, and meaningful, at least to a point. Some think that dreaming is pure noise. But this is wrong. I'll explain why this is false, even though Mother Nature did not *select* for dreams. She selected for sleep and sleep-cycling. Dreams came along as a free rider.

Five Philosophical Problems about Dreams

There are two famous philosophical problems about dreams: (1) *How can I be sure I am not always dreaming?* (Descartes's problem; also Plato's and Cicero's), and (2) *Can I be immoral in dreams?* (Augustine's problem).[1]

After his transformation from philandering pagan to an ascetic Christian, Augustine proposed a theory for how dreams might contain sinful content without being sins. His proposal, in modern terms, was that dreams are happenings not actions. Augustine wrote:

> You commanded me not to commit fornication. . . . But when I dream [thoughts of fornication] not only give me pleasure but are very much like acquiescence to the act. . . . Yet the difference between waking and sleeping is so great [that] I return to a clear conscience when I wake and realize that, because of this difference, I am not responsible for the act, although I am sorry that by some means or other it happened in me.[2]

A third problem emerged in the twentieth century in the hands of Norman Malcolm and Daniel Dennett,[3] a natural sequel to the prominence of verificationist ideas generally. The question was (3) *Are dreams experiences?* Or are so-called dreams just reports of experiences we think we had while sleeping but which in fact are, insofar as they are experiences at all, constituted by certain thoughts we have while waking or experiences we have while giving reports upon waking?

The answers to the first three dream problems are these: (1) Rest assured, you're not always dreaming; (2) Augustine's right that committing adultery, murder, and so on in dreams is not sinful; (2) You can be immoral while dreaming, but it is hard to pull off, requires planning, effort, and skill—roughly, it involves a complex project of character deformation through self-hypnosis; (3) Dreams *are* experiences that take place during sleep.[4] But dreams are not a natural kind. The unity dreams possess consists in this alone: they comprise the set, or the dominant set, of experiences that take place while a person is asleep.

Given that dreams are experiences that take place while sleeping, a fourth dream problem suggests itself: (4) *Is dreaming functional?* And if it is functional, in what sense is it so?

My answer to the fourth dream problem is this: Although there are credible adaptationist accounts for sleep and the phases of the sleep cycle itself, there is reason to think that the mentation—the phenomenal mentation—that occurs during sleep is a bona fide example of a byproduct of what the system was designed to do during sleep and sleep-cycling. If this is right, then there is a sense in which dreaming, phenomenally speaking, is an example of "automatic sequelae,"[5] a spandrel,[6] an exaptation.[7]

I'll first rehearse my argument for this answer to the fourth dream problem and then go on to talk about the fifth dream problem: (5) *Can dreams fail both to be a natural kind and fail to have a adaptationist evolutionary explanation but still make sense, still be identity expressive and identity constituting?* The answer is yes.

Constructive Naturalism and the Natural Method

I raise the epiphenomenalist suspicion about dreams not as another skeptical philosophical exercise. It is intended as a serious proposal that I've been led to in my work on consciousness within the framework of two general assumptions: (1) *Consciousness has depth, hidden structure, hidden and possibly multiple functions, and hidden natural and cultural history;* (2) *Conscious mental states are heterogeneous in kind.*

Consciousness has a subjective surface structure. But the subjective aspects of consciousness (call these *phenomenal aspects*) do not exhaust the properties of consciousness. The hidden structure of conscious mental states includes their neural realization. Call the neural realization of conscious mental states the *brain aspects* of these states.

From the first personal point of view consciousness only has *phenomenal aspects*. So with respect to dreaming all we know about first personally is *phenomenal dreaming*. The story of the brain side—of *brain dreaming*—as it were, will need to be provided by the neuroscientists, and the functional-causal role(s) of dreaming (now taking both the phenomenal and brain sides together) will need to be nested in a general psychological cum evolutionary (both natural and cultural) account.

The idea here is to deploy *the natural method;* that is, coordinate as best one can, phenomenological, psychological, and neuroscientific data and theory.[8] Now this procedure will, I claim, yield success in understanding consciousness if anything will. The expectation that success is in store using this method is what makes my kind of naturalism *constructive* rather than *anticonstructive*, as is the naturalism of philosophers like Colin McGinn, who thinks that although consciousness is a natural phenomenon, we will *never* be able to understand it.[9]

The troika of phenomenology, psychology, and neuroscience, despite playing the initial and central role in the explanatory procedure I favor, are not enough. Evolutionary biology and cultural and psychological anthropology are also crucial, as the case of dreams makes especially clear. Embedding the story of consciousness into theories of evolution (biological and cultural), thinking about different forms of consciousness in terms of their ecological role, and in terms of the mechanisms of drift, adaptive selection, and free riding will be an important part of understanding what consciousness is, how it works, and what, if anything, it is good for. As consilence and reflective equilibrium emerge, if they do emerge, from these different informational sources, we will understand the nature of consciousness more deeply. Even claims about how things *seem* can change as our views about how things *are* change.[10]

Dreams: A Double Aspect Model

I've said that phenomenal dreaming is a good example of one of the heterogeneous kinds of conscious experience, and it is at the same time, given neuroscientific evidence and evolutionary considerations, a likely candidate for being given epiphenomenal status from an evolutionary point of view. Phenomenal dreaming is an interesting side effect of what the brain is doing, the function(s) it is performing during sleep.

To put it in slightly different terms: phenomenal dreams, despite being experiences, have no interesting biological function—no evolutionary proper function. The claim is that phenomenal dreams (and possibly even rapid eye movements after development of the visual system is secured) are likely candidates of epiphenomena. Since I think that all mental phenomena supervene on neural events I don't mean that phenomenal dreams are nonphysical side effects of certain brain processes. I mean in the first instance that phenomenal dreaming was probably not selected for, that phenomenal dreaming is neither functional nor dysfunctional in and of itself, and thus that whether phenomenal dreaming has a function depends not on Mother Nature's work as does, for example, the phenomenal side of sensation and perception. It depends entirely on what we as a matter of cultural inventiveness—*memetic selection*,[11] one might say—do with phenomenal dreams and phenomenal dream reports. We can, in effect, create or invent functions for dreams. Indeed, we have done this. But as temporally significant aspects of conscious mental life, they are a good example, the flip side, say, of awake perceptual consciousness, which is neither an evolutionary adaptation nor ontogenetically functional or dysfunctional until we do certain things with "our dreams"—for example use them as sources of information about "what's on our mind," utilize dream mentation in artistic expression, and the like.

Despite being epiphenomena from an evolutionary perspective the way the brain operates during sleep guarantees that the noise of phenomenal dreams is revealing and potentially useful in the project of self understanding. Thus many things stay the same on the view I am staking out. But there is a paradox: phenomenal dreams are evolutionary epiphenomena, noise that the system creates while it is doing what it was designed to do, but because the cerebral cortex is designed to make sense out of stimuli, it tries half successfully to put dreams into narrative structures already in place, structures which involve modes of self-representation, present concerns, and so on. But the cortex isn't designed to do this for sleep stimuli, it is designed to do it for stimuli, *period,* and it is ever vigilant. The idea is that it did us a lot of good to develop a cortex that makes sense out of experience while awake, and the design is such that there are no costs to this sense-maker always being ready to do its job. It works during the chaotic neuronal cascades of part of the sleep cycle that activate certain sensations and thoughts. So phenomenal dreams despite their bizarreness, and epiphenomenal status, are meaningful and interpretable up to a point.

What Is a Dream?

I've been using *phenomenal dreaming* so far to refer to any mentation that occurs during sleep. But the term *phenomenal dreaming* despite being useful for present purposes, ultimately won't carve things in a sufficiently fine way. An example will help see why: Until I started working on dreams a year or two ago, I often woke up remembering and reporting dreams like this: "A late tenure letter (ten years late) was just received by the provost, it was negative, and my tenure has been taken away." Now to say that this is a dream is to use the term "dream" as it is commonly used to refer to any mentation occurring during sleep. But research has shown that this sort of perseverative fearful thought is most likely to occur during non-REM (NREM) sleep, the sleep standardly divided into four stages that occupy about 75 percent of the night. Sleep-walking, sleep-talking, and tooth-grinding are also NREM phenomena— and no one knows for certain whether we should say persons walking and talking in sleep are *phenomenally-conscious* or not.

Night terrors, a common affliction of young children are very puzzling since the child seems totally awake, eyes wide open, running about speaking alternately sense and nonsense, but almost impossible to comfort and wake up entirely and, on most every view, suffering terrifying hallucinations (which, even if the child is finally awakened, are remembered much less well than hallucinatory REM dreams). But, and here's the anomaly, the terrorized child is almost certainly in stage III or IV NREM sleep.

The first point is that mentation occurs during NREM sleep as well as during REM sleep, and we report mentation occurring in both states as "dreams." Now, since the discovery of REM sleep and its close association with reports of vivid fantastic dreaming, some have simply identified dreaming with REM-ing or with mentation occurring during REM sleep.[12] But this goes against the grain of our folk-psychological usages of the term "dream."

So much the worse for the folk-psychological term, one might say. But if one wants to regiment language in this way, the stipulation must be made explicitly and there are costs with the explicit stipulation. To the best of my knowledge, only one dream research team has made any explicit sort of definitional maneuver along these lines. Allan Hobson's group at Harvard (sometimes) defines "dreams" as the bizarre, fantastic, image-rich mentation that occurs during REM sleep. Hobson's group leaves the logically perseverative tenure dream, worries about tomorrow's agenda, that the car needs gas first thing in the morning, and the like, on the side of *conscious but nondreaming mentation* associated with NREM sleep.[13] This definitional maneuver cleans things up and helps in general to draw a useful distinction between different kinds of phenomenal mentation. We can imagine people—I now do this—reporting as *real* dreams only the really weird sleep mentation, and thinking of the recurring thought of failing the exam as NREM mentation—a "dream" in raised-eyebrow quotes. But the definitional maneuver has costs, for it doesn't deal well with the NREM states, like night terrors, that (probably) involve hallucinations and bizarre mentation. These will turn out to be *nondreams* because they occur during NREM sleep, but, at the same time, *dreams* because they are bizarre and hallucinatory. And there are, of course, daydreams, which, at least phenomenally, may be closer to the old wish fulfillment model than the mentation of NREM or REM sleep. So everything doesn't become neat and tidy once we use the natural method to make principled distinctions. One reason is that terms that have their roots in folk psychology, although often helpful, are not designed to specify scientific kinds or natural kinds, if there are such kinds in the science of the mind.

Having recognized the benefits and costs of the definitional maneuver, it will do no harm for present purposes if I continue to use *phenomenal dreams* to refer to any mentation occurring during sleep, recognizing full well that since mentation occurs in all stages of NREM and REM sleep, phenomenal dreaming isn't precise enough ultimately to type mentation during sleep from either a phenomenological or a neuroscientific point of view.

Sleep

Now some of the essential questions that any good theory of sleep and dreams will need to explain are these:

1. Why (and how) despite involving vivid experiences do phenomenal dreams involve shut-downs of the attentional, motor, and memory systems and (relative) insensitivity to disturbance by external stimuli.
2. Why do the phenomenology of NREM and the phenomenology of REM mentation differ in the ways they do?
3. What function(s) does sleep serve, and how do the clocklike cycling of NREM and REM sleep contribute to these functions?

There are numerous additional questions that need addressing, but these are the ones that are both somewhat tractable at the present time and most useful for pressing the epiphenomenalist suspicion.

The short answers to (1) and (2) are these: Sleeping in general is controlled by a clock in the *suprachiasmatic nucleus of the hypothalamus*—the hypothalamus is an area importantly implicated in the manufacture of hormones and thermoregulation. This clock gets us into NREM sleep, a hypometabolic form of sleep, and moves us through its four stages. There appears to be a second clock in the *pons* (the pontine brainstem) that sets off REM movements and its accompanying mentation.

In REM sleep, pulsing signals originate in the brainstem and reach the lateral geniculate body of the thalamus. (When you are awake, this area is a relay between the retina—on certain views, part of the brain itself—and visual processing areas.) Other pulses go to the occipital cortex—the main visual processing area of the brain. These pulses are called *PGO waves* (for *pons, geniculate,* and *occipital cortex*) and are the prime movers of REMing. This much accounts for the saliency of visual imagery in the dreams of sighted people. But the PGO noise goes to lots of different places and reverberates every which way. This is why people who work at remembering dreams will report auditory, olfactory, tactile, kinesthetic, and motor imagery as well as visual imagery. There is a nice convergence of neuroscientific and phenomenological data here. Brain-imaging studies indicate that mentation during sleep utilizes the same brain regions as does awake perception.[14] But the main point is that PGO waves are dominant during REM sleep and quiescent during NREM sleep, giving us the best available explanation why the mentation of REM sleep involves vivid, bizarre, and multimodal imagery.[15]

The answer to another piece of the puzzle, namely, why we don't in fact get up and do or try to do the things we dream about doing, has to do with the fact that a certain area in the brainstem containing the bulbar reticular formation neurons sends hyperpolarizing signals to the spinal cord, blocking external sensory input and motor output. People with certain brainstem lesions sometimes do get up in the middle of the night and act out dream episodes. Needless to say, this is not good.

The Fourth Dream Problem and Functional Explanation

So far, I've tried to answer the questions about the differences between REM sleep and NREM sleep and the accompanying mentation. The answer to question (3)—the question of the function(s) of sleep and sleep-cycling is not as well understood as some of the matters just discussed. From my reading, I have compiled a list of over fifty distinct functions that have been attributed to sleep and dreams in the last decade alone. Using the best-theory-in-town principle, here is how things look to me regarding the function question.

First, some facts. (1) Fish and amphibia rest but do not sleep at all. The most ancient reptiles have only NREM sleep, while more recently evolved reptiles and birds have robust NREM sleep and some REM sleep. All mammals save one, the egg-laying marsupial echidna of Australia, have REM sleep. (2) In creatures that REM, REMing is universally more frequent at the earliest stages of development. So for humans, newborns are REMing during half the sleep cycle, this drops to 33 percent at three months and at puberty REM sleep comprises about 25 percent of all sleep. It decreases in relative amount as we age, as does stage III and IV NREM sleep.

The fact that NREM is the oldest form of sleep and is hypometabolic suggests the following hypothesis: NREM sleep was selected for to serve restorative and/or energy conservation and/or body-building functions. Now some people find this hypothesis empty—akin to saying that sleep is for rest, which, although true, is thought to be uninformative. But things are not so gloomy if we can specify some of the actual restorative/conservatory/building mechanisms and processes in detail. And we can. The endocrine system readjusts all its levels during sleep. For example, testosterone levels in males are depleted while they are awake, regardless of whether any sexual or aggressive behavior has occurred, and are restored during sleep—indeed, levels peak at dawn. Pituitary growth hormone does its work in NREM sleep. Growth hormone promotes protein synthesis throughout the body—new cell growth helps with tissue repair—for example, cell repair of the skin is well known to be much greater while one is sleeping than when one is awake. Protein synthesis in the cerebral cortex and the retina follow the same pattern, having a faster rate in sleep than in waking. And, of course, the amount of food needed for survival is lowered, insofar as metabolic rate is. To be sure, much more needs to be said (and can be found in medical textbooks) about the restorative/conservatory/building processes that are fitness-enhancing and associated with NREM sleep.[16]

Regarding REM sleep, two functions suggest themselves. First, the much larger percentage of REMing in the early development stage across mammals suggests that REM sleep is important in helping build and strengthen brain connections, particularly ones in the visual system, that are not finished in utero. If, on the other hand, the orthodox Freudian account of dream function was true, then one would expect there to be less REM sleep the earlier in development one looks. The reason is simple. Dreaming, according to psychoanalysis, involves the release of socially unacceptable wishes and whatever gratification such release brings. Thus adolescents bubbling over with vivid and new socially unacceptable wishes should REM a good deal. And they do. But they REM much less then newborns. The trouble is that it is hard to imagine exactly what sexual and aggressive fantasies newborns have, or even less credibly, what fantasies thirty-week-old fetuses have who, according to some experts, go through phases of REMing twenty-four hours a day.

The second function of REM sleep relates to the significant differences among waking, NREM sleep, and REM sleep in terms of the ratios of different types of neurochemicals, modulators, and transmitters in the soup. In particular, the ratios of cholinergic and aminergic neurochemicals flip-flop. Neurons known to release serotonin and norepinephrine (noradrenalin) shut off in the brainstem during REM sleep, when neurons secreting acetycholine are on.

What good could this do? Here's one possible answer. The best theory of attention, namely Posner and Peterson's,[17] says that norepinephrine is crucial in getting the frontal and posterior cortical subsystems to do a good job of attending. Furthermore, both norepinephrine and serotonin are implicated in thermoregulation as well as in learning, memory, and attention; and dopamine has been shown to play an essential role in learning, at least in sea slugs. Now what happens in REM sleep that is distinctive, in addition to the dream mentation part, is that there is a complete shift in the ratios of certain classes of neurochemicals. In particular, in waking, serontonin is working hard, as are dopamine and norepinephrine. The aminergic neurons that release these neurochemicals quiet down in NREM sleep and turn off during REM sleep—this helps explain why memory for dreams is degraded. Meanwhile, cholinergic neurons, for example, those releasing acetylcholine, turn on. Here is a credible hypothesis for why this might be: By a massive reduction in firing during REM sleep, the neurons releasing the neurochemicals most directly involved in attention, memory, and learning get a rest. While resting, they can synthesize new neurotransmitters. The evidence points to a major function of REM sleep as "stockpiling" the neurotransmitters that the brain will need in the morning for the day's work.[18]

Another hypothesized function of sleep, and of REM sleep in particular, that I haven't yet mentioned is that something like disk maintenance, compression, trash disposal, and memory consolidation take place.[19] These seem like good things for the system to do. But it's pie-in-the-sky hypothesizing until some mechanism is postulated that could do the job. How could such memory consolidation or junkyard functions work? What sort of mechanism could govern such a process or processes? One idea is this: For memories to be retained they must be converted from storage in the halfway house of distributed electrical patterns into stable protein structures within neurons, in particular at the synapses. To get a feel for the need here, imagine your computer crashing and the difference *save* makes. The idea is that memory reactivation involves the reactivation of the neural networks whose synaptic strengths have been altered. What happens during REM sleep is that the cholinergic neurons that are on and releasing acetylcholine interact with the temporary but connected electrical synaptic hot spots that constitute a memory from the day and change those hot spots to a more stable form—to some sort of protein structure.[20]

Natural Functions

Enough theory and data are now on the table to show how I intend the argument for the hypothesis I floated at the beginning of the essay to go. The hypothesis can be formulated somewhat more precisely, given what has been said so far. It is that sleep and the phases of the sleep cycle—NREM and REM sleep—were selected for *and* are maintained by selective pressures. They are *adaptations* in the biological sense.[21] However, the mental aspects of sleep, the thoughts that occur during NREM sleep, as well as the dreams and lucid dreams (dreams that contain the awareness that one is dreaming) that occur during REM sleep are probably epiphenomena, in the sense that they are serendipitous accompaniments of what sleep is for.

Now some things that were originally selected for to serve a certain function, end up being able—with some engineering modifications—to serve another function. Selection pressures then work, as it were, to select and maintain the adaptation because it serves both purposes; or to put it another way, both the original phenotypic feature and the extended one, serve to increase fitness. For example, feathers were almost certainly selected for thermoregulation, but now selective pressures work to maintain feathered wings because they enable flight. Insect wings are an even better example, since it is known that it was aerodynamically impossible for the first wings to serve to get insects aloft. Initial selection was for thermoregulation.

It is standard in evolutionary biology to say of some "automatic se-quelae," pleiotropic or secondary characteristics, that they are *nonadapta-tions* only if they are concomitants of traits that were selected for and if in addition no concurrent positive selection or independent modification operate on those traits.[22] So the capacity to fly may have been a sequela of selection pressures to design efficient thermoregulation, but feathered wings are an adaptation because despite being a secondary characteristic they were (and are) subject to positive selection and modification pres-sures. But the human chin and the color of blood are common examples of sequelae that are nonadaptations.

The biological notion of an *adaptation* and even a *nonadaptation* needs to be marked off from the concept of *adaptiveness* or *functionality*. The bio-logical notion is tied to selection pressures which contribute to reproduc-tive success in a particular environment or set of environments.[23] But we also say of mechanical devices, intentional human acts or act types, and of cultural institutions that they are *adaptive* or *functional*. Here we mean that the device, act, act type, institution *does what it is designed to do*.[24]

We need to draw one further distinction within the nest of meanings of the terms *function* and *functional:* this between the sense of function as a causal contribution and the sense of functional versus dysfunctional. So, to use Kitcher's example, mutant DNA causing tumor growth is functioning as it is supposed to from the point of view of the relevant cell lineages; it is making the causal contribution we expect. But it is also dysfunctional—bad biologically and psychologically for the organism in which the tumor is growing.

Now my argument is this: sleep and sleep-cycling is an adaptation for reasons given above—it restores, conserves, and builds, and we can specify some of the specific things it does and the mechanisms these are done by.[25] There is some reason to wonder whether REMing and NREMing, that is the moving or nonmoving of eyes, is an adaptation. And there is very good reason to be dubious about the adaptive significance of the phenomenal experiences that supervene on REM and NREM sleep. Dreaming, broadly construed, is pleitropic, an automatic sequela, a spandrel. It is doubtful that dream consciousness, once in play as a sequela of causal processes originating in the brain stem that tickle the visual areas producing REMs, was subjected to positive selection pressures and modification. I should put it this way: For reasons discussed earlier, the brainstem is designed to activate the visual system to finish building it during the first year of life. Once the system is built, the continuation of the activation of the visual system serves no obvious further developmental function. Furthermore, whereas the PGO waves of REM sleep are implicated in the processes of stockpiling neurochemicals for the next day's work, for making what is learned more stable so that it can be remembered, and possibly for trash disposal, there is no reason to believe that these jobs require mentation of any sort.

Assuming, tentatively, that the stabilizing idea is right, there is no phenomenological evidence that, as electrical patterns are transformed into protein structures, the associated mentation involves the activation of the thoughts worth remembering. People remember nonsense syllables better after sleep than if tested right after learning but before sleep. But, to the best of my knowledge, people never report phenomenal dreaming about nonsense syllables. Nor do students of mathematics work through the proofs of the previous day in dreams. It may well be that the proof of the Pythagorean theorem would go in one ear and out the other if we didn't sleep in between. But I would place large bets that one will have trouble getting any phenomenological reports of sophomore geometry students dreaming through the steps of the theorem in REM sleep. The point is that PGO waves are causally implicated in the neurochemical stockpiling of amines (serotonin, norepinephrine, etc.) and in setting acetylcholine and its friends to the task of bringing stability to what has been learned. But there is no reason, so far as I can see, to think that the mentation caused by the PGO waves is causally relevant to these processes. The right circuits need to be worked on, but no mentation about the information that those circuits contain is needed; and typically such mentation does not occur. The visual, auditory, propositional, and sensory-motor mentation that occurs is mostly noise. One might be drawn to a different conclusion if the mentation was, as it were, about exactly those things one needs to stabilize for memory storage, but phenomenologically that seems not to be the case.[26] It can't be the actual thoughts that occur during the bizarre mentation associated with REMing that the system is trying to stabilize, remember, or store—most of that is weird. Of course, some is not weird, and the so-called day's residue makes occasional appearances in dreams. It would be surprising if it didn't. It's on your mind. The incorporation of external stimuli is also easily explained—the system is designed to be relatively insensitive to outside noise, but it would be a pathetic survival design if it was completely oblivious to outside noise. So dripping faucets, cars passing on the street outside, are being noticed but in a degraded way, they won't wake you, but a growling predator at your campsite will.

Phenomenal dreams are a special but by no means unique case where the epiphenomenalist suspicion has a basis. Phenomenal dreaming is to be contrasted with cases where phenomenal awareness was almost certainly selected for. Take normal vision, for example. It is, I think, a biological adaptation. Blindsighted persons who have damage to a specific area of the visual cortex get visual information but report no phenomenal awareness of what is in the blindfield. They behave in degraded ways toward what is there if asked to guess what is there, or reach for it, which is why we say they are getting some information. But the evidence suggests that the damage that is essentially implicated in phenomenal visual awareness explains why the performance is degraded.[27] And this suggests that the phenomenal side of vision is to be given an adaptationist account along with, and as part of, an adaptationist account of visual processing generally. This is not so with phenomenal dreaming.

Invented Functions

The phenomenal aspects associated with sleeping are nonadaptations in the biological sense. The question remains, does phenomenal dreaming serve a function? If it does, it is a derivative psychological function constructed via mechanisms of cultural imagination, utilizing the fact that, despite not serving a direct biological or psychological function,[28] the content of dreams are not totally meaningless. (This has to do with what the system is trying to do during sleep and sleep-cycling.) Thus dreams can be used to shed light on mental life, on well-being, and on identity. What I mean by the last remark is this: *The cortex's job is to make sense out of experience and it doesn't turn off during sleep.* The logically perseverative thoughts that occur during NREM sleep are easy for the cortex to handle since they involve real, but possibly "unrealistic" ideation about hopes, worries, and so on. Indeed, from both a phenomenological and neuroscientific perspective, awake mentation and NREM sleep mentation differ more in degree than in kind: worrying and wondering and problem solving while awake are less likely than their NREM kin to get caught in perseverative ruts or involve running around in circles. The point remains: we express ourselves, what's on our mind, when we wonder and worry and plan and rehearse. This is something we just do (as, for example, when NREM mentation automatically, but unproductively, extends ordinary thinking episodes) or that we *learn* to do (as, for example, when we work while awake or just before sleep on strategies to move dream mentation in certain directions).

Thinking comes in handy while awake, and apparently the costs of doing so while asleep don't exceed the benefits, unless of course perseveration is keeping us from sleep, in which case we do need to learn how to prevent or control the thinking.

REM mentation is a different story. It differs in kind from ordinary thinking. Phenomenologically and brainwise, it is a radically different state—closer to psychosis than to any other mental-state types. Still, the cortex takes what it gets during REM sleep and tries to fit it into the narrative, scriptlike structures it has in place about how my life goes and how situations go, for example, restaurant scenes, visits to amusement parks, to the beach, and so on.

Consider Sigmund Freud's famous dream of "Irma's Injection." The dream makes sense, possibly the sense assigned to it by Freud, but it requires none of the psychoanalytic apparatus: no orthodox manifest-latent content distinction, no repressive "dream work," and certainly no symbols requiring Lamarckian transmission. Here is Frank Sulloway's summary account of the dream of "Irma's Injection."

> The immediate circumstances associated with this famous dream were as follows. Irma, a young woman who was on very friendly terms with Freud and his family, had been receiving psychoanalytic treatment from Freud in the summer of 1895. After several months of therapy, the patient was only partially cured, and Freud had become unsure whether he should keep her on. He had therefore proposed a solution to her, but she was not inclined to accept it. The day before the dream, Freud was visited by his friend "Otto" (Oskar Rie), who had been staying with the patient's family at a summer resort. Otto reproved Freud for his failure to cure Irma of all her symptoms. That evening Freud wrote out Irma's case history so that he might present it to "Dr. M." (Josef Breuer) in order to justify his treatment of the case. Later that night Freud dreamt that he met Irma at a large party and said to her, "If you still get pains, it's really only your fault." Irma looked "pale and puffy," and Freud wondered if she might not have an organic disease after all. He therefore examined his patient and detected white patches and scabs in her mouth. Otto and Dr. M., who were also present in the dream, then examined the patient for themselves; it was agreed by all that Irma had contracted "an infection." The three physicians further determined that the infection had originated from an injection previously given to the patient by Otto, who had apparently used a dirty syringe.
>
> Upon interpretation the next morning, Freud's dream revealed the fulfillment of at least two unconscious wishes. First, the dream had excused him of responsibility for Irma's pains by blaming them on Otto (Oskar Rie). Simultaneously the dream had exercised revenge upon Otto for his annoying remarks about Freud's unsuccessful therapy.[29]

This dream presupposes the following: a life, an unfolding history, a sense of self, fairly normal insecurities about whether one is doing one's job well, various defensive strategies. What it does not require is "two unconscious wishes." To be sure the dream is not a simple read. What is? We think in scripts, prototypes, and stories; and metaphors and metynomic extension abound. We are storytelling animals, and we think and say things before we know what they mean, or perhaps more familiarly, we know what we think only once we have expressed ourselves. Freud's dream sounds more

REM-like than NREM-like, but, that aside, it is no harder to interpret than a variation on my "tenure dream" would be, one that involves (a) the painful death of the negative and tardy letter writer and (b) a thought about some (lesser) harm coming to the provost for giving me the bad news. In neither case is there any "unconscious wish" in the sense Freud came to soon after the "Irma dream." The Irma dream, as dreams go, is in need of interpretation. But it is hardly difficult to interpret.

Hobson's group is now studying the underlying *grammar of dream mentation* and the evidence is fascinating.[30] *Settings* and scenes are fairly unconstrained, *plot* is intermediate, and *characters* and *objects* tend to be transformed in the most gradual ways. So one's true love might be in Japan one second and in France the next. There will be some work to make the plot coherent, which will be hard, so what she's doing in Japan and France might involve an odd plot shift but not a completely incoherent one. But you may also find that she has turned into an old true love, but probably not into a sofa, in the transcontinental scene shift.

Now mentation about one's current true love and one's old true love, might be informative about what's on your mind, or it might be uninformative, just the best story line the cortex can bring to the materials offered up, but this could be true and such a dream could still be a good place to start from in conversation with a psychiatrist if your love life is going badly, or if you are suffering from any psychosocial malady. This may be because the content itself is revealing—remember there is a top-down/bottom-up struggle going on between the noise from below and the cortex, which is trying to interpret the noise in terms of narrative structures, scripts, and self-models it utilizes in making sense of things while awake. It could be that the dream is uninterpretable, or is meaningless as an intentional narrative construct, or that it has nothing like the meaning we are inclined to assign, but is nonetheless a good conversation starter for someone trying to figure out the shape of his life.

Your cortex (but not it alone) is expressing what's on your mind, how you see things. Your dreams are expressions of the way you uniquely cast noise that someone else would cast differently. This view leaves plenty of room for dream symbolism and even for something like the distinction between manifest and latent content. During REM sleep, the cortex must, insofar as it can, work up a story that builds largely on the contents activated by the PGO waves. But these contents are hardly the building blocks a teller of literal tales would start with. These contents will enter into the dream narrative, but it will be up to the cortex to determine what, if anything, the image of, for example, the Empire State Building means (and the limbic system will have a say in how the image "feels") and this will be determined and will be interpretable (if it is interpretable) by seeing how this image is situated within the larger narrative structure of which it is a part.

So things remain the same; phenomenal dreams make a difference to your life. They may get you thinking in a certain way upon waking. You may find yourself in a hard-to-shrug-off mood despite learning that the imagined losses of loved ones causing that mood were dreamed and didn't really happen.[31] You may be inspired to write a poem or a mystical text, and you may work at the project of interpretation. This is not silly. What you think while awake or while asleep is identity-expressive. The project of self-knowledge is important enough to us that we have learned to use the serendipitous mentation produced by a cortex working with the noise the system produces to further the project of self-knowledge and identity location. This is resourceful of us.

Another piece of evidence about dreams and self-expression involves the technique of dream splicing. Hobson and his colleagues have tried two different techniques involving *third-party* judgments about the meaning, in particular the thematic integrity of dream reports (approximately 80 percent REM mentation reports). In one situation, subjects were given spliced dreams, that is, dreams cut at mid-point and connected to the dream of which they were a part *or* to some other individual's dream report, as well as intact reports. Subjects correctly scored 82 percent of spliced and intact reports, and over 50 percent were correctly scored by all five judges. In the second situation, subjects were provided with abridged but not spliced dreams. An abridged dream consisted of the first five and last five lines of an account with a 50 percent or greater missing midsection. Abridged dreams are correctly identified as such in only 25 percent of the cases. This suggests to Hobson and his colleagues that dreams are self-expressive and have narrative structure. But the noise created, randomly enough, for the plot line is such that something like Seligman and Yellen's "principle of adjacency"[32] is deployed. That is, the rule for the dream narrator is to make sense in terms of what was just made sense of. This is hardly the Freudian line about night-long thematic continuity. But it allows for two things that I would insist on: (1) that dreams be allowed meaningfulness and significance, even if only prima facie, meaningfulness; (2) that we keep alive the possibility that ordinary awake thought does not simply satisfy some principle of self-expression of who I really am—some principle much stronger than adjacency, for example.

I am attracted to the idea that there is no way we really are until we engage in the project of self-narration. Once begun, a self-model is kept as a complex dispositional structure of the brain and is involved (and updated) to some extent in subsequent thinking. So what I think about myself helps constitute who I am, and what I think is made up within various systems of constraints as I go along. Dreams both reflect and participate in the project of self creation. Perhaps they have less overall causal importance to how my life goes and seems than awake thinking. We don't know at present how to perform this crucial experiment. But it is not silly to end up wondering about the meaning and significance of ordinary *thought*— "cognition," as we now say. For, surely, ordinary thought is not self-expressive always, nor is it all the result of direct biological selection pressures. Some kinds of thinking, for example, thinking about what is in your visual field (or better, just perceiving it), may well be analyzable as either directly selected for or as an automatic sequela of selection for vision. But some kinds of thinking, for example, thinking about which house to buy, requires as a condition of its very possibility the existence of certain social practices and much contingency about one's location in a particular culture and historical time. Such thought, we might say, is a tertiary sequela. Exercising—jogging, swimming, doing aerobics—is similar (as are doing calculus, science, and developing a refined taste for fine wines). To be sure, exercising is functional physiologically and psychologically speaking. But thinking, dreaming, and exercising may all well be best viewed as *social* "practices," as ways of being within a certain form of life. Certainly, we couldn't do any of these if our biology didn't allow them. But none of these are natural kinds. Furthermore, what is permitted and what is required are as different as night and day. And there is a world, a natural and social environment, that antedate *this* organism. I'll express what is on *this* organism's mind, but as I go along—as I figure it out. Self-expression is ubiquitous. But you get the idea: The self is an *objet d'art*—the self is made, not born. Dreams sometimes express aspects of you. But not always. When they do, and when they don't, they can be used as grist for the interpretative mill or as meaningless stimuli for further thought. Read your diary or look at a dot on the wall. It is by no means obvious which leads or would normally lead to better self-exploration or deeper self-knowledge. But surely, and this is perhaps the main point, *thinking* (awake, REM, NREM) is identity-expressive. It is processed by and through me, this organism, this thinking thing. This thing with a history— a life; a life whose shape and content and contours I know something about. In the end, it is no more surprising that I, this thinking thing, should have its own and only its own experiences, than it is that this thinking thing should express in its thoughts its nature; should express it*self*. There is something that it is like to be me, and I can sometimes experience, even on occasion say, what it is like. In this way I express who I am, what matters to me, where I locate meaning, significance, and worth. Neuroscience allows that much. This seems like enough to me, enough meaning for valuing and respecting oneself and others to occur, but not so much as to breed fantasies of transcendent meaning. This seems like a good, realistic, and stable place to end up, neither dismissive of the self, or meaning, or valuing; but, on the other hand, not too fantastically wishful.

Notes

Acknowledgments—An earlier version of this chapter was published in the *Journal of Philosophy* (1995) under the title "Deconstructing Dreams: The Spandrels of Sleep." The earlier version began as the presidential address for the meeting of the Society for Philosophy and Psychology, June 1994, in Memphis, Tennessee. Other versions were given at the University of Arizona, Cornell University, Stanford University, and East Carolina University. The present version was first presented at the International Institute for Advanced Study in Kyoto, Japan, in September of 1994. Deborah Stahlkopf has been a great help listening to my ideas and helping me sort through the literature on the function question. Thanks also to J. Allan Hobson, Greg Cooper, Robert Brandon, Patricia Churchland, Daniel Dennett, Gail Marsh, Larry Rosenwald, and David Sanford.

1. See G. B. Matthews, "On Being Immoral in a Dream," *Philosophy* 56 (1981): 47–54.

2. Augustine, *Confessions*, trans. R. S. Pine-Coffin (New York: Penguin, 1961), 233–34.

3. Norman Malcolm, *Dreaming* (London: Routledge and Kegan Paul, 1959); Daniel Dennett, "Are Dreams Experiences?" *Philosophical Review* (1976): 151–71.

4. But Malcolm and Dennett are right to express the worry that dream reports are poor evidence that this is so. We need a neuroscientific account to shore up the phenomenological confidence that dreams are experiences that take place while asleep. We now, I claim, have such a theory (see discussion in chapter 2); also see J. A. Hobson, *The Dreaming Brain* (New York: Basic Books, 1988) and *Sleep* (New York: Scientific American Library, 1989) for the theory called AIM, which I depend on). Some of the most recent work on AIM has been published in *Consciousness and Cognition* 3, no. 1 (1994). Dreams turn out to be experiences on that theory and thus to belong to the heterogeneous set of experiences we call "conscious."

5. S. J. Gould, "Covariance Sets and Ordered Geographic Variation in *Cerion* from Aruba, Bonaire and Curacao: A Way of Studying Nonadaptation," *Systematic Zoology* 33, no. 2 (1984): 217–37.

6. S. J. Gould and R. C. Lewontin, "The Spandrels of San Marco and the Panglossian Paradigm," *Proceedings of the Royal Society of London*, ser. B, 205 (1979): 217–37.

7. S. J. Gould and E. Vrba, "Exaptation: A Missing Term in the Science of Form," *Paleobiology* 8 (1982): 4–15.

8. O. Flanagan, *Consciousness Reconsidered* (Cambridge: MIT Press, 1992). See discussion on the natural method in chapter 2.

9. C. McGinn, "Can We Solve the Mind-Body Problem?" *Mind* 98 (1989): 349–

66, reprinted in C. McGinn, *The Problem of Consciousness* (Oxford: Blackwell, 1991).

10. If we ever come to have really good theoretical reasons for thinking that dreams were not experiences, they might well seem less like experiences. It is hard to imagine giving up the idea that there are perceptual experiences, since such experiences take place in the specious present (or so it strongly seems); but even dreamers will admit that they are remembering both the alleged experience and the content of the alleged experience. See the exchange between Kathleen Emmett, "Oneiric Experiences," *Philosophical Studies* 34 (1978): 445–50, and Daniel C. Dennett, "The Onus Re Experiences," *Philosophical Studies* 35 (1979): 315–18.

11. See R. Dawkins, *The Selfish Gene* (Oxford: Oxford University, 1976).

12. The exciting work of researchers in the late 1950s led to the identification of "dream mentation" with REM sleep. M. Jouvet, "Récherches sur les structures nerveuses et les mécanismes résponsables des différentes phases du sommeil physiologique," *Archives Italiennes de Biologie* 100 (1962): 125–206; E. Aserinsky and N. Kleitman, "Two Types of Ocular Motility Occurring in Sleep," *Journal of Applied Physiology* 8 (1955): 1–10; and W. Dement, "The Occurence of Low Voltage, Fast, Electroencephalogram Patterns during Behavioral Sleep in the Cat," *Electroencephalography and Clinical Neurophysiology* 10 (1958): 291–96. But this, it appears, is a mistake: NREM sleep is also associated with reports of mentation, and although the phenomenological content of such mentation is mundane and fairly nonbizarre, involving such things as worries about something that needs to be done the next day, subjects do not say they were just thinking about what they needed to do the next day, but that they were dreaming about it: J. H. Herman, S. J. Ellman, and H. P. Roffward, "The Problem of NREM Dream Recall Reexamined," *The Mind in Sleep,* ed. A. Arkin, J. Antrobus, and S. Ellman (Hillsdale, N.J.: Lawrence Erlbaum Associates, 1978). Indeed, if one thinks that mentation is dreaming only if it occurs during REM sleep then people are even more disastrously bad at giving dream reports that most have thought: for many reported dreams are of the "I was supposed to do *x,* but didn't" sort and the evidence points to greater likelihood that such mentation occurs during NREM sleep than during REM sleep. It was Foulkes—see D. Foulkes, *Dreaming: A Cognitive-Psychological Analysis* (Hillsdale, N.J.: Lawrence Erlbaum Associates, 1985)—who led the credible movement, not yet won, to disassociate the virtually analytic connection that had been drawn and continues to be drawn by most researchers between REM and dreaming. Indeed, someone—I can't remember who it was—founded "The Society for the Prevention of Cruelty to NREM Sleep." The idea was to let dreaming be, as a first pass, any mentation that takes place during sleep, and go from there. The frequency of NREM mentation casts doubt on the idea that dreaming is a natural kind, although we may well be able to discern differences between NREM mentation and REM mentation. Nonetheless, some researchers (Herman, Ellman, and Roffward, "The Problem,") suggest that the conclusion to be gained from expanding the concept of dreaming is that "[t]he hope that one stage of sleep, or a given physiological marker, will serve as the sole magic key for vivid dream mentation has all but faded from view" (92). The overall point is this: Phenomenal

dreams, as we normally think of them, include both the perseverative, thoughtlike mentation of NREM sleep and the bizarre and fantastic mentation of REM sleep; however, the foregoing scientific considerations suggest reasons for restricting the use of the term "dreams" for certain scientific and philosophical purposes only to REM mentation, though there are some reasons against doing this—for example the hallucinatory night terrors of stage III and IV NREM sleep. A further issue is this: Since we are always either in NREM or REM sleep or awake it is possible that we are *never* unconscious. Alternatively, it is possible that there are times in both NREM and REM sleep when virtually nothing thoughtlike is happening—or perhaps we are informationally sensitive (this could explain how sleepwalking without awareness could be possible—rather as blindsight patients process some information about what's in the blind field without being phenomenally aware of, or experientially sensitive to what's in that field). No one knows for sure.

13. J. A. Hobson and R. Stickgold, "Dreaming: A Neurocognitive Approach," *Consciousness and Cognition* 3 (1994): 1–15.

14. Llinás and Paré, "Of Dreaming and Wakefulness," *Neuroscience* 44, no. 3 (1991): 524. This helps explain why prosopagnosiacs don't report dreaming of faces and why people with right parietal lobe lesions who can't see the left side of the visual field report related deficits in their dream imagery. On the other hand, it tells us something about memory that visual imagery sustains itself better both in the dreams and the awake experiences of people who develop various kinds of blindness in later life.

15. Once such imagery is overrated, dreaming is equated with REMing, and the sensorily dull, but thoughtlike, mentation of NREM sleep is overlooked. This then leads to the assumption that NREM sleep, especially stage IV NREM sleep, is a period of unconsciousness.

16. See M. H. Kryger, T. Roth, and W. Dement, *Principles and Practice of Sleep Medicine*, 2d ed. (London: W. B. Saunders, 1994).

17. M. I. Posner and S. E. Peterson, "The Attention System of the Human Brain," *Annual Review of Neuroscience* 13 (1990): 25–42.

18. Hobson, *Sleep.*

19. See, e.g., F. Crick and G. Mitchison, "The Function of Dream Sleep," *Nature* 304 (1983): 111–14; J. J. Hopfield, D. I. Feinstein, and R. G. Palmer, "'Unlearning' Has a Stabilizing Effect in Collective Memories," *Nature* 304 (1983): 158–59; Steriade, McCormick, and Sejnowski "Thalamocortical Oscillations."

20. See Hobson, *Sleep.*

21. See Mary Jane West-Eberhard, "Adaptation: Current Usages," 13–18; and Richard Burian, "Adaptation: Historical Perspectives," both in *Keywords in Evolutionary Biology*, ed. Evelyn Fox Keller and Elisabeth Lloyd (Cambridge: Harvard University Press, 1992), 7–12. Also see Philip Kitcher, "Function and Design" (forthcoming), and Peter Godfrey-Smith, "A Modern History Theory of Functions," *Noûs* 27 (1994): 344–62.

22. West-Eberhard, "Adaptation: Current Usages."

23. R. Brandon, *Adaptation and Environment* (Princeton: Princeton University Press, 1990).

24. Kitcher, "Function and Design," argues that this idea unifies attributions of *function* across biological and nonbiological contexts.

25. I haven't even mentioned some of the other systems that are being worked on in sleep, e.g., the immune system. People who are kept from sleeping die, not from lack of sleep as such, but from blood diseases. Without sleep the immune system appears to break down.

26. Rats that have learned that certain spatial tasks have the relevant neural circuits worked on during sleep. Why the rat would need to be thinking the "right" spatial thoughts in addition to having the "right" circuits worked on is utterly obscure: a tempting inference, but totally unwarranted, as best I can tell. See M. A. Wilson and B. L. McNaughton, "Reactivation of Hippocampal Ensemble Memories during Sleep," *Science,* in press, and "Dynamics of the Hippocampal Ensemble Code for Space," *Science* 261 (20 August, 1993): 1055–58.

27. See N. Block, forthcoming in *Brain and Behavioral Sciences,* for an objection to this sort of reasoning; and see my response in *Consciousness Reconsidered,* 145–52.

28. I need to be clear here that the very same processes that produce phenomenal dreaming as an effect produce the switch in neurotransmitter ratios that do serve an important psychological function. But phenomenal dreams don't serve this function.

29. Frank Sulloway, *Freud: Biologist of the Mind* (New York: Basic Books, 1979), 327–28.

30. R. Stickgold, C. D. Rittenhouse, and J. A. Hobson, "Constraint on the Transformation of Characters, Objects, and Settings in Dream Reports," *Consciousness and Cognition* 3 (1994): 100–113, and "Dream Splicing: A New Technique for Assessing Thematic Coherence in Subjective Reports of Mental Activity," *Consciousness and Cognition* 3 (1994): 114–28.

31. I have talked very little about the activation of limbic areas during dreams. Hobson's group finds that emotions and moods are coherently coordinated with dream content. This, it seems to me, is good evidence of cortical domination of the plot line and of limbic cooperation.

32. M. Seligman and A. Yellen, "What Is a Dream?" *Behaviour Research and Therapy* 25 (1987): 1–24.

4

Neuroscience, Agency, and the Meaning of Life

Where Am I?

It seems as if I do things. It would undermine, possibly destroy, the meaning and significance of my life if I am not an agent, if who and what I am is in no way the result of choices I make. It matters that I am not just along on some ride that the cosmos, for some absurd reason, is taking. And yet if I am just an animal, if what I think and do is just the emergent product of what the world outside, my body and its brain jointly produce, then it is hard to see what sense there is to the ideas that I am an agent, that I am self-productive, and that I create or cocreate some of the meaning my life has. These are reasonable worries. But they are not rational.

The Ghost in the Machine

In 1949 the Oxford philosopher Gilbert Ryle wrote:

There is a doctrine about the nature and place of minds which is so prevalent among theorists and even among laymen that it deserves to be described as the official theory. Most philosophers, psychologists, and religious teachers subscribe, with minor reservations, to its main articles and, although they admit certain theoretical difficulties in it, they tend to assume that these can be overcome without serious modifications being made to the architecture of the theory. . . . [T]he official doctrine, which hails chiefly from Descartes, is something like this. . . . [E]very human being has both a body and a mind. His body and mind are ordinarily harnessed together, but after the death of the body his mind may continue to exist and function. Human bodies are in space and are subject to mechanical laws. . . . But minds are not in space, nor are their operations subject to mechanical laws.[1]

Even great brain scientists have fallen prey to the charms of "the official doctrine." In 1975, the year before his death, Wilder Penfield wrote: "After years of striving to explain the basis of mind on the basis of brain-action alone, I have come to the conclusion that it is simpler . . . if one adopts the hypothesis that our being does consist of two fundamental elements."[2] The mind, Penfield thought, was immaterial but did possess energy. How this is possible, he did not explain. Nor has anyone since.

The Mind's Will

The concept that the mind is nonphysical—incorporeal, as philosophers say, was developed within the context of a faculty theory of mind: The mind had among its faculty two main ones: *reason* or *understanding* on the one side and *will* or *volition* on the other. In *involuntary action* the mind and its faculties have no involvement. The body functions as a closed system in which stimulation at the periphery leads to nerve activation, which leads to the release of distilled particles of blood ("animal spirits") from the pineal gland at the base of the brain, which lead to the appropriate physical or motor response. Pupil contractions, knee jerks, pulling a limb away from fire were, Descartes thought, subject to physical law—fully explicable in causal terms.

Voluntary action, on the other hand is action involving the incorporeal mind and, in particular, the faculties of *reason* and *will* and it is *not* subject to natural law. *Reason* surveys the possible actions available to agent, decides on the best course, and the unconstrained *will* generates or creates a volition to carry out *reason's* command. Descartes writes, "But the will is so free in its nature, that it can never be constrained. . . . And the whole action of the soul consists in this, that *solely because it desires something*, it causes a little gland to which it is closely united to move in a way requisite to produce the effect which relates to this desire."[3]

The contemporary philosopher Roderick Chisolm puts the view this way: "If we are responsible . . . then we have a prerogative which some would attribute only to God: each of us, when we act, is a prime mover unmoved. In doing what we do, we cause certain things to happen, and nothing—or no one—causes us to cause those events to happen."[4]

Why The Official Doctrine Appeals

The reasons why the official doctrine of the ghost in the machine was found attractive are numerous: it fits nicely with a theology committed to the idea that persons have a spiritual part that can control their actions and their lives. Possession of this part enables the assumption of metaphysical free will, of complete responsibility for actions generated by free will, and of the possiblity of personal immortality. It also secures the justice of a good God who rewards and punishes persons in accordance with whether they use their will to choose the right or the wrong path. The doctrine of the ghost in the machine was, as it were, one of the elements needed to provide a unified doctrine of free action, personal responsibility, God's goodness, and personal immortality.

But the question arises: Why has this idea of metaphysical freedom of the will lasted even until today, and even among thinkers who have no stake in the relevant theological doctrines? There are, I think three sources for the persistence of the doctrine, one reasonable, the other two not.

First, whatever our thoughts about God, life after death, and personal immortality, most thoughtful persons have thought that there is something to the idea of free action and to the distinction between voluntary and involuntary behavior. And indeed there is. Furthermore, our practices of ascribing responsibility for action seem to depend on some such notion. And they do. The distinction between the voluntary and involuntary is one we cannot do without. Our ideas of free choice, our conception of moral responsibility, our notions of diminished responsibility, and our developing theory of excuses depend on the preservation of some sort of distinction between voluntary and involuntary. The mistake to avoid is thinking that the involuntary is subject to causal law, the voluntary not. Both voluntary and involuntary action are caused. But they are caused by different sorts of causal processes. Descartes and Penfield were right about that. Where they went wrong is in thinking that the processes governing voluntary action were not within the domain of science, and that the proximate mechanisms governing free action were outside the domain of brain science in particular.

The second, even more seductive, but in the end less defensible, reason for the persistence of the idea that free action must involve a metaphysical "wonder works"—a mental unmoved mover—has to do with the fact that we give too much weight to "the way things seem" from the first-person point of view.

How do they seem from the first-person point of view? Well, we seem impotent when it comes to our control over reflexes and the like, but we sometimes seem to have complete control over certain of our actions. Control involves reasoned volitions that move the body in intentional action *but seem to be themselves unmoved.* I decide to lift my right arm and do so (how does my will know about arms, movement, and right versus left?) The root problem here has its sources in a second idea that Cartesianism also made popular: the idea that the nature of mind is transparent to its owner. So if things mental seem a certain way, then they are that way.

The idea that the mind is transparent to itself is of course another myth worth abandoning. The advent of the human sciences, psychology and sociology, in the nineteenth century, undermined the myth somewhat by analyzing distal causes of behavior. The myth didn't have to yield completely however, because social and psychological causes could always be treated as "mere influences," as fodder for the rational will, information at its disposal, as it were, but not as causes moving the rational will. The big advance in destabilizing the transparency myth has come from neuroscience, for we now understand that the human mind is a system that is not only in imperfect touch with external influences, with distal causes, but it is quite out of touch with the manifold, largely unconscious, massively parallel, soupy neural processes that immediately precede instances of voluntary choice. We typically have no accurate and ongoing personal access to proximate causal antecedents of conscious acts of thought and choice, and this can produce a "user illusion" that unmoved volitions precede and guide acts.

The third and most compelling cause of worry over the possibility that we might lack metaphysical freedom of the will lies in the concern I voiced at the start. It seems as if I dissolve as an agent, if I am not the prime mover, myself unmoved, of my thoughts and actions, if *I* do not exist, or do not exist as a genuine agent, then I am simply a cog in some grand cosmic accident, one that produces an illusion in the space "I" occupy. So I am nothing, the cosmos is a surd, and my life is not mine at all. As such it can have no meaning for me who is not, and who does nothing. Cogito, therefore I am eradicated.

Naturalizing Agency

Fortunately, there is a conception of free action that does the jobs we need it to do in everyday social life, in ethics, and in the law, and that is at the same time compatible with the naturalistic assumptions made in the human sciences generally and brain science in particular about the nature of persons. By naturalism I simply mean the view that all phenomena are natural and subject to causal principles. Mind, consciousness, human volition are like other phenomena in that they are made of natural stuff, have natural histories, and are explicable in terms of natural law.

So the question is: Once we give up on the myth of the ghost in the machine, and of the mind as transparent to its owner, and think of a human person as an organism subject to complex natural law, what can be saved of the notions of agency and free and responsible action? The answer is, a surprisingly large amount. Let me explain.

The first thing I should point out is that the view I espouse is not new nor is it particularly complex philosophically. It goes back at least as far as Aristotle, to the fourth century B.C. In the *Nichomachean Ethics,* Aristotle drew the involuntary-voluntary distinction this way: "What is involuntary is what is forced or is caused by ignorance. What is voluntary seems to be what has its origins in the agent himself when he knows the particulars that the action consists in" (3.18).

What Aristotle had in mind was something like this: An action is involuntary if it results from some sort of compulsion against which effort and thinking are impotent, or if the agent in no way knows or grasps what he is doing. Voluntary action, on the other hand, involves the agent knowing what action it is that she is performing and acting from reasons and desires that are her own.

This analysis is *silent* on the issue of the origin of the capacities to think and act with reason. But this silence should not be taken for neutrality on the existence of natural causal origins for these capacities. For Aristotle, and for many post-Cartesians, like David Hume, John Stuart Mill, John Dewey, and many others, the assumption is that the capacities in question are distinctive, but perfectly natural, human capacities with perfectly ordinary natural histories. The position that the reality of voluntary action is fully compatible with an analysis of such action *as caused* is called "compatibilism." By those who would disparage it, it is called "soft determinism."

To get the basic flavor of the view one might look at John Dewey's 1894 paper "The Ego as a Cause."[5] Here, Dewey claimed that the main question facing the science of the mind was whether we can "carry back our analysis to scientific conditions, or must we stop at a given point because we have come upon a force of an entirely different order—an independent ego as an entity in itself?" His answer was that the myth of a completely self-initiating ego, an unmoved but moving will, were simply indications of our ignorance of the causes of human behavior. And his main point was that there was no need to have the notion of a metaphysically unconstrained will or of an independent ego as an unconstrained primal cause to have a robust conception of free agency. Dewey rightly noted that "[w]hat men have esteemed and fought for in the name of liberty is varied and complex—but certainly it has never been metaphysical freedom of the will."[6]

As I have said, what is needed is to show that the ingredients necessary for free action are compatible with causation. What are the ingredients necessary for free action? Well, they are such things as *the ability to pay attention, the causal efficacy of conscious deliberation, reasons sensitivity, the capacity to act in accordance with desires, the capacity to consciously monitor and guide action.* The fear is that being a natural creature, an organism subject to natural law—to causation—will rule out these things. But that is the big mistake. Far from ruling out causation, the concepts of control and self-control *are* causal notions. This is vivid in Daniel Dennett's analyses of the meanings of "control" and "self-control":[7]

According to Dennett, we can define control as follows:

DF. CONTROL: A Controls B if and only if the relation between A and B is such that A can drive B into whichever of B's normal range of states A wants B to be in.

This definition captures most of what we mean when we say "A controls B" when A and B are separate entities. What about when B is a part of A? This would involve self-control: Which we can define as follows:

DF. SELF-CONTROL: For some integrated system S, some subsystem S_a *controls subsystems* S_1 . . . S_n if the relation between S_a and S_1 . . . S_n is such that S_a can *drive* S_1 . . . S_n into the states S_a *wants* them to be in.

The concepts of control and self-control construed in this way are silent about where the causal powers attributed to the controlling mechanisms themselves originate, but the characterizations are thoroughly compatible with there being some such causal antecedents, both ontogenetic and phylogenetic.

Folk Agency

It should be clear, and at the same time somewhat worrisome, that the notions needed to salvage a conception of free thought and action are imprecise folk-psychological ones, for example, attention, conscious deliberation, belief, desire, interest, self-control, and so on. I think we know for sure that neuroscience is not going to find any place for *metaphysical freedom of the will*, since that would involve the neuroscientific vindication of the hypothesis that there is a faculty that initiates thought and action without itself having causal antecedents. The question arises, however, whether there is reason to believe that neuroscience will allow mappings of some sort of the capacities of attending and reasoning and desiring and self-controlling, and so on, that are needed to preserve the naturalistic conception of free action I have been recommending.

Certain philosophers, the eliminative materialists, think that neuro-science spells doom for all our commonsense notions of mind. But that to me seems unlikely. And if it is unlikely, and we are able to give explanations of the capacities of conscious thought and deliberation, of reasons sensitivity, of action guidance, and so on, in neuroscientific terms, the naturalistic conception of voluntariness will be refined but not diminished.

The Epiphenomenalist Suspicion

Besides the eliminative materialist move that suggests that none of com-monsense psychology will withstand the maturing of brain science, there is a somewhat more specific challenge that is raised against the compatibilist view of freedom that I have been defending. I call this challenge "the epiphenomenalist suspicion"—the basic idea is that the conscious mind *must* be causally efficacious for the compatibilist view to get off the ground. But, it is claimed, neuroscience spells doom for that notion of conscious-ness, for a picture of consciousness as causally efficacious. Consciousness, according to some, is a useless epiphenomenon, a noticeable but ineffec-tual side effect of causally more interesting processes taking place within the system. One experiment often cited in making this claim is by Benjamin Libet (1985).[8]

Libet's experiment has been thought by some to prove dualism and by others to secure the case for materialism. I am interested in it here only as it relates to the issue of free, consciously initiated action. If it undermines the idea that there is such a thing, then in addition to worries from tradi-tional metaphysicians, we would have worries internal, as it were to neuro-science, to abandon the idea of free, consciously initiated action as I have defended it so far.

The experiment works as follows: First, subjects are hooked up to elec-troencephalographs, which measure "the readiness potential" in the corti-cal area that is thought to subserve hand movement, and to electromyo-graphs, which measure onset of activity in the hand muscles. Second, subjects are told to spontaneously flex their right hand whenever they feel like it. They are also told "to pay close introspective attention to the instant of the onset of the urge, desire, or decision to perform each such act and to the correlated position of a revolving spot on a clock face (indicating 'clock time'). The subject is also instructed to allow such acts to arise 'sponta-neously,' without deliberately planning or paying attention to the 'pros-pect' of acting in advance."[9] The findings were these: First, in cases where subjects experience no preplanning, the consciousness of an intention to flex occurs about 350 milliseconds after the onset of the readiness potential and about 200 milliseconds before muscle activation. Second, in cases where the subjects reported a feeling of preplanning, of getting ready to spontaneously flex a few seconds before they flexed, they still were able to distinguish this preplanning stage from the immediately following urge to flex. The finding that the readiness potential precedes conscious intention or urge, which precedes muscle movement, was confirmed. Libet writes, "Onsets *of* RP regularly begin at least several hundred ms before reported times for awareness of any intention to act in the case of acts performed ad lib. It would appear, therefore, that some neuronal activity associated with the eventual performance of the act occurs before any (recallable) conscious initiation or intervention. . . . This leads to the conclusion that cerebral initiation of the kind studied . . . can and does usually begin *unconsciously.*"[10] Libet asks, "If the brain can initiate a voluntary act before the appearance of conscious intention, that is, if the initiation of the specific performance of the act is by unconscious processes, is there any role for conscious function?" He answers, "Conscious control can be exerted before the final motor outflow to select or control volitional outcome. The volitional process, initiated unconsciously, can either be consciously permitted to proceed to consummation in the motor act or be consciously 'vetoed.'"[11]

Libet argues that so long as there is veto power, conscious triggering would be redundant. That is, the mind allows the action to proceeed to consummation unless it has reason to stop it. So long as it can stop a motor movement before it occurs, it does not need to actively trigger it.

This experiment is interesting, but one wonders why it generates such surprise and why it is taken by many to be so deflationary, so bad for consciousness. In the first place, the strong evidence that subjects can consciously veto flexion in the two hundred milliseconds between the urge or intention to flex and the response indicates that consciousness can play an important functional role in this particular motor routine. So consciousness is hardly shown to be epiphenomenal by this experiment. Second, it is hard to see what causes surprise at the fact that brain processes precede conscious experience, unless it is, as I suspect, a lurking Cartesian intuition that in voluntary action our conscious intentions are prime movers, themselves unmoved (except possibly by prior intentions).

From a naturalistic perspective, this intuition, familiar as it is, gives rise to a set of deep illusions to be avoided at all costs. According to the naturalist, only some neural activity is conscious. All conscious processes occur in complex causal networks in which they both supervene on certain neural processes and are caused by and cause other mental processes (also supervenient on the neural), some of which are conscious but most of which are not. It would be completely unexpected if all the causal antecedents of conscious mental processes were themselves conscious. In other words, conscious mental processes emerge out of the neural processes that give rise to them. It would be absurd to expect these emergent conscious neural processes to precede the neural processes they arise from.

Analogously, freezing occurs in collections of water molecules whose mean molecular kinetic energy has slowed to thirty-two degrees Fahrenheit. Freezing is caused by water reaching that temperature. But getting to that temperature involves a process of cooling, and it would be absurd to expect freezing to antedate the process that brings it about.

In addition to misunderstanding the nature of emergent properties, the picture of the mind as conscious of all that goes on in it falls prey to a further difficulty. It involves a very inefficient design. The "buzzing confusion" that James (probably incorrectly) thought constituted the experiential world of the infant would be our lot for life if we were aware of everything happening in our nervous system! Third, there is a problem with the interpretation of the experiment. The experiment and most of the discussion about it ask us to picture the experiment this way:

1. Readiness potential (500 ms) → conscious awareness of urge to flex (200 ms) → flexing.

The trouble with this way of conceptualizing things is that it leaves out of view the fact that the subjects are first asked *to make a conscious effort* to let flexion occur spontaneously. To do so, the subjects have to load from conscious awareness an instruction to perform a certain complex task. Perhaps the instruction could be given subliminally to comatose patients or to normal persons in deep sleep. The fact is that in the actual experiment the instructions are given to fully conscious individuals who agree to comply with the experimental instructions and who make an effort to do so. How we load such instructions and get ourselves to do such things is completely closed off to introspection (to mine, anyway). But the power of complex intentions or plans to be carried out once the initial steps have been taken is made vivid in cases where individuals suffer petit mal seizures while driving to some destination and then, while "unconscious," complete the drive to that destination! Once they have reached the destination, they just stop, unless they come out of the seizure-induced sleeplike state. It is a matter of utmost importance that Libet's experiment begins with a discussion of the task and the conscious agreement on the part of the subject to perform as instructed. The right picture, then, is this:

2. Conscious awareness of instructions and conscious self-instruction to comply → (minutes later) flexing readiness potential (500 ms) → conscious awareness of urge to flex (200 ms) → flexing.

The upshot is that conscious processes are not causally inconsequential, even on (1), the narrow description of the experimental situation. Conscious processes serve as the middle link in a three-term chain, and they have the power to inhibit (or veto) the motor response being readied, if the agent so desires. It may be that occurrence of the awareness of the urge to flex two hundred milliseconds before flexion is not part of the cause of flexion in the case where flexion is allowed to go forward. But the fact that flexion can be stopped by a conscious veto strongly suggests that awareness of impending flexion plays the role of broadcasting information about the system that the system can then use to change its course. On (2), the wide description, conscious processes appear at two different stages: first, when instructions are given and the effort to comply is made; second, when the instructions loaded at the first step are actually carried out.

I conclude that Libet's results, far from offering solace to the individual suspicious about the causal powers of conscious intention making processes, are precisely the sort of results one would expect if one believes that conscious processes are subserved by nonconscious neural activity, and that conscious processes play variable but significant causal roles at various points in different cognitive domains.

Brainy Agents

In the end, we can salvage the notion of free thought and action so long as neuroscience does not force us to abandon completely or radically revise the picture of ourselves as creatures who can deliberate, who are sensitive to reasons for and against actions, who have interests and desires, and who can acquire complex views. Since, to the best of my knowledge, there is nothing in neuroscience as it has evolved so far, which calls the reality of these features into question, "the varieties of free will worth wanting," to use Dennett's phrase, are safe. We can safely preserve the notions we need for ascriptions of voluntariness and responsibility. Here are three of the features that need to be preserved; there may well be others. An organism is an agent capable of free action if:

1. *The organism is reasons-sensitive:* An agent is free just in case the agent could have done otherwise if there had been good and sufficient reason.
2. *The organism can self-adjust behavior:* An agent is free just in case the organism is capable, that is, has the ability, to monitor and adjust its current behavior in response to changing thoughts and desires, or of "learning" to respond differently in the future.

3. *The organism is responsible:* An organism is free and subject to attributions of agency and responsibility (praise, blame, etc.) insofar as it has the ability (the relevant capacities) to respond differently in the future than it does now or just did. The capacity to learn is key.

Meaning, Again

Agency, causation, free-action, responsibility, and a meaningful life, are not conceptual enemies but are, in fact, required to make sense of each other. The coevolution of neuroscience, cognitive psychology, psychiatry, and our philosophical and legal conceptions of persons will lead to refinement all around. Our theories of moral and legal judgment cry out for more specific knowledge of the etiology of certain types of action and behavioral patterns. We have already accommodated some of the little we know into our theories of excuses, and our modes of grading varying degrees of responsibility. Some day we may well have the help of a mature neuroscience in helping us to see whether, and to what degree, some individual is incapacitated in his or her ability to exercise conscious choice and guide action by reasons. It will then be up to us to use our best judgment of the neuroscientific facts *and* of the function and purpose of responsibility-ascribing practices in moral life and in the law to decide how to treat the incapacity in question. The neuroscientific facts alone won't tell us what to do with them. That will take what Aristotle called phronesis—knowing how to do the right thing in the right way at the right time, based on an accurate appraisal of the facts. No easy task.

The good news is that there is nothing in our current neuroscience, no implicit core commitments or potential discoveries looming on the horizon, that will remotely suggest that human agency, self-expression, self-control, free action, and the possibility of a meaningful life, a life worth living, ought to be removed from the ontological table of elements. Indeed, neuroscience as it develops will yield deeper understanding of how these capacities are realized and work. It will help us see more clearly what the voluntary-involuntary distinction comes to, and it will yield insight, as it is already doing, about how the biochemistry and functional architecture of different brains subserve both positive and negative attitudes toward oneself and one's life.

Notes

Acknowledgments—This essay began as an invited address to the Society for Neuroscience, Anaheim, California, November 1, 1992.

1. Gilbert Ryle, *The Concept of Mind* (Chicago: University of Chicago Press, 1949), 11.

2. Wilder Penfield, *The Mystery of the Mind* (1975).

3. René Descartes, *Passions of the Soul* (1649), 350, in *The Philosophical Works of Descartes,* eds. E. Haldane and G. Ross (Cambridge, Cambridge University Press, 1968).

4. Roderick Chisolm, *Human Freedom and the Self,* The Lindley Lecture, University of Kansas, 1964, reprinted in *Free Will,* ed. G. Watson (Oxford: Oxford University Press, 1973), 34.

5. John Dewey, "The Ego as a Cause" (1894), reprinted *Philosophy, Psychology, and Social Practice,* ed. J. Rattner, (New York: Capricorn, 1963).

6. John Dewey, *Human Nature and Conduct* (New York: Henry Holt, 1957), 303.

7. D. C. Dennett, *Elbow Room: The Varieties of Free Will Worth Wanting* (Cambridge: MIT Press, 1984), 52–73.

8. See Owen Flanagan, *Consciousness Reconsidered* (Cambridge: MIT Press, 1992).

9. Benjamin Libet, "Unconscious Cerebral Initiative and the Role of Conscious Will in Voluntary Action," *Behavioral and Brain Sciences* (1985) 8: 529–66.

10. Ibid., 536.

11. Ibid., 536–37.

5

Multiple Identity, Character Transformation, and Self-Reclamation

Multiple Identity and Multiplex Identity

Consider the following propositions:

Proposition 1. We abide by a "one self to a customer" rule.[1] Normally, each body houses one person, one self. Having one and only one self is normative for us.

Proposition 2. But identity is scalar. It admits of degrees. Our conception of personal sameness allows for change and transformation. Indeed, our norms of personal and moral development require that the self changes.

Propositions 1 and 2 might seem to conflict. We want each individual to have one and only one self. But we want this self to be malleable enough to undergo even radical changes. We want the self to maintain its identity over the course of a life, and yet we want and expect the self to become complex and multifaceted, and to change, modify, and adjust itself, sometimes radically, over this course.

The prima facie conflict or tension between these two propositions can be reduced by accepting a third proposition:

Proposition 3. The conditions governing personal sameness require not strict identity or absolute sameness but rather that certain relations of psychological continuity and connectedness obtain. We require that there be *narrative connectedness* from the first-person point of view, that I be able to tell some sort of coherent story about my life.

65

In addition, we expect the following to hold:

Proposition 4. The narrative connectedness that obtains is caused in part by active *authorial work* on the agent's part: by working at integration[2] and working at making one's plans and projects materialize.[3]

The overall idea is to think of personal identity as a scalar relation of psychological continuity and connectedness caused in part by the agent's own activity in light of his plans and visions for his own development. Thinking about identity in terms of agency makes sense of future concern, and thus of self-adjustment, reclamation, transformation, and the like. It allows the possibility that I may participate authorially in the creation of a changed person to whom I am nonetheless narratively connected at each point in the reclamation or transformation project.[4]

Augustine's *Confessions* is an autobiography; it is the story of single *self*. This is established in part because Augustine is able to produce an account that narratively links up the multifarious episodes of his life from the first-person point of view. What events he remembers are *all* events in *his* life, and the changes he undergoes from philanderer to Bishop of Hippo are changes that involve, at each point, deployment of his own developing sense of the kind of person he wants to be. Augustine is often thought to be atypical because his transformation was so radical. And indeed it was. But Augustine is also typical because his character is complex and his plans, projects, and desires are multifarious—and they are, to a certain extent, in tension with one another both synchronically and diachronically.

I will refer to a single self that is like this as a *multiplex self*. Normal selves are multiplex. When a single individual experiences herself or expresses her being with different narrators who cannot grasp the connection between or among the narratives or narrative segments, the individual is a *multiple*.

Individuals with multiple personality disorder (MPD) present multiple narrators, multiple selves. These different selves sometimes display different allergies and immunological reactions and have different visual acuity. True believers in MPD think the multiple narrators reflect multiple, functionally and qualitatively distinct selves inside a single body. Skeptics about MPD see suggestible individuals who are capable of mimicking various socially available personas. It seems to me that in either case—whether the individual really experiences what it is like to be each self she displays or is merely adept at simulating or feigning multiplicity—there is a problem. I'm not going to try to resolve the thorny question of exactly in what sense multiplicity exists. I assume only that there are cases in which persons actually become different selves in the sense that there is something it is like for them to be the different selves they display, *or* that there are cases in which individuals feign or mimic alternative selves while under some sort of delusion or misapprehension that they are, in some sense, the self they mimic. Perhaps both kinds of multiplicity exist. It is interesting that the titles of the two newsletters written by MPD patients, "Speaking for Ourselves" and its successor "Many Voices," display, one might say, a certain ambivalence over whether to tie speaking in different tongues to bona fide different selves or merely to represent the phenomenon as involving speaking in different tongues.

I focus on MPD cases because of their special vivacity. But I want it to be clear at the start that I think that MPD cases represent only one of the ways in which the process of identity formation, development, and maintenance can go awry. My aim is to see how the idea of the self as a narrative construct can shed light on multiplicity and the process of transformation from a multiple to a multiplex self, and conversely, to use the phenomena of multiplicity to help us think more clearly about ordinary multiplex selfhood and identity. It might be thought a bad idea to try to analyze and refine two obscure notions in tandem. But for better or worse, that is my strategy. Whether illumination results is for the reader to judge.

Narrative Self-Representation

Many thinkers have converged on the insight that a narrative conception of self is the "essential genre" of self-representation.[5] One useful way of conceiving of the self is as a kind of structured life, structured in part by its temporal components—its beginning, middle, and ending—and by the relations among the various characters who figure in our lives.[6]

Although personal identity proper can be grounded in the thinnest thread of biological or psychological continuity, the sort of connectedness that constitutes a normatively acceptable self or life is the sort that makes for a contentful story that involves an unfolding rationale for the shape it takes.

Why is narrative structure natural? Several reasons come to mind. First, human life in fact has the property of being lived in time. Second, our memories are powerful. We possess the capacity to appropriate our distant past and draw it into the present. Life and consciousness can be as streamlike as you want, but if memory is weak, if the present thought is not powerfully "appropriative" of what has gone before, then no narrative can be constructed. There is simply the here and now. Third, as beings in time, we are navigators. We care how our lives go. Successful concern requires attentiveness to the long term. We look toward the future, attentively both planning insignificant things and making monumental life plans, and we do so with a grasp of our present beliefs and desires and a grasp of who we are, given our past.[7] Fourth, we are social beings. We live in society and in predictable and unpredictable interaction with other people. Characters abound to fill out the complex story of our lives. Fifth, because the story of any individual life is constituted by and embedded in some larger meaning-giving structure and because it is only in terms of this larger structure that a life gains whatever rationale it has for unfolding in the way it does, a life is illuminated, both for the person who lives it and for others, by seeing it against the background of this larger structure.

Although numerous characters appear in our life stories, each of us has but one character that constitutes one's self. With narrative selves the basic principle is, as I have said, "one to a customer." Multiple chapters, novel twists and turns, even radical self-transformations are allowed. But these have to be part of the life of a single self. A self can change, but the changes, we prefer, should make sense. I need to understand your conversion from a hedonist to an ascetic Buddhist in a way that locates *you* both before and after the conversion. In those rare cases where this is not possible, we say that some individual is no longer the same person. From the insider's and outsider's point to view, different judgments may be rendered about narrative flow and personal sameness. Despite my judgment that you are no longer *you*, you may well judge otherwise and see your radical transformation as part of the perfectly coherent narrative of your life.

Oneness reigns when it comes to selves. It makes sense to have one and only one inner persona, given the complexities of rationally guiding action in a complex and ever-changing social world.[8] Severe amnesiacs have less than one full self, whereas persons suffering from multiple personality disorder have too many selves. Normally, persons suffering from MPD can represent the self that is in the driver's seat. Since they are wholly or partly amnesiac of other personalities they house, they cannot represent these selves until they, so to speak, become them.[9] The sort of self that severe amnesiacs have too little of and MPD patients have too many of is the self that is "the center of narrative gravity."[10]

We narratively represent our selves in part in order to answer certain questions of identity. It is useful to distinguish two different aims of self-representation that in the end are deeply intertwined. First, there is self-representation for the sake of self-understanding. This is the story we tell ourselves to understand ourselves for who we are. The ideal here is convergence between self-representation and an acceptable version of the story of our actual identity. Second, there is self-representation for public dissemination, whose aim is underwriting successful social interaction. The two are closely connected. Indeed, the strategic requirements of the sort of self-representation needed for social interaction, together with our tendencies to seek congruence, explain how self-representation intended in the first instance for "my eyes only," and thus, one might think, more likely to remain true, could start to conform to a false projected social image of the self, to a deeply fictional and far-fetched account of the self.

Self-represented identity, when it gets things right, has actual identity (or some aspect of it) as its cognitive object. Because representing the self is an activity internal to a complex but single system, it does not leave things unchanged. The activity of self-representation is partly constitutive of actual identity. This is true in two senses. First, even considered as a purely cognitive activity, self-representation involves the activation of certain mental representations and cognitive structures. Once self-representation becomes an ongoing activity, it realigns and recasts the representations and structures already in place. Second, the self as represented has motivational bearing and behavioral effects. Often this motivational bearing is congruent with motivational tendencies that the entire system already has. In such cases, placing one's conception of the self into the motivational circuits enables certain gains in ongoing conscious control and in the fine-tuning of action. Sometimes, especially in cases of severe self-deception, the self projected for both public and first-person consumption may be strangely and transparently out of kilter with what the agent is like. In such cases, the self as represented is linked with the activity of self-representation but with little else in the person's psychological and behavioral economy. Nonetheless, such misguided self-representation helps constitute, for reasons I have suggested, the misguided person's actual full identity.

One further point is worth emphasizing. Although self-represented identity is identity from the subjective point of view, it invariably draws on available theoretical models about the nature of the self in framing its reflexive self-portrait. We represent ourselves by way of various publicly available hermeneutic strategies. Psychoanalytically inspired self-description is most familiar in our culture. But genetic and neurobiological models are increasingly visible in the self-understandings of ordinary people. When multiples (MPD patients) present "alters," they invariably present themselves as characters from the historical and contemporary stock of characters known about by persons in their culture.

The Center of Narrative Gravity

The self that is "the center of narrative gravity"[11]—the self that answers questions about who a person is, what that person aims at and cares about—is a complex construct. It is both expressed and created in the process of self-representation. The self in this sense, what I call "self-represented identity," is a causally efficacious part of the whole system, and it affects both the cognitive content and the qualitative character of new experiences. The causal efficacy of a representation of the self is fairly obvious when a person is actively engaged in self-representing. It is also plausible to think that once a complex model of the self has been constructed and is in place, it exists as a complex dispositional structure in the brain and is often involved in structuring experience, albeit unconsciously. That is, the causal-efficacy-of-the-self model is compatible with its making only infrequent and partial appearances in consciousness and with its having differential effects in different situations from behind the phenomenological scenes.

The construction of a self begins in earliest childhood as parents try to shape the emerging character of the charges they love. Since we abide the "one self per customer" rule, we try to assist the child in building an integrated self that comprehends basic social norms and is equipped with a system of beliefs, desires, and values that will help it to live successfully and well. The "one self to a customer" principle is not just an arbitrary social construction. Productive relations with a single body favor minimal cognitive dissonance and maximal integration at the level of conscious thought and action guidance (although harmony at the top may well belie all sorts of disagreement and competition among lower-level processors).[12]

In both normal and abnormal cases, the process of constructing the self starts in interaction with elders, and it begins well before the child uses language. There is some evidence that the child, if given social interaction, may be innately disposed to develop a theory of mind, a theory of its own mind and those of others, a theory primed by evolution to frame the self and other selves as single integrated intentional systems.[13] The parents provide models for constructing the self in what they do and say and in how they express their own formed beings. Increasingly, as time proceeds and especially with the development of speech, a child engages her parents with her own emerging self as *agent* and modifies their attempts to shape her. With language, time, maturity, and elaborate and multifarious interactions with others, there emerges the self, a relatively autonomous and integrated self.

The construction and maintenance of the self involves many players. Whether I know it or not, "others made me, and in various ways continue to make me the person I am."[14] Our selves are multiply authored. Lest this sound too deflationary, it is important to emphasize that normally we are one of the main authors of our identity. Once our character is well formed and we have a good grasp of it, our powers of self-authorship increase dramatically. We gain the power to guide our life more self-consciously in terms of our model of who we are and who we want to become. We modify and adjust our self-conception unconsciously and effortlessly in response to social feedback, as well as consciously, with effort, and with mixed success in response to our judgment of the fit between who we are and who we aspire to be.

Coming eventually to consciously grasp one's self does not require—at least in the early stages—that there already is a full-blown self in place. There is wide agreement among psychologists and philosophers who have thought carefully about identity formation that it proceeds largely unconsciously and that many aspects of identity never come into view for the agent who has that identity.[15]

The main point is that selves are just like most other things. They are complex effects that do not in any way precede their causes. They don't need to. They emerge naturally in complex interactions with the world and other persons. And they acquire autonomy and increased causal efficacy as they develop, mature, and come to constitute character and personality.

Self-represented identity is emblematic. Multiplex selves in complex environments display different parts of their narrative to different audiences. Different selves—my philosopher self, my baseball-coach self, my religious self, my parental self—are played for different audiences. Different audiences see who we are differently. Different selves surface in different interpersonal ecological niches. Displaying a self and getting my audience (or myself) to posit one or the other as my center of narrative gravity is, in a sense, to produce a sort of illusion, since to me, in the first person, my different selves are part of an integrated and unified narrative that contains, as proper parts, the different selves that I sometimes display in isolation. What distinguishes a multiplex self from a multiple self is, first and foremost, the fact that a multiplex self is not amnesiac with respect to these selves, they permeate each other in ways the selves of multiples typically do not. Furthermore, I draw my selves together, through the force of narrative gravity, and I comprehend my self in terms of a single, centered narrative in which they all fit together (but not without tension, various confusions, and much second-guessing). Taken together and consciously interwoven, they give my life what I take to be its unique qualitative character.[16]

The self is an extemely complex construct. Indeed, it is multiplex. Different portions or aspects of the self are played in different environments. Nonetheless, there are pressures to coordinate and bring into reflective equilibrium the different ways of conceiving the self. I speak, therefore, of the *self model* to refer to the highest-order model of the self that contains the various components of the self as proper parts or aspects. We can think of the self model as a construct that draws functional distinctions among various roles, characteristics, and personas, but recognizes these as part of one self and experiences the self as a qualitative whole. Thinking of the self model as involving recognition of functionally distinct aspects of a qualitatively integrated self allows us to think of the model as a complex construct without advancing the dubious idea of true proliferation of the self. The effects of different *aspects* of the self can explain everything that several different selves can explain without undermining the phenomenological sense of coherence of the self that most people experience. Most people, but not people with MPD perhaps, experience qualitative wholeness of being across time.

The person for whom my narrative self plays is I, a whole emotionally rich information-processing system from which the narrative self emerges and for which it plays a crucial role. Often I express and grasp snatches of my narrative self and utilize these representations in monitoring and guiding my life. This way of thinking about our reflexive powers makes matters fairly unmysterious. I am a system constituted in part by a certain narrative conception of self. Sometimes I hold that conception in view as I think about things. I, being more than my narrative self, can comprehend it, utilize it, and, in concert with outside forces, adjust it. What am I? This organism. This thinking thing.

The Fictional and Nonfictional Self

I have suggested that the self is constructed. Dennett is committed to the stronger thesis that the self that is the center of narrative gravity is a fiction, a useful fiction, but a fiction nonetheless. "Centres of gravity" are "fictional objects . . . [that] have only the properties that the theory that constitutes them endowed them with."[17] The idea that the self is a fiction is, in part, a way of expressing the fact that it is, for the reasons given, a construction. Mother Nature does not give us a robust self. She starts us off caring about homeostasis, and she equips us with the equipment to distinguish "me" from "not me." But she hardly wires in a personality or an identity. Identity is the joint production of many sources, including one's own evolving self.

To conceive of the self as a fiction seems right for four reasons: it is an open-ended construction; it is filled with vast indeterminate spaces, and a host of tentative hypotheses about what I am like, that can be filled out and revised post facto; it is pinned on culturally relative narrative hooks; and it expresses ideals of what one wishes to be but is not yet.

But there are two important respects in which the analogy of the self with a piece of fiction is misleading. First, there is the issue of constraints. The author of a true piece of fiction has many more degrees of freedom in creating her characters than we have in spinning the tale of our selves. Despite the indeterminacies operative in construction of the self and despite the fact that different narrative emphases will be reinforced in different communities, there are more firm and visible epistemic constraints in construction of the self than in ordinary construction of fiction. There are, after all, the things we have done, what we have been through as embodied beings, and the characteristic dispositions we reveal in social life. Third parties will catch us if we take our story too far afield. We may also catch ourselves. There are selection pressures to keep the story that one reveals to oneself and to others in some sort of harmony with the way one is living one's life.

Second, some people, of course, are massively self-deceived. Self-deception only makes sense if selves are not totally fictive, that is, only if there are some facts constraining what is permitted in our self narrative. So real selves are fictional to a point. But they are less fictional than fictional selves because they are more answerable to the facts. The self can be a construct or model, a "center of narrative gravity," a way of self-representation, without being a fiction in the problematic sense. Biographies and autobiogtraphies are constructs. But if they are good biographies or autobiographies, they are non-fictional or only semifictional. For Dennett, there are, it seems, only normal fictive selves and invasive fictive selves, such as those suggested by abusive caretakers who posit imaginary selves for the abused child.[18] One father gave his daughter Old Testament names, displaying at once his anti-Semitism and his need to sanctify his great sinfulness. Not surprisingly, this sort of abuse is sometimes causally effective in giving multiplicity a foothold. That said, there is considerable and increasing controversy, as yet empirically unresolved, over the degree to which MPD depends on actual abuse.[19]

The distinction between fictive and nonfictive selves is important, but its application in the case of multiples is exceedingly tricky. On one plausible interpretation, multiples qualitatively feel, and therefore first-personally are, the self they narratively posit, for the time of the posit. Whether the posited self is real or fictive depends, among other things, on whether the narratively posited self has the features and has done the deeds that the narrator claims, and on whether third parties recognize the posited self as having historical standing from the objective point of view.

Alters on equal qualitative footing from the first-person point of view will not have equal status from the third-person point of view. Not surprisingly, the differences between first- and third-person judgments about the realism and the historical validity of various alters will determine the direction of therapy.

Unmaking Multiplicity

We are in a better position now to address directly the issue of how modification of the self might work, even in extreme cases where there are several or many selves in one individual. One thing we have seen so far is that we needn't frame the task as one of how a multiple can regain unity, since in a certain sense no one is a unity. Selves, even very normal selves, are multiplex. The project is to move from multiplicity to mutiplexity. Multiplex selves live lives that are continuous, connected, functionally coherent, and qualitatively more or less homogeneous. Multiplex selves are integrated.[20] Or to put it another way, even if multiplex persons are perceived as unintegrated by some third-party norms, they are integrated if they are in control of their own mode of organization of disorganization. Individuals with MPD are unintegrated, despite there being a certain amount of integration within each alter" "Alters who claim (and appear) to be aware of another alter's mental states and actions, typically refer to them as 'his' or 'hers', not as 'mine.'"[21] Furthermore, there is no center of control.

How might a multiple become whole again? There are two senses of wholeness that seem relevant. The first is the multiple becomes whole in the sense of reexperiencing himself or herself as a single qualitatively integrated self, as a single qualitatively integrated center of narrative gravity. The second is that the multiple becomes whole in the sense of having something like a complete personality. The notion of a complete personality is a normative concept, and it can be satisfied in multitudinous ways.

The overall idea is that the individual experience himself or herself as whole in the first sense and, in addition, that his or her personality display the kind of fullness or completeness that we deem necessary for attributing a full *character* in the second, normative sense.

The question of how a multiple might become whole *again* makes sense for the first sense of wholeness, for multiples presumably once experienced themselves as single centers of self-consciousness and were once single centers. Indeed, even as multiples, they often experience wholeness of being in this sense. The trouble is that they experience themselves as qualitatively distinct centers of self-consciousness at different times. The aim, then, is to have the multiple regain the sense of a single center of self that is the same center over time. Third parties definitely prefer that persons they deal with be whole in this first sense. Multiples, once multiplex, prefer it as well.[22]

The question of how a multiple might become whole *again* makes less sense for the second sense of wholeness, character wholeness or personality wholeness. This is because multiples often begin to dissociate at a very early age. They were never whole or complete in the normative sense of having achieved a stable, mature, full character.

This last point suggests that if a multiple becomes whole *again,* it cannot usually involve becoming who he or she "really" is or was beneath or behind the multiplicity of selves he or she displays. This is because there is no self he or she "really" is or was before multiplicity took hold. This suggests that thinking of self-reclamation in any literal sense may be misleading, since it suggests getting back again what one once was or had.

To explain this point and extend reflection on the transformation from multiplicity to multiplexity, it will be useful to say a little more about the etiology and progression of multiplicity. According to the philosopher Stephen E. Braude,

> Multiple personality has two main causal determinants. The first is the capacity for profound dissociation; in fact MPD patients tend to be highly hypnotizable. The second is a history of (usually severe and chronic) childhood trauma—typically, a combination of emotional, physical, and sexual abuse. The significance of high hypnotizability (in this case, really, *self*-hypnotizability) is that MPD patients have a coping mechanism at their disposal not available to victims of abuse or trauma who do not become multiples. To put it roughly, through dissociation the subject is able to avoid experiencing or dealing with an intolerable episode by turning it over to an alternate personality (or *alter*) who undergoes those experiences in his place.[23]

Modern multiples average between six and sixteen personalities. One author reported a patient with 4,500 alters. Not surprisingly, the proliferation of alters appears to give them a certain ghostly shape. So Braude writes that many alters "are perhaps better described as personality *fragments,* since their functions tend to be highly circumscribed, and because they do not exhibit the more extensive range of traits and dispositions found in more personality-like alters".[24] But clinicians agree that even the more "personality-like alters" are "two-dimensional compared to normal persons, even a very young child."[25]

It is not at all surprising that a person with powers to do so might create an alter to fend off the pain of abuse and the recognition that someone he or she loves is an abuser. But it is obscure why there is so often proliferation beyond one alter. One hypothesis is that proliferation is a complex effect of therapeutic suggestion, involving the therapist's belief in multiplicity and his conveying to the patient the possibility of fitting the description (indeed, a savvy patient may well know that multiplicity is a genuine and increasingly popular way to be damaged or express damage). This is why one leading worker in the field thinks that MPD is "grossly overdiagnosed [especially among females] . . . and is heavily dependent upon cultural influences for both its emergence and its diagnosis."[26] Aldridge-Morris recommends that one "should only diagnose multiple personality when there is corraborative evidence that complex and integrated alter egos, with amnesiac barriers, existed prior to therapy and emerge without hypnotic intervention by clinicians."[27] Braude is less skeptical about the existence of MPD, but he is skeptical about determining the exact nature and character of the predissociative self and of there being some determinate number and types of personalities a given MPD patient has even if they have not, so to speak, shown themselves yet. "It is far more reasonable to maintain that a multiple's array of alters *at any time* represents merely one of many possible dissociative solutions to contingent problems in living."[28] The philosopher Ian Hacking thinks that "many, or most, but not all, of the panoply of alters, up to 100 in number, are a product of a therapy."[29] Hacking rejects the idea that the "entire array of alters is a real part of the patient's structure of personalities." And he thinks that there is no answer to the question of how many alters a multiple has before he or she displays them. Multiplicity is potentiality. How many and what type of multiplicity develops depends on the nature of the therapy, the cultural availability of alter types, the patient's knowledge of these types, individual capacities to dissociate, and so on. Just as it is neither true nor false that there is a good lacrosse player inside me now (I've never played), even if, after trying lacrosse, I become good at it, so too it is neither true nor false that some multiple has at time t_1 the alters that he or she displays for the first time at t_2.

In any case, there is considerable and increasing controversy, as yet empirically unresolved, over the degree to which MPD depends on actual abuse,[30] on therapeutic suggestion, or on an individual's knowledge of the possibility of adopting this form of sickness or defense and their powerful abilities to self-hypnotize.[31] Commitment to both the reality of MPD and the assessment of it as a pathological solution to problems of living are compatible with a certain agnosticism about its exact causes. What seems fairly clear is that some cases of MPD are caused by actual abuse.

The question arises, When a person who has had her identity mutilated during personality formation, who has been so deflected in the normal project of finding or maintaining a unified personality, tries to gain unity or tries to transform herself, *toward which self, old or new, is she trying to transform herself?* And if she is a multiple, which self, if any, orchestrates the change? To answer this question, we need to clarify the nature of what, in the literature, is called the *host* personality or the *primary* personality, since one obvious thought is that the host orchestrates the change.

Indeed, until very recently it was thought that the project of therapy with multiples involved reintegrating the alters with the host. One trouble with conceptualizing things in this way is that the host is usually a very emotionally flat self, and many of the alters have chatacteristics that one should not much want. The integration of a host with all its alters gets you a radically transformed but more or less unified personality. However, it also gets you a limited self, normatively speaking. Remember, the host is at best a very damaged root system, and the alters are all creations to maintain damage control in a radically unhealthy environment. Furthermore, even if such a reintegrated self has resources to go on, that is, even if the victim, once reintegrated, possesses the agentic capacities to try to make a better life for herself, these resources are, for the same reasons, likely to be very poorly developed and malformed. To be sure, such persons can be helped. But we would be less than honest if we denied that in many such cases the damage is both real and irremedial.

Another trouble Braude puts as follows:

> One striking feature of the recent literature on MPD is that one sees almost no references to *primary* personalities. By contrast, around the turn of the century it was commonplace to refer to alters as either primary or secondary. There seem to be two main reasons for the current reluctance to designate an alter as primary. First, within the personality system discovered by the clinician, there may be no personality whose *role* within the system is primary in any deep way. . . . One might think that the *presenting* personality should be considered primary. But that alter often turns out to be relatively recent and fairly peripheral in the multiple's total system of alters. Similarly, there might be an alter who acts as *host* for the others, or who initially shows his or her face to the world before yielding to alters awaiting their appropriate times to emerge. And there might be alters who—for a time, at least—dominate the multiple's life. But host personalities might serve no vital function other than serving as 'masters of ceremonies' (so to speak), and both they and dominant personalities generally may be replaced by others who dominate for a while or act as host.[32]

Traditionally, the term "primary personality" referred to the personality that had historical primacy, the one that was there before multiplicity took over. The trouble with this way of conceptualizing things is that although there was normally some single center of self-consciousness prior to multiplicity, there is no basis, for the reasons just given, to think that there was anything like a complete personality in place prior to multiplicity. If all splitting took place in late adolescence or adulthood, then it would be possible that there was. But because dissociation typically begins in childhood, there is no reason to think that there is usually a bona fide personality in place that was historically primary and might be regained or, what is different, is worth regaining.

Indeed, there is little justification for regarding any active personality as the historically primary one, even if we presume that there was a complete personality in place prior to becoming a multiple. This is because, even when there was some single, historically memorable character in place prior to multiplicity, "rarely (if ever) does an alter seem to be *that* personality, or any clear evolution or descendant of that personality."[33]

The principle reason for this has to do with the functional specificity of alternate personalities and a pair of related phenomena called *attribute distribution* and *attribute depletion*. In general, clinicians believe that as alters are created to deal with quite specific traumas, the traits and abilities manifested by or latent in the predissociative personality begin to get distributed throughout the members of the personality system. Moreover, as alters proliferate, they apparently become increasingly specialized, and one is less likely to find any personality having the complexity or range of functions that might have been (but usually were not) possessed by the subject prior to the onset of splitting or that have the shape of a whole self.

How might a person overcome the damage to her identity after suffering from physical or sexual abuse as a child and developing an identity scarred by this abuse and taking the defensive route of multiplicity? One image is this: The abused person consciously accepts that these awful things have happened to her, have ruined her self-esteem, have made her identify with certain unworthy values and characteristics of her abusers, and have, in engendering multiplicity, created massive identity confusion in her. Armed with this recognition, she simply decides—by executive fiat, as it were—to move on, to reclaim her "real self" or make a "new" self, and to allow the scarred and mutilated self or selves to pass into oblivion.

But this view is much too Panglossian. First, there is the problem of finding a self with the power to set out and execute such orders. Second, there is the problem mentioned earlier with the idea of reclaiming a "real self." Besides the problem of attribute depletion and distribution and problems with the ideas of a host or primary personality that is most "real," there is also the problem that if one accepts that a self is a center of narrative gravity, then a multiple has to engage in the project of *self-dissolution*. Since self-dissolution is a bad and dangerous project in normal cases, it is hard to see why it wouldn't constitute yet another form of damage to a multiple to have to undermine and dissociate from selves she has come to identify with to various degrees.

Perhaps this is why the standard way of thinking about curing multiplicity is framed as involving *integration* or *reintegration,* although for reasons we have seen, the picture cannot be one of drawing all the dissociated selves back into the single narrative center of some host self (except in a sense to be explained shortly) or into some historically primary self. Furthermore, since alter selves often possess conflicting traits, desires, and values, hate each other, and so on, they cannot simply be reunited—at least not without undergoing constitutional changes, allowing various successions, and reaching certain peace treaties.

There is another reason that the aim of therapy or integration or reclamation of self cannot involve bringing into a single unified center of narrative gravity the "lives" lived by each alter. This is because some, indeed many, of these lives are utter confabulations, involving confabulated persons with confabulated lives. For example, many multiples typically become good at telling what they have been up to since their last appearance as a narrative center. But to lay claim to frequent visits to Disneyland and to consorting with Madonna, because that is what one of my alters says he has been doing while not making appearances, is to allow my unified narrative to be guided too much by the shape of other narratives that are perhaps in some sense notionally lived but are, in large measure, fictive.

We want the eventual integrated center of narrative gravity of a multiple to seek convergence with his or her actual full identity. This will require recognition of what it felt like to be the various alters and of what the alters did and thought they did. But it will not, indeed it should not, involve appropriating the memories of all the alters as true memories. Among other things, there will be chaos and too many overlapping, incompatible events if this is allowed. Nor can the move from multiple to multiplex personhood involve retaining the autonomous feel of each alter if there really is to be a return to a single narrative center. This, I admit, is a thorny issue. I am not saying that a multiple should remember *all* that he or she thinks he or she was and did as each alter and disclaim what he or she did not do. It is probably best if a lot is forgotten. What I am claiming is that insofar as the individual remembers being certain ways, having certain traits, and having done certain things, that individual will need to mark off certain acts and traits as *alien* and *undesirable* and certain memories as false. Living out a narrative makes certain things true, but not everything. Normal multiplex selves face the problem of making their narrative self cohere with their actual identity and shedding undesirable characteristics. Multiple selves face this problem in spades. They not only need to see certain contentful acts as misattributed; they must also come to see some of the selves who allegedly did the things that never really happened as *alien*, fictive, unwanted, and undesirable in some strong sense. It will not be a mistake to think that they once felt or thought in certain ways or even believed that they did certain things. It will just be that they will want to disengage from certain alters and deny that some of the things the alter thought it did were done. In cases where the alters did in fact do things that are not consonant with the projected ideal, these will need to be accepted as done, but by one of the individual's now conceptually *alien* selves.

The proposal to which this is leading is this: Something like integration is part of what it takes to move from being multiple to multiplex. But not all aspects of all alters can or should be integrated. The therapeutic process will involve some disidentification, some dissolution of self. This is a bad thing because it is alienating. But it is not unconditionally bad. It is usually worse being a multiple or living lies. Furthermore, the alienation involved in shearing alters is mitigated somewhat when a multiple comes to see the ways in which certain of his or her alters are understandable as defensive maneuvers but are not the sort of selves one should want to be.

What I have said so far leaves open the question of which self orchestrates the process of change. Since I have expressed skepticism about the idea of a host or primary personality or a single "real self" beneath the manifold clutter, it becomes hard to say which self orchestrates the difficult transformation required. My view is that no particular self is necessary as orchestrator, so long as some self seizes executive control and projects a model, even an inchoate one, of a healed multiplex self. This self model held in view and encouraged in therapy, as it certainly is socially by the "one self to a customer" principle, can lead, especially in highly suggestible (hypnotizable) persons, to the breakdown of amnesiac barriers and can engender the various compromises, dissolutions, and integrations required for personal wholeness in the two senses discussed earlier.

The idea that active consciousness of self and modeling an improved self can be causally efficacious is not mysterious.[34] We needn't even think of some single self as in charge of working over a family of alters. Let every self be an alter. It makes no difference, so long as some alter comes forward with the strong desire for the system to become whole, and so long as the circumstances of that individual's life afford him or her the therapeutic environment to do the work required.

It is not even necessary to think that once the process of becoming multiplex begins, the alter who puts forward or embraces the plan to become whole again stays in place as orchestrator. The picture of one self at the head of a council table talking over matters with various ghostly selves, each in turn abandoning their seat at the table and entering the self at the table's head, is misleading in a variety of ways. Among other things, it stays too close to the picture of an alter with primacy, as if the host's shape and character set down the basic parameters or guidelines for the operation of making the person whole again. Indeed, some alters are easier to work with than others (both first-personally and third-person-ally), and there may be certain traits of the alter who announces the plan to become whole that are maintained throughout. But there is no self, especially once multiplicity is deemed undesirable from the first-person point of view, who isn't in certain respects ghostly or at least a candidate for being booted out of the club. The project is to have some alter announce an action plan based on the normative ideal of multiplex wholeness and then to have the cognitive system, in conjunction with a therapist, work out a way of conforming both the narrative center and the actual life to the envisioned ideal. Since the multiplex self at the end of therapy did not exist at the beginning of the effort to become whole, there is a sense in which it is new. But because becoming that self involves an active, agentic working over of possibilities, ideals, and narrative structures available in the multiple, there is, in a certain sense, continuity and authorial connect-edness. Multiplicity ends when a single multiplex narrative center is achieved. The multiple has recovered in the sense that he or she has gotten better. But the multiple has not recovered any self that he or she once was or that was lying beneath the surface wholly integrated and waiting to emerge. The whole process is a complex one involving at once some recovery and reclamation, some evolution, some transformation, and some creation. While a multiple is a multiple, it is fair to say that she is not the same person she was before she became a multiple. This is because when a multiple is a multiple, she is a cluster of narrative fissions, many of which, indeed too many of which, are the closest continuer of whatever antecedent self there was before fissioning took place. Paradoxically, however, when a multiple becomes multiplex again, we *can* think of the individual as the same person throughout her life. This is because in regaining a single center of narrative gravity, the individual will regain memory connections to her premultiple life, as well as memories about her alters during her life as a multiple. Furthermore, and as important as the memory connections, the individual will achieve multiplex wholeness through efforts involving active consciousness of self and projection of who she wants to become—recognizing incompletely at first, what she is like now.[35]

Authorship of Self, Therapeutic Rage, and Moral Luck

One way such passing from multiplicity to multiplexity in therapy of multiples involves anger, rage, and fury at the abuse. This rage may pass;

perhaps it is even best that it eventually pass. But experiencing it and directing it at the perpetrator of one's abuse is typically a necessary condition for moving on. If this is right, then what P. F. Strawson called the reactive attitudes are backward-looking but at the same time are essential components of moving forward, of identity reclamation, transformation, and so on. Certain authorial transformations may *require* blame, fury, anger, and rage at the victimizer. When the blame, anger, and rage are vivid, consciously recognized, and actively orchestrated by the victim, the work of overcoming is most likely to succeed. In such cases where the agent engages her own reactive attitudes and uses them to excise damage, it is also safe to say that we have the same person on the other side of the transformation. When the process works more unconsciously and with little agent involvement, it is less clear what to say about sameness of identity.

So far I have been thinking of cases where moving forward requires shearing aspects of self-identity that are unworthy, unwanted, and imposed without the agent's own involvement. What is shorn is guided in some important respect by some image of the self the agent intends to reclaim or become. In cases of multiple personality disorder, unlike some other identity disorders, venting all one's anger at the external source of one's malformation is straightforwardly justified. Parental abuse is a paradigm case in which the parent or caretaker has grossly violated moral norms and has caused the malformation. Any complicity that the child or her grown-up self may feel is inappropriate.[36] The trouble is that philosophical or legal clarity about where fault lies is of little help to a damaged person who feels as if she has been party to her own ruination. Indeed, it is partly constitutive of her ruination that she feel this way. There is some reason to believe that such cases are made more difficult for victims because the culture at large has problematic views about complicity, and thereby makes it harder for victims to overcome these feelings. We know this is true in the case of rape. This suggests that more refined views widely shared by philosophers, legalists, therapists, and the public at large could change the climate of assumptions about complicity and thereby help victims not to be so tempted to blame themselves for what they in no way deserve. But this is easier said than done.

One final concern is this. I've been focusing on MPD as a problem of individuals to be solved in concert with professionals. But it is important to keep in mind that MPD reflects and raises problems that transcend individuals: problems of communal responsibility and of social practices with deep historical roots that lead to the malformation of many persons. In almost every case of abuse, there is a point to rage at the abuser. Such rage is a necessary part of moving forward, of identity repair and reclamation. The problem, however, is that any close look at almost any abuser will suggest an explanation in that abuser's life history that will explain why they themselves are so awful and why they did what they did.[37]

This point seems to me to raise some especially difficult problems. Victims of oppression and abuse need to feel and express rage at the perpetrators of that abuse, and they need to blame these individuals for the harm these individuals have caused them. One might think that it is the rage that is important and not what it is directed at, and thus that it could just as well be directed at the larger context of what caused one's abuser to be the way he is rather than at the abuser himself. I have trouble thinking this is true. The overall view does seem, as Gary Watson puts it, to simultaneously demand and preclude that we regard perpetrators of evil as victims. If we allow the considerations that preclude directing rage and blame at some individual to win out, we are in danger of losing focus on the very capacities of agency that give the victimized the power, courage, and confidence to try to go on. But if we give in to the considerations that direct *all* the blame at the perpetrator, then we are in a sense simply blaming another victim. So we seem to need to keep both points of view in mind at once, despite the tension between them.

This is a familiar plight, once philosophical reflection reaches a certain depth. But it is nonetheless troubling. One way of making it less troubling is to think of what could happen that would require less use of this cognitively dissonant solution of both blaming particular agents for the harm they cause and seeing the harm they cause as something they are caused to do. One thing that would reduce the need for the cognitively dissonant solution is there being less evil, less harm, less personality malformation, less abuse and exploitation. How could there be less of these things? I admit that I have little in the way of a detailed plan about how to reduce these things. But I do know that it requires collective work to change the forms of life in which evil flourishes. At this point work on identity, agency, and ethics must yield to the work of politics, to the work of political action designed to change poisonous social structures. This, it seems to me, is where the solution lies, but it involves the hardest work of all.

Notes

Acknowledgments—I began thinking about some of the issues discussed in this chapter when I was invited to comment on Claudia Card's paper "Responsibility and Moral Luck" at the Eastern Division Meetings of the American Philosophical Association in December 1989. I am grateful to George Graham and Lynn Stephens for their immensely perceptive and helpful comments on several earlier versions of this chapter. Jennifer Radden and Ruth Anna Putnam also provided especially close critical readings. My colleagues at Wellesley helped when they read the chapter for our departmental seminar, as did audiences at Oberlin, Wake

Forest, the University of Utah, Clemson, and Syracuse. Virgil Aldrich, Michael Lynch, Todd May, Philip Peterson, and Peter van Inwagen made especially helpful points. Steven Braude neatly identified the main difference between us as involving the need to posit some sort of "transcendental ego" in order for self-construction to get going. Braude thinks we need such an ego; I think not. It should be said that MPD is currently being called DPD (dissouative-personality disorder).

1. D. C. Dennett, "The Origins of Selves," *Cogito* 2 (1989): 163–73.

2. I want to emphasize from the start that when I speak of integration, I do not posit some particular model of a "well-integrated person." The crucial thing is that whatever form integration takes, there is a first-person qualitative unity of the experience of the self and this integration (which can come in very disorganized forms) is in some large measure under one individual's control capacities.

3. Christine Korsgaard writes, "Authorial psychological connectedness is consistent with drastic changes, provided these changes are the result of actions by the person herself or reactions for which she is responsible [1989]." "Personal Identity and the Unity of Agency: A Kantian Response to Parfit." *Philosophy and Public Affairs* 18 (1989): 101–32.

4. Throughout this chapter I am using terms like "self" or "person," even "I," to mean that which grounds or constitutes personality, rather that whatever is denoted by "I" in its strict indexical use. Issues like MPD, as treated within philosophy of psychology, have important implications for questions of personal identity, including metaphysical questions of numerical identity over time. But it is best if we leave the issue of the meaning and reference of the essential indexical "I," in its strict metaphysical sense, to one side here.

5. J. S. Bruner, *In Search of Mind: Essays in Autobiography* (New York: Harper and Row, 1983); J. S. Bruner, *Actual Minds, Possible Worlds* (Cambridge, Mass.: Harvard University Press, 1986); D. C. Dennett, "Why Everyone Is a Novelist," *Times Literary Supplement* (September 16–22, 1988): 1016–22; D. C. Dennett, "The Origins of Selves," *Cogito* 21 (1989): 163–73; F. Kermode, *The Sense of an Ending: Studies in the Theory of Fiction* (New York: Oxford University Press, 1967); A. MacIntyre, *After Virtue* (Notre Dame, Ind.: Notre Dame University Press, 1981).

6. D. Spence, *Narrative Truth and Historical Truth: Meaning and Interpretation in Psychoanalysis* (New York: W. W. Norton, 1982), thinks that continuity, coherence, and comprehensiveness are the ideals of narrative explanation. I favor more emphasis on correspondence truth in thinking about narrative selves, and I think that our expectations about comprehensiveness are moderate.

7. M. Bratman, *Intentions, Plans, and Practical Reason* (Cambridge, Mass.: Harvard University Press, 1987).

8. Dennett, "The Origins of Selves," 171.

9. This is true of "unreclaimed" multiples but not of "reclaiming" multiples, who can, indeed must, represent the different selves they house. Furthermore, even "unreclaimed" and "unreclaiming" multiples sometimes speak of or write about alters, but they do so from the third-person point of view and often without the knowledge that the alters are their alters.

10. Dennett, "Why Everyone Is a Novelist."

11. Ibid.

12. Dennett writes, "There is in every country on earth a Head of State. . . . That is not to say that a nation lacking such a figurehead would cease to function day-to-day. But it is to say that in the longer term it may function much better if it does have one. . . . The drift of the analogy is obvious. In short, a human being too may need an inner figurehead—especially given the complexities of human social life" ("The Origins of Selves," 171).

13. H. M. Wellman, *The Child's Theory of Mind* (Cambridge, Mass.: MIT Press, 1990).

14. M. Sandel, *Liberalism and the Limits of Justice* (New York: Cambridge University Press, 1982), 143.

15. E. H. Erickson, *Identity: Youth and Crisis* (New York: Norton, 1968); J. Kagan, *The Nature of the Child* (New York: Basic Books, 1984); J. Kagan, *Unstable Ideas: Temperament, Cognition, and Self* (Cambridge, Mass.: Harvard University Press, 1989); M. Sandel, *Liberalism and the Limits of Justice* (New York: Cambridge University Press, 1982); D. Stern, *The Interpersonal World of the Infant* (New York: Basic Books, 1985); C. Taylor, *Sources of Self: The Making of Modern Identity* (Cambridge, Mass.: Harvard University Press, 1989).

Erickson writes that the process of identity formation is "a process taking place on all levels of mental functioning. . . . This process is, luckily, and necessarily, for the most part unconscious except where inner conditions and outer circumstances combine to aggravate a painful, or elated, 'identity-consciousness,'" (*Identity*, 22–23). Furthermore, our innate temperamental traits (Kagan, *Unstable Ideas*), our differential natural intelligences (Howard Gardner, *Frames of Mind: The Theory of Multiple Intelligences,* New York: Basic Books, 1983), are productive forces in identity formation from the start. These aspects of our self may never be seen very clearly in the first-person in self-representation, but they are indispensable pieces of the puzzle of who we are. They are causally efficacious aspects of our actual full identity.

16. This is why we should be wary of William James's claim *"A man has as many social selves as there are individuals who recognize him* and carry an image of him in their mind. To wound any one of these images is to wound him. . . . We may practically say that he has as many different social selves as there are distinct *groups* of persons about whose opinion he cares" (*Psychology: The Briefer Course,* New York: Harper and Row, 1961, 46 First published 1892).

17. Dennett, "Why Everyone Is a Novelist," 1016.

18. Dennett, "The Origins of Selves."

19. See G. K. Ganaway, "Historical versus Narrative Truth: Classifying the Role of the Exogenous Trauma in the Etiology of MPD and Its Variants," *Dissociation* 2, no. 4 (1989): 205–20.

20. "Although non-multiples may dissociate in any number of ways, and even experience amnesia, they tend nevertheless to retain only one center of self-consciousness. No matter how differently a non-multiple might act, think, or feel about himself on separate occasions, those changes generally 'refer' or apply to the same center of self-awareness, even from the person's subjective point of view. That is, not only would an outsider say that the changes were changes *in* the same

individual, but that person generally experiences the changes in that way and would refer to successive states as 'mine'" (Stephen Braude, *First Person Plural: Multiple Personality and the Philosophy of Mind*. [New York: Routledge, 1991], 70).

21. Ibid., 71.

22. Braude writes, "In all the cases I know of where a multiple has been integrated extensively enough to feel what it is like to be a person with different and often conflicting desires, preferences, and interests, the integrated state has been preferred. Granted, the internal group of friends may have disappeared, but the integrated multiple recognizes that their distinctive quality tends to remain. In fact, the integrated multiple will tend to experience those qualities in a somewhat enhanced and enriched way, as they blend for the first time with and become augmented by other attributes previously limited to specific alters" (*First Person Plural*, 46). This claim that multiples always prefer integration (once they have achieved it) is controversial. There is also the question of what a preference, for what one is *now* like, proves.

23. Braude, *First Person Plural*, 39. One of the first widely discussed cases of multiplicity was that of Mary Reynolds (1793–1854). Miss Reynolds case was described by S. Weir Mitchell, and William James quotes his report at length in volume 1 of his *Principles* (1890). Miss Reynolds had two distinct personalities, each of which displayed the classical amnesiac symptom with respect to the other. Miss Reynolds regularly remained a distinct self for a month or more, while alternating selves over the course of fifteen years.

24. Braude, *First Person Plural*, 41.

25. Ibid., 59.

26. R. Aldridge-Morris, *Multiple Personality: An Exercise in Deception* (Hillsdale, N.J.: Lawrence Erlbaum Associates, 1989), 4.

27. Ibid., 109.

28. Braude, *First Person Plural*, 127.

29. I. Hacking, "Two Souls in One Body," *Critical Inquiry* 17, no. 4 (1991): 860. Also see I. Hacking, Rewriting the Soul: Mutiple Personality and the Sciences of Memory (Princeton: Princeton University Press, 1995), which appeared as this book was in press.

30. Ganaway, "Historical versus Narrative."

31. Aldridge-Morris, *Multiple Personality;* Braude, *First Person Plural*.

32. Braude, *First Person Plural*, 56.

33. Ibid., 57.

34. W. H. Calvin, *The Cerebral Symphony: Seashore Reflections on the Structure of Consciousness* (New York: Bantam, 1990); K. Craik, *The Nature of Explanation* (Cambridge: Cambridge University Press, 1943); Dennett, "Why Everyone Is a Novelist"; O. Flanagan, *Varieties of Moral Personality: Ethics and Psychological Realism* (Cambridge, Mass.: Harvard University Press, 1991); O. Flanagan, *The Science of the Mind,* 2d ed. (Cambridge: MIT Press, 1991); O. Flanagan, *Consciousness Reconsidered* (Cambridge: MIT Press, 1992); P. N. Johnson-Laird, *Mental Models* (Cambridge, Mass.: Harvard University Press, 1983); P. N. Johnson-Laird, *The Computer and the Mind* (Cambridge, Mass.: Harvard University Press, 1988); G. L. Stephens and G. Graham, "Voices and Selves," in *Philosophical Perspectives on*

Psychiatric Diagnosis Classification, ed. J. Sadler et al. (Baltimore: Johns Hopkins University Press, 1994).

35. Virgil Aldrich pointed out to me that although we are inclined to speak of "multiple personalities" in the same body, we are not inclined to speak of "multiple persons" in the same body. This is right, and one reason for it, I think, is that bodily continuity is important to us in ascribing personhood. So Jane is one person with many personalities because "Jane" names this continuous organism. She is not a multiple person; she is an individual with many different personalities. The importance of bodily continuity in thinking about the identity of persons helps to explain why, when multiplicity yields to multiplexity, we are willing to think that we have the same person we had before multiplicity took hold, even though we do not think this when the person is in the full grip of MPD. During multiplicity, standards of psychological continuity and connectedness are rightly most weighty and undermine the ascription of personal identity.

36. One MPD patient who was repeatedly raped by her father was confused by the fact that she had played along with certain of what her father called "daddy games." This father, perhaps to reduce his own cognitive dissonance, suggested a new name for his daughter when they played "daddy games." I have come across another case in which the abusive father actually laid the ground for alters to take hold in his daughter by providing names for them (N. Humphrey and D. Dennett, "Speaking for Ourselves," *Raritan: A Quarterly Review* 9 [1989]: 69–98).

37. Gary Watson provides a vivid example. Watson first describes the case of Robert Harris, a reckless and unfeeling murderer capable of enjoying his lunch immediately after pumping two innocents full of bullets. He needed their car to commit a bank robbery after lunch. Harris, according to his sister, "cared about nothing." He was born to a mother sent into labor from the hemorrhaging caused by a beating that she, six-and-a-half months pregnant, suffered at the hands of her alcoholic husband. Harris's father was convicted several times of sexually abusing his daughters, and his mother also eventually became an alcoholic and was arrested several times, once for bank robbery.

Watson writes, "The fact that Harris's cruelty is an intelligible response to his circumstances gives a foothold not only for sympathy, but for the thought that if *I* had been subjected to such circumstances, I might well have become as vile. What is unsettling is the thought that one's moral self is such a fragile thing. . . . The awareness of moral luck, however, taints one's own view of one's moral self as an achievement, and infuses one's reactive attitudes with a sense of irony" (Gary Watson, "Responsibility and the Limits of Evil" in *Responsibility, Character and the Emotions,* ed. F. Schoeman, Cambridge: Cambridge University Press, 1987, 276–77). Watson goes on to write, "Harris both satisfies and violates the criteria of victimhood. His childhood abuse was a misfortune inflicted upon him against his will. But at the same time (and this is part of his very misfortune) he unambivalently endorses suffering, death, and destruction, and that is what (one form of) evil is. With this in focus, we see him as a victimizer and respond to him accordingly. *This ambivalence results from the fact that an overall view simultaneously demands and precludes regarding him as a victim*" (ibid., 275, my emphasis).

6

I Remember You

A Childhood Fantasy

When I was twenty-six, I returned to New York from Cambridge for a Thanksgiving feast with my parents and my five siblings. Over dinner one of my sisters asked my parents a question about the anxieties of being young parents of young children. My mother reported that one of her most worrisome times was when she, my father, my sister, and I returned from a three-year stint in Puerto Rico, so that my father could take a new job in the States, and so that I could start first grade. Her worry was that at age five, without the experience of kindergarten, and coming from Puerto Rico where I "had no playmates," I might have trouble adjusting to school.

I was incredulous and reminded my mother of my deep and important friendship with Billy Fletcher with whom I had played "all the time." My mother looked at me as if I was crazy, then at my father, whose face expressed similar bewilderment. She explained that Billy Fletcher was the son of a business relation of my father's who had visited Puerto Rico for a few days and had spent *one* afternoon at our home, during which time I had indeed played with him.

Childhood confabulation of this sort is not all that uncommon. There were lots of photos taken that momentous afternoon, and no doubt looking at them helped fill out my imaginary friendship with Billy. The fact remains, had my mother gone to her grave without telling me the true story, I would have believed my version—I might even still be working on it.

There are three points I want to make with regard to this autobiographical tale. First, what I remembered about my early years was, in one significant respect, straight-out false. Second, the misremembering, the confabulation, is best explained as involving a germ of truth planted in an *autosuggestible* host. Perhaps I was lonely. Whatever the reason I was, without doubt, fertile ground for the elaboration of the story, prepared to spin out the tale of my friendship with Billy. My mother was not complicit. She never said at any time after the momentous afternoon, "Now, Owen why don't you go play with Billy Fletcher for a while. Dinner will be ready soon." Third, it may well be (I'm sure it is, but cannot prove it) that my temporally extended fantasy of playing with Billy was in fact identity-constitutive in two respects: I was *really* Billy's friend and playmate, *and* being his friend and playmate (even though only in imagination) prepared me for getting along adequately with other children when first grade began. Memory is a funny thing.

Alien Abduction

In a two-part *New Yorker* article, "Remembering Satan," Lawrence Wright,[1] quotes a therapist, Michael Nash, who gave this account of his work with a patient who "remembered" an abduction by aliens: "I successfully treated this highly hypnotizable man over a period of three months. About two months into this therapy, his symptoms abated: He was sleeping normally again, his ruminations and flashbacks had resolved, he returned to his usual level of interpersonal engagement, and his productivity improved. What we did worked. Nevertheless, let me underscore this: he walked out of my office as utterly convinced that he had been abducted as when he walked in. As a matter of fact he thanked me for helping him 'fill in the gaps of my memory.' I suppose I need not tell you how unhappy I was about his particular choice of words here."

Positive Illusions

Believing utter nonsense about oneself and one's life can make things go better than they otherwise would. Positive illusions are ubiquitous and multifarious in kind.[2] When such illusions have costs, the bearers of these costs typically include not only the individual but his or her relations as well—family, friends, and coworkers. Even when an illusion is seemingly costless—suppose I discount all the well-known base rates in assessing the probability that I will someday develop cancer—an epistemically zealous bystander, a jealous guardian of *the truth,* come what may, might worry that *Truth* itself has paid, even if neither I nor any of my relations may have. After all, the fact is that my chances are one in three or four of getting cancer, and if I think otherwise I am simply unknowing or self-deceived.

Perhaps such guardians of truth overrate truth. I think they do. Whether this is right or not, one thing is clear: Feeling good or bad about myself hardly requires that my self-understanding tracks truth, in the first case, or falsity, in the second. We can learn things while engaged in fantasy, confabulation, and misremembering. This is one lesson of my relationship with Billy Fletcher.

Memory and Identity

Memory is intimately linked to identity. John Locke famously proposed that subjectively speaking I am what I remember my self being. Who I am is importantly constituted by both the content of my memories and by the manner in which I remember things—by how I fit them into the narrative of my life and by the spin I put on the events I remember.

But what of lost memories? And what of false memories? Do lost memories affect identity? Or does it depend on why they are lost; whether they simply wane and are forgotten because they matter so little, or whether they are actively buried because they matter so much? And what of memories that are false—what of misrememberings and disguised memories? The patient who thinks he was abducted by aliens has incorporated a set of alien-abduction scenes into the way he thinks of and represents his self, his life. In some perfectly reasonable sense he is a man whose abduction by aliens is constitutive of his identity, despite the fact that he was never in fact abducted by aliens.

Despite the fact that Billy Fletcher and I did not spend nearly as much time together as I thought, or do almost any of the things I remember us doing together, my relationship with Billy changed my life, and this despite the fact that my Billy existed mostly only "notionally."

Why do otherwise seemingly well-put-together people remember things that didn't happen—sometimes things that could not have possibly happened? And why do certain memories come flooding in long after the fact?

Psychoanalysis and Repression

There are theories about these matters. Psychoanalysis is the most well known. Suppose the psychoanalytic theory of repression, the theory that painful memories are repressed, buried as memories, but are also at the same time of utmost causal importance in personality development, is false; or, what is different, suppose it is not remotely well grounded. Does it matter? And if it does matter, how, why, and when does it matter?

Many psychologists and philosophers think it does matter. One idea is that the psychoanalytic theory of repression is seriously deficient, even though it is widely believed. Neither the psychoanalytic theory of personality, a theory whose main tenet is the theory of repression, nor the associated therapeutic theory whose main tenet is that the road to mental health involves remembering what is true but repressed, is well supported.

One critical argument is simplicity itself. Psychoanalysis claims confirmation for its theory of repressed memories, the basis of its theory of personality, because of the success of the therapeutic treatment that deploys that theory. "Actual *durable* therapeutic success guarantees *not only* that the pertinent analytic interpretations *ring* true to the analysand, *but also* that they *are* indeed veridical. . . . Collectively, the successful outcomes of analyses do constitute *cogent* evidence for all that general psychoanalytic theory tells us about the influences of the unconscious dynamics of the mind on our lives."[3] The key idea is the "tally argument."[4] Positive change, the overcoming of certain neuroses, even health itself, occur only if what the troubled individual remembers tallies with what is true. The troubled person and an analyst might converge on a certain story. But a two-way tally will make the restoration of mental health possible only if there is a third ingredient—the interpretive convergence of analyst and analysand must also tally with the truth, with what *really* happened, with what is *truly* at the root of the problem.

The "tally argument" is testable. Notoriously, psychoanalysis bases its credibility on clinical success, and the "tally argument," although widely accepted within the orthodox community, has not been well-tested. The possibility of placebogenic effects that owe nothing to features of the theory, its associated therapy, or hitting upon what is true but until now was hidden, has hardly been ruled out.

This is not a situation where one can say, "Well, sure, anything is possible. But why *really* entertain the possibility that the therapeutic effect of psychoanalysis is any more likely placebogenic or due to suggestibility than that it is due to the intercession of angels?" The answer is that there is a huge amount of independent evidence from psychopharmacology, from psychology, and from the very tradition from which psychoanalysis itself emerged, that placebogenic effects are ubiquitous, and that many people, some more than others, are highly suggestible. There is no independent evidence for the intercession of angels, nor have there been in the history of psychoanalysis any systematic independent checks of the truth of what patients remember; nor have there been any systematic checks of the bases of therapists' confidence in the causes of the outcomes they observe.

This matters, because there exists independent evidence of causal misattribution, sampling biases, an availability bias (thinking that what one notices or thinks is salient is salient), of bloated confidence ratings, of the corrigibility of first-person psychological reports. But most important of all, there is good evidence that it is easy to get people first to entertain that they did certain things or that certain things happened to them (e.g., that they were lost in a large shopping center as a small child), then to remember the false implanted memory with the same confidence that true memories have, and finally to elaborate on the implanted episode, filling it out in plausible directions.

Good experimental work in psychology, as well as good work in naturalistic epistemology and the philosophy of science converge to render the verdict that psychoanalytic theory and therapy not only lack a sound evidential base but in fact stand jeopardized by experimental work in the science of the mind.

There are three responses to such a claim—equally common and equally unsatisfactory. The first is that Freud himself recognized the phenomenon of false but identity-constitutive memories. Indeed, he himself shifted from thinking that memories of childhood seduction were veridical reports to the view that they were often something else—fantasies, he thought. This is true but irrelevant, since the issue is not whether Freud recognized the problem of false remembering or memory reinterpretation. The issue is how he proposed distinguishing veridical from nonveridical memories, and here the point is that Freud proposed that true memories would be given high confidence ratings by both analyst and analysand and that durable improvement would only track true remembering, not false remembering. It is this tandem that remains unconfirmed.

The second response to the critic is that of the eclectic. The eclectic can be virtually any kind of theorist or clinician who claims to have sorted credible tenets of psychoanalytic theory and practice from less credible or incredible tenets, and to have retained, possibly in modified form, the credible tenets. Despite a widespread impression to the contrary, electicism is not good in and of itself. The eclectic is picky, he is discriminating, he has standards and doesn't accept any old view. But it hardly follows that the eclectic is particularly discerning. How does he decide what to believe and what not to believe? If it is on the basis of what his mentors say is credible, and if what they say is credible is based on musings from the armchair, or from the thrill of therapeutic successes with novel techniques, the same problems about (excessively) liking one's own theories and the possibility of placebogenic effects need to be ruled out. Eclecticism in and of itself hardly moves one to high ground.

The third response is that skepticism about repressed memories is an unwarranted philosophical luxury. Evidence of the causal efficacy of repressed memories abounds, and memories exhumed through hypnosis, free association, or just sitting around are familiar occurrences. Everyone knows that the theory of repression is true. This much is just common sense.

To be sure, many of the major tenets of psychoanalysis are part of contemporary folk psychology, part of the way contemporary persons understand themselves and each other. But widespread acceptance hardly bespeaks credibility, let alone that rare commodity, truth. So there is work to be done if psychoanalytic theory and practice are to be defended.

Is such defense of consequence only to psychoanalysis, its institutes, and its offshoots—fodder for clever but inconsequential debate among various therapeutic schools, experimental psychology, and the philosophy of science? Surely, the status of psychoanalysis has some consequences for certain styles of literary and art criticism, biography, and many aspects of intellectual life in the West. Perhaps one could think that psychoanalysis is rubbish, but also think that the psychoanalytically inspired practices of intellectuals are harmless, lubricate the mind and the spirit, attune us to the complexity of mind and identity, and so on.

Life and culture, but not as we know them, could survive the demise of psychoanalysis. But psychoanalytic theory, or central aspects of it, are at present deeply embedded in common sense—even the common sense of the most unlikely sorts—officers of the law, judges, and ministers of God. And this is the reason why the status of psychoanalysis is not simply a matter of concern internal to the lives of intellectuals, and why it has practical consequences beyond the monetary exchanges between therapists and clients. The theory of repression is now part of cultural common sense, and it is causing trouble as I write.

Theory Contamination

Lawrence Wright's article, "Remembering Satan," chronicles the story of a family and a community unraveled by charges of sexual abuse against a respected sheriff by his daughters. Paul Ingram, the man charged, did not initially remember any episode of abuse. But he reached the conclusion that he was guilty as charged as an inference to the best explanation. After several hours of questioning, Ingram said, "I really believe that the allegations did occur and that I did violate them and abuse them and probably for a long period of time. I've repressed it." When asked why he was confessing to things he did not remember doing, Ingram cited the fact that his daughters wouldn't lie about such matters. Furthermore, there was some indirect evidence: the girls, now twenty-two and eighteen, had not been acting normal, and Ingram said, "I have a hard time hugging them, or even telling them that I love them, and uh, I just know that's not natural."

Ingram was assured by the detective in charge that now that he had confessed he would in fact start to really remember his sins. Ingram was a member of a Protestant fundamentalist church and prayed that his repressed memories would be restored. The daughters for their part had started to remember episodes of sexual abuse at church retreats. But none of these memories—at least initially—involved their father. After instruction in techniques for retrieving repressed material, and reassurances from the family's minister that God would only allow true memories, Ingram built a story involving a Satanic cult, group sex, infanticide, and human sacrifice. The church grapevine, aided by an appearance of the younger daughter on a Geraldo Rivera TV special, "Devil Worship: Exposing Satan's Underground" (Rivera's show is among the slimiest and most popular talk shows in America), led to the elaboration of the story in the hands of many alleged participants and victims.

The important points for present purposes are that the stories of no two persons ever matched, and that every single mental health professional called in to aid the prosecution or the alleged victims believed in the theory of instant memory repression. So widely held was this belief that a detective involved in the case confidently explained to Dr. Richard Ofshe, a Berkeley social psychologist, who was called in to testify, that the daughters' failure to remember repeated rapes by their father over a decade and a half were due to the "well-known mechanisms of repression." This lesson in the well-known mechanisms of repression was provided by the detective to the psychologist on the ride to Olympia from the airport.

Ofshe was able to get Ingram to remember a story of abusive behavior that he, Ofshe, fabricated from thin air. Ofshe proceeded over time to try to convince Ingram to drop his guilty plea, since he concluded that the problem was not one of repressed memories but of a highly suggestible person. By the time Ingram saw fit to change his plea, it was too late, and he is now serving a twenty-year sentence. Meanwhile, one of the undersheriffs involved in the case has become a registered counselor working at exhuming the repressed memories of victims of abuse.

The issues here are bicoastal. A documentary (July 1993) on the American Public Television show *Frontline* is another gripping and depressing tale of the way in which the belief in the theory of repression so contaminated the investigation into allegations of sexual abuse, that barring new independent evidence (videotapes, perhaps) it seems impossible to have any confidence that abuse did occur, despite the fact that it might have occurred. In Edenton, North Carolina, the proprietor of the Little Rascals Day Care was sentenced to twelve consecutive life sentences, one for each child he allegedly abused. The defendant may be guilty. But no one may ever know. Not one child in the case produced any memories (except one of a slapping) without being actively prodded by police, parents, and therapists. The police officer who interviewed the children with anatomically correct dolls didn't know the first thing about how to use them, although she surely "knew" about repressed memories and that silence, confusion, denials, and fantastic tales are evidence of abuse. The therapists who interviewed the children showed no sensitivity to the phenomenon of suggestibility—instead they gave the children "homework" involving elaborating the tales of abuse with their parents at home between sessions. The idea that these children were becoming messed-up due to the contagion of the parents, police, and therapists and not due to abuse at the daycare center seems not to have crossed anyone's mind. Nor did the fact that the children *eventually* remembered sexual abuse, as well as abductions by aliens and episodes of infanticide at the daycare center give anyone much pause.

The explanation of what happened at Edenton is very complex. But no matter how one assesses the relative importance of various factors the following played a role: the belief in the theory of repression, an insensitivity to the phenomenon of suggestibility, and a complete lack of insight into the working of the confirmation bias—for example, behavior initially assigned to the category of "the terrible twos" was subsequently seen as evidence of abuse, as were all manner of ordinary childhood medical complaints.

Sir Karl Popper was the first philosopher of science to see how common the confirmation bias was. Psychoanalysts (and Marxists, he thought) see confirmations everywhere and disconfirmations nowhere. On this point Popper's contribution can be read as anticipating a major thesis of T. S. Kuhn, with whom he is usually contrasted. Logical relations between a hypothesis and its implications might yield insight into potentially falsifying (or corroborating) tests, but scientists generally are disinclined to subject their theories to hard, potentially undermining tests, and strongly inclined to ignore anomalies and see confirmations abounding.

The patient mentioned at the beginning who left therapy better off but with the filled-in memory of his abduction by aliens does no harm. Subjectively speaking he is the self whose abduction memories are partly constitutive of who he is. My mother straightened me out about Billy Fletcher. But in a way the truth came too late—too late to defeat "the Untrue," that is. Still my imaginary friendship is not, and will not be causally implicated, in any harm I have done or do. I'm fairly certain of this.

The memories of the children and adults of Olympia, Washington, and Edenton, North Carolina, have been incorporated into their self-images. True or false, these memories have already harmed all those involved. The true and the false, the good and the bad can go in different directions.

John Locke thought that God would straighten memory out at the Final Judgment—like my mother at Thanksgiving. Unlike an omniscient God or attentive parent, we misremember and misappropriate, but we can hope that we are not led to misremember and misappropriate because those who should know better pay too little attention to the phenomena of suggestibility, thought contagion, the confirmation bias, and the perseverance of false belief. An immoderate version of the theory of repression zseems to have spread like a virus among ordinary people, lawyers, judges, and ministers of God, and the psychoanalytically inspired therapeutic community seems, by and large, to have little interest in containing the spread. To be sure, there are insights of psychoanalysis, including components of the theory of repression, that can be accommodated in modified form by experimental psychology, cognitive science, neuroscience, and psychopharmacology. But unless the psychoanalytic community joins the rest of mind science, it will be guilty of the charges that it lacks epistemic integrity and does moral harm.

Concluding Unscientific Postscript

Since I wrote the review on which this essay is based, an enormous literature on false memory syndrome—pro and con—has come into print.[5] This spate of literature makes me want to clarify and distinguish my position from certain views currently afloat. First, my point is that we can't know when, where, or how often sexual abuse of very young children takes place until all the professionals involved stop engaging in memory contamination and suggestibility exercises. But second, no one can know at this point whether sexual abuse is over- or underreported. And the reason is that the data is putrid. Some say that it must be vastly overreported because the various survivors' movements claim that such abuse is ubiquitous, the cause of all sorts of psychosocial problems, and engage in inducing false memories. Furthermore, it is pointed out that victims of other kinds of awful trauma, for example, concentration camp survivors and survivors of Hiroshima and Nagasaki and Dresden do not—sometimes despite great effort to do so—forget the atrocities they underwent.

But the situations are disanalogous in several respects. First, those traumatized in Japan and Germany were linguistic beings at the time of the trauma and memory is well known to be tied to linguistic competence, as well as to a fully developed hippocampus and prefrontal cortex. To be sure, there were prelinguistic survivors of the terrible events of the Second World War who were told the relevant tales and who as they grew observed the aftereffects of the awful events. Community was fostered by remembering. Furthermore, it was in no one's particular interest to deny the trauma, largely because the victims were not the perpetrators. The situation is different in many of the established cases of child abuse. Sometimes, perhaps, abuse occurs to linguistic novices, but even when it does not, it is always in the interest of the perpetrator to deny playing the role of abuser. Furthermore, because there is often love and affection between victim and perpetrator, there is bound to be some tendency on the part of the victim to interpret the event in a way that does not undermine these feelings. We have reliable memories to a point, but many variables count toward what we think, reduction of cognitive and affective dissonance among them.

My considered view then is that we know very little about the causes or frequency of sexual or physical abuse of children, and we are all to blame. Our theories and our data are mixed up internally, and social forces of various sorts, the recovered memory movement, and the extreme reaction it has spawned, have made everything but the basic questions unclear.

There is nothing decisive or comforting to say. I conclude with this. "I remember you" is a paradigmatic I-thou, me-you thought or utterance. It is natural to think that the "remembered you" is an other—a not-self. However, remembering one's own life is not obviously easier or subject to radically different epistemic conditions than knowing another. Remembering Billy Fletcher involves remembering (if it involves remembering at all) my own ideas, not Billy at all.[6] My ideas seem like more than that. But Mother says they are not. And Mother knows best.

Notes

Acknowledgments—An earlier version of this essay appeared as a review in the *Times Literary Supplement* (October 29, 1993): 3–4, of Adolf Grünbaum's *Validation in the Clinical Theory of Psychoanalysis: A Study in the Philosophy of Psychoanalysis*, intro. by Philip S. Holzman (Madison, Conn.: International Universities Press, 1993).

1. The article appeared in the May 17 and 23, 1993, issues of the *New*

Yorker. It is now available as a book, *Remembering Satan* (New York: Knopf, 1994).

2. See S. Taylor, *Positive Illusions: Creative Self-Deception and the Healthy Mind* (New York: Basic Books, 1989); and S. Taylor and J. Brown, "Illusion and Well-Being: A Social Psychological Perspective on Mental Health," *Psychological Bulletin* 103 (1988): 193–210.

3. Grünbaum, *Validation,* 185.

4. The "tally argument" is a central focus of Grünbaum's earlier book, *The Foundations of Psychoanalysis: A Philosophical Critique* (Berkeley: University of California Press, 1984).

5. See Frederick Crews, "The Revenge of the Repressed," *New York Review of Books* 41 (November 17, 1994): 19, and "The Revenge of the Repressed: Part II," *New York Review of Books* 41 (December 1, 1994): 20. Also see Peter Lomas, "How Far Is Freud to Blame? The Limitless Vulnerability of the Human Mind to Suggestion," *Times Literary Supplement* (December 2, 1994): 13–14. Among the published books, see Lenore Terr, *Unchained Memories: True Stories of Traumatic Memories, Lost and Found* (New York: Basic Books, 1994); Elizabeth Loftus and Katherine Ketcham, *The Myth of Repressed Memory: False Memories and Allegations of Sexual Abuse* (New York: St. Martin's, 1994); Lawrence Wright, *Remembering Satan* (New York: Alfred Knopf, 1994); Ellen Bass and Laura Davis, *The Courage to Heal: A Guide for Women Survivors of Child Sexual Abuse,* 3d ed. (New York: Harper Perennial, 1994); Richard Ofshe and Ethan Watters, *Making Monsters: False Memories, Psychotherapy, and Sexual Hysteria* (New York: Scribner's, 1994); Mark Pendergrast, *Victims of Memory: Incest Accusations and Shattered Lives* (New York: Upper Access, 1995); Charles R. Kelley and Eric C. Kelley, *Now I Remember: Recovered Memories of Sexual Abuse* (Vancouver, WA: K/R, 1994). For recent research see the special issue of *Consciousness and Cognition* (December 1994) 3, nos. 3/4, on *The Recovered Memory/False Memory Debate.*

6. The example allows me to emphasize something about the distinction I draw between self-represented identity and actual full identity, namely that the distinction is not pure. One might think that the narrative with Billy as my playmate is only part of my self as narrated, but not part of my actual self as seen from the God's eye point of view. But this would be wrong since the actual structure and shape of my life are determined, as this case shows, not only by what in fact happens or happened to me, but also, possibly as much by how I think of things— even when these are things that did not happen. One might think of the point here as a corollary of familiar ones about the nature of intentional systems.

7

Children, Other Minds, and Honesty

Epistemic and Moral Issues

Two philosophical issues arise persistently in discussions of children and lying. First, there are epistemic issues—issues of what sort of knowledge the child must possess in order to lie. Second, there are issues of moral psychology—issues of how and when children learn that it is wrong to lie, and in what they understand the wrongness of lying to consist. My argument is this: On the epistemic side, lying is a type of action that requires a rich understanding of other minds, of the connections between belief and action, and in particular, of the way mental representations can be transformed into misrepresentations. Children can lie without being able to correctly define the term *lie*. But they cannot lie without having solved the philosophical problem of other minds.

What I call a *minimal lie* requires that the perpetrator believes that X but does something (or omits to do something) with the intention of making another think "not X." Being a minimal lie is not sufficient for being a bona fide lie. Many practical jokes satisfy the two conditions set forth but are not lies. Furthermore, if I believe "X" and try to make you believe "not X" whereas unbeknownst to me "not X" is, in fact, true, then I have satisfied the conditions for a minimal lie. But I have not lied, only attempted one. Although being a minimal lie is not sufficient for being a bona fide lie, it is necessary. The purpose of marking off the concept of a minimal lie is to capture the idea that *at a minimum* we require of bona fide lies that *mental* misrepresentation be intended.

Children who have not yet reached the point where they possess the knowledge that (a) other persons have beliefs and (b) they themselves possess causal powers to create false beliefs in others can simulate lies. But they cannot even produce minimal lies. A child may be able to mislead others so long as he or she has correctly surmised how to do certain things that have the effect of misinforming and misleading others. That is, before a child has learned to lie he or she can aim to mislead. Producing this behavioral effect may normally require producing a false belief in one's audience. But children need not intend to produce this false belief, even though in fact they do so. Before children know what false beliefs are, or that they have the capacity to produce them, they may *know how* to produce them. Those who have learned to lie know what a false belief is, intend to create a false belief in their audience, and know how to do so.

With regard to moral psychology, things are substantially more complicated than is acknowledged in the literature devoted to lying. It is standardly thought that children are taught that lying is wrong, *simpliciter*. But that is not true. To put things in the most contentious way, it would be better to say that children are taught norms of politeness, privacy, reticence, and loyalty that teach them that there is no categorical obligation to tell the truth. We hear that honesty is the best policy. But "honesty" has a complex meaning for us. And the policy is by no means set forth as a categorical one. Rational self-interest, the need for privacy, self-esteem, and self-respect compete with honesty and are thought, in some cases, to override the requirement to be honest. Kindness, politeness, tact, and the demands of friendship and loyalty also compete with honesty, and they too, in certain cases, override the requirement to be honest. Socialization in honesty involves the acquisition of what Aristotle called *phronesis*—practical wisdom. The honest person is the person who knows when to tell the truth and does so in the right circumstances, in the right way, and to the right persons. There is no known algorithm that can be taught and that will produce the requisite set of moral sensitivities.

The Semantics of 'Lie'

What does the child need to know in order to tell a lie? The answer to this question depends in part on what is meant by *lie*—by the semantics of the term. The semantics specify what conditions must be met for an action to be a bona fide lie. Once the relevant conditions are specified, psychologists can tell us whether children satisfy the relevant conditions. What are the relevant conditions.

It is tempting to think that in order to lie the child must know what a lie is, and that this is equivalent to saying that the child must possess the concept of a lie. But a trap lurks in this way of speaking. A child no more needs to have the concept of a lie in order to lie, than he or she needs to have the concept of consciousness in order to be conscious. Certainly, the child needs to be capable of engaging in acts that satisfy our concept of a lie in order to lie, but he or she herself need not possess the relevant concept.

What is our concept of a lie? The classical view is that the extension of a concept consists of a set of conditions that are jointly necessary and sufficient for the correct application of the concept. A child lies just in case he or she meets the necessary and sufficient conditions. This idea has two problems. First, like most concepts, the concept of a lie does not admit of characterization in terms of jointly necessary and sufficient conditions. One might think that expressing a falsehood, knowing it is false, and intending to mislead by expressing this known falsehood are jointly necessary and sufficient conditions for lying. The trouble is that a speech act can express a falsehood, be known by the speaker to express a falsehood, be intended to deceive and not be a bona fide lie. Practical jokes, as I have said, are examples.

Actually, even the assumption that a lie must involve a speech act is problematic if one sticks to the straight and narrow in characterizing speech acts. The philosopher Sissela Bok, for example, defined a lie as "an intentionally deceptive message in the form of a statement."[1] But surely pointing someone in the wrong direction can count as a lie, even though no statement is involved at all.

The problem of defining *lie* is like the problem of defining *knowledge*. For centuries, philosophers thought that Plato had succeeded in providing a definition of knowledge in terms of necessary and sufficient conditions. *S* knows that *X* if and only if *S* believes that *X*; *S* is *justified* in believing "*X*"; and "*X*" is *true*. But in the 1960s a series of counterexamples to the justified-true-belief analysis of knowledge created a philosophical industry of seekers for the additional necessary condition. No satisfactory additional condition was ever discovered that, together with justified true belief, was immune to counterexamples.

Wittgenstein's idea that conceptual structure is normally rooted in family resemblance rather than necessary and sufficient conditions helps explain why exceptionless definitions for nontechnical terms almost never exist. The psychological theory of prototypes has vindicated the core idea. Indeed, even concepts such as "even number," which do have strict necessary and sufficient conditions, display prototype structure, that is, 2 is a better exemplar of an even number than 1,224, in the mind of an ordinary speaker.

With lies, all the putative necessary conditions—saying something false, knowing that it is false, and intending by one's utterance to deceive— matter in our determination of some act as a lie. But these conditions can be satisfied and a lie not be told because of subtle features of the context or to the speaker's overall intentional state. Again, certain jokes fit this mold straightforwardly. More counterintuitively, one can tell a lie by telling the truth. Indeed, one lying strategy is to tell an abridged version of the truth knowing that one's audience will elaborate its meaning in exactly the wrong direction. If one's concept of "lie" has as a necessary condition the requirement that one says what is false, then such lies are not real lies. The concept of a minimal lie can accommodate lies that involve speaking the truth, since the characterization given involves the intention to create a false belief. The means of generating the false belief are left unspecified. This is why I have some hope that the notion of a minimal lie captures a necessary but not a sufficient condition for a bona fide lie, where by a "bona fide lie" I mean "lie" as construed by experts, say, by moral philosophers. The core idea that, at a minimum, a lie requires intent to deceive does not capture a necessary condition of the concept "lie" as used by all ordinary speakers because some speakers, especially young children, think of objective falsehood as the most important feature of a lie. Intent to produce false belief figures negligibly, in some cases not at all, in their understanding of the concept of "lie." This is true, for example, of children who think that mistakes are lies. The claim that intent to produce false belief is a necessary condition of a bona fide lie is a normative semantic claim, not a descriptive sociolinguistic claim.

With lying, unlike with knowing, moral features are relevant in the determination. So-called *benevolent lies* will be thought by some to not be *real* lies at all. The best explanation for this is that for some individuals bad moral intent is the most important determinant of a lie. Inasmuch as a benevolent lie is a false utterance intended to mislead with good moral intent, it is not really a lie. But our semantic intuitions pull in both directions here. We might be tempted to say of a speech act intended to save a life that it is not a real lie or, equally sensibly, that it is a lie but is excusable.

The upshot is this: Knowing what counts as a lie is no simple matter of knowing a definition. Lies have prototypical structure.[2] Almost all the research shows that objective falsity has greatest saliency in determining whether something is a lie for very young children, and thus that for them mistakes are considered lies.[3] Furthermore, contrary to one standard expectation, neither preschoolers nor older children seem to lay much stock in whether a falsehood is believed or not in determining whether a lie has been told. Stating a falsehood is normally enough for the ascription of a lie.[4]

Definitions and ascriptions come apart in important ways. Coleman and Kay found that objective falsehood was the main feature given by adults when asked to define *lie*.[5] But it "turned out consistently to be the least

important element by far in the cluster of conditions" in actually determining whether a lie is ascribed.[6] Other important elements in the cluster
of conditions relevant to the determination of whether some act is a lie
include believing the opposite of what one says and intending to deceive.
All the research shows that both of these factors increase in saliency over
time in determining whether a lie is attributed, despite the fact that they
do not display similar saliency in attempts to give definitions of the word
lie. For many adults, objective falsehood reigns supreme for the definitional task, even as its power wanes in determining ascriptions. Suppose
that I, unaware that my partner in crime has changed the location of your
pilfered fortune, suggest that you might look in the right, rather than in
the wrong, direction. Have I lied or not? Our semantic intuitions tug in
two directions. I have said what is true while I intended to say what is false.
If objective falsehood is the main determinant, I have not lied. But if
intention to deceive and belief that what I said is false are more salient,
then I lied but failed to mislead.

Learning the semantics of a term involves learning in the first instance
how to use it, rather than how to define it. We might wonder whether
children will ascribe lies, something they are taught is wrong, when there
are countervailing pressures to do what are, under normal circumstances
good things, for example, obeying adults and being loyal to friends. The
answer appears to be that they will. Haugaard and Reppucci found that
most young children correctly attributed a lie when they were given a
vignette in which a child protected a classmate who violated an order to
stay in from recess.[7] On the basis of this study and several related ones,
they have concluded that "most young children understand that a child
who purposefully makes an inaccurate statement, either at the request of a
parent or in order to protect a friend, is telling a lie." The evidence
suggests that the ability to use the term *lie* correctly, and to ascribe lies on
the basis of a complex set of properties—even when these properties occur
in situations that might be thought to undermine their saliency—matures
earlier than the ability to define a lie in terms of these very properties.

What about self-ascription of lies? Attribution theory provides good
evidence of a self-serving bias. The self-serving bias warrants the prediction that third-person attributions of lies and self-attributions will diverge
in identical circumstances. Not surprisingly, children powerfully tempted
to transgress some rule will do so, but will deny that they have done so.
Children who peek at a toy lie when asked if they did.[8] It is unlikely that
the children think that they did not peek. In fact, it is well known that both
children and grown-ups often construe certain circumstances as mitigating in their own case (which would not be mitigating for others), and thus
offer self-serving construals of their own lies as not real lies. The child who

is caught in a lie and says sheepishly, "I was only kidding," may well believe her own, after-the-fact self-attribution to a far greater extent than perfect memory of her actual prior intent would permit.

The upshot so far is that an individual can possess, as it were, first-order competence at lying, and even attribute lies correctly (especially third-personally), without being able to provide a definition in terms of jointly necessary and sufficient conditions (there are none), nor even a definition that captures what properties that individual thinks, in practice, constitute the most important factors in the determination of whether some act is a lie. Competent use of the term *lie* is best measured against the preferred prototype in the linguistic community in contexts where ascription, rather than definition, is called for. Ability to define the term *lie* is a bad test for adults as well as for children.[9] That said, the evidence indicates that the preferred prototype in which belief in something other than what is conveyed and intent to deceive have greater weight than objective falsehood is not fully acquired until the teenage years—and even then it is somewhat unstable.[10]

Why does intent eventually take top billing in our conception of a lie? It has to do, I think, with the distinctively moral character of lying. Lying is asymmetrical with truth telling in this respect. That is, even though we are taught that it is right to tell the truth and wrong to lie, all lies are moral violations, whereas most truthful utterances have nothing to do with morality. To inform another truly about the weather, one's health, what's on TV, or the latest finding about neurotransmitters, is not conceived of as doing something that falls within the domain of the moral. If you lie about these things, you do what is morally wrong. But the converse is not true: When you say what is true in these domains, you do not do something morally good or praiseworthy. You simply do what is expected.

Focusing on the moral component of our prototype helps explain one respect in which practical jokes differ from lies. When you say something false with the intention of deceiving me in order to get me to open the door with the bucket of water on top it, you satisfy the conditions of intent, belief, and falsehood. The temptation to say that you have not really lied comes from the fact that you intend fun, not harm.

The general semantic model I favor is a network theory. We possess elaborate cognitive models for terms, with nodes and links to other terms, which themselves have elaborate connections to other concepts. The holism of conceptual structure explains why subtle or novel features of a situation can kick off novel semantic intuitions. Strictly speaking, any unmarried male is a bachelor. But "Is the pope a bachelor?" is a question that produces in many a mental cramp. Similarly, a white lie is a lie; it has "lie" as a proper part of its name, after all. But if I say of your disgustingly gaudy new dress—"Oh Jane, what a colorful new outfit!"—fully intending to make you think I like it, have I lied? Our semantic intuitions tug in two directions, producing a cramp similar to the question about the pope.

Paradigm case lies involve speech acts. Is intentionally pointing someone in the wrong direction a speech act? If it is, then doing so is a lie. If it is not a speech act, then doing so is not a lie. What counts as a lie depends on how things are fitted together in our semantic network. Normally, there will be a significant amount of shared structure and thus shared meaning within a relatively homogeneous linguistic community. But identical terms will often diverge somewhat in meaning even within a relatively homogeneous community of speakers. The fact that the concept of "lie" is bound up with a moral conception suggests a special complication. The moral conceptions that the term is tied to may well differ among speakers of the same language. Insofar as meaning is rooted in the overall semantic relations of a term, the meaning of *lie* will have a different meaning for different speakers depending on their moral background theory. Imagine a strict Kantian for whom all intentional falsehoods are lies and for whom no lies are excusable. For such a person, "benevolent lies" are just as good exemplars of bona fide lies as are straightforward self-serving lies, and both are equally bad. If one disagrees with the usage of the term *lie* of this strict Kantian, it is tempting to revert to sociolinguistic facts about preferred usage (as I have done at several points), and claim that she doesn't understand the meaning of *lie*. But we should be clear, when we do so, that all we have then done is pointed to where linguistic power lies. We have not hashed out the real issue that involves a substantive disagreement about morality.

The upshot is simply that to know what *lie* or any other term in the language means, and to understand how to ascribe it correctly, involves possessing an elaborate theory, not just of lies and lying but of *all* their semantic relations besides. In the case of "lie," these relations include connections to an elaborate moral theory. There are no purely semantic facts about the meaning of "lie" that stand sequestered from our views about substantive moral matters.

Indeed, despite whatever heterogeneity in background moral conception affects use of the term "lie," it seems fair to say that the term has a moral component for all speakers. A lie requires that the perpetrator of the intentional falsehood intends harm. The Kantian simply has very strict criteria of when harm is intended.

So far we have isolated several components of our shared prototype: falsity, belief, intent to deceive, intent to produce harm by this deception. To be a competent liar, a child needs to know how to express falsehoods, he or she must be capable of believing "X" while expressing or otherwise indicating "not *X*." One must be capable of intending to deceive another, and one must be capable of intending, as part of the deception, to do moral harm (i.e., to protect oneself from being caught in some rule violation, to evade responsibility, to inconvenience or injure another, etc.). To possess this competence, to be capable of telling a *moral lie,* requires more than does the capacity to tell a minimal lie because it requires in addition to the intent to deceive the intent to do harm by this deception. I return to the more specifically moral dimensions of lying after saying something more specific about the epistemic competencies required for successful lying.

Lying and Knowledge of Other Minds

When does the child know enough to really lie? The answer, I said at the start, is when he or she has solved the problem of other minds. Of course, I was exaggerating because the problem of other minds is, in one sense, a problem no one ever solves. Other minds never lose all their opacity. Furthermore, insofar as we do solve the problem of other minds, that is, insofar as we learn to treat others as mental beings and to make inferences about their mental states, we do not solve the problem all at once. Indeed, it is a lifelong project to become better and better at reading other minds. Nonetheless, there is a clear, but attenuated, sense in which lying requires solution of the problem of other minds. This comes out by reflecting on what sort of knowledge needs to be imputed for a minimal lie to be ascribed. A minimal lie requires that the perpetrator believes that *X*, but intends to make another think "not *X*." A minimal lie requires that one intends to produce in another the effect of *mental* misrepresentation. To intend to produce some effect *E*, requires that one comprehends the nature of *E*, in this case the nature of mental misrepresentation, at least to some degree. The construct of a minimal lie is meant to highlight the fact that in order to lie the child must know something about the nature of false beliefs and about how to produce them.

Misleading does not require possession of this knowledge about false beliefs. A child can know how to mislead by pointing, by sabotage, by laying false tracks, and so on, without comprehending how he or she is producing this desired effect.[11] Susan Leekam rightly points out that "the use of a deceptive strategy does not always entail *intention* to influence *belief* at the time of the deception."[12] As she points out, children may have lots of rules of thumb, such as to "say 'no' if accused of a misdeed." They may recognize that these rules of thumb have some degree of success but not have a clue as to how they produce these successes. Insofar as young children think that certain generalizations obtain, they might think of them as straightforward generalizations linking certain behaviors on their part with certain behaviors on the part of others. The child might operate on the basis of purely behavioral generalizations without being fully consciously aware of these generalizations, and more importantly, without entertaining any views whatsoever about what mediates the behavior of his or her audience—indeed without any idea that there is reason to posit mental representations in the audience. According to the distinction between minimal lies and misleading, the same speech act, for example, "No, I didn't look at the toy when you were out of the room," motivated by the same self-serving intention, may be a case of misleading (with no intention to create a false belief) or a lie (with that intention).

Leekam suggests that in mature lying the "speaker might not only have an intention about the listener's *belief* of the *statement*. She might also have an intention about the listener's *belief* of her own *intention* or *belief*."[13] This seems right. Being a good liar requires competence both at producing false belief in one's audience and in making the audience think that one is being helpful and cooperative and speaking the truth. To be capable of producing a minimal lie one needs only to be capable of believing "*X*" and intending to make one's audience believe "not *X*." But one can produce a minimal lie, in this sense, without being at all successful at duping one's audience. Success at lying requires that one have some understanding of how others read faces, voices, and bodily gestures in testing for sincerity. Unless one realizes that one's audience is assessing what one says in the context of how one says it, as well as in the context of the current situation—is the situation ripe for acts of self-protection?—and in terms of an overall assessment of one's character, one will not be good at lying.

The competencies required for successful lying require a very elaborate understanding of other minds. Children must understand that other persons are repositories of intentional states, such as beliefs and desires, and that beliefs can be manipulated. They must also understand that they themselves are being read for sincerity, reliability, and motivational state by their audience, and must know what markers need to be deployed to give the desired impression of these things. Saying what is false with the intention of producing false belief is rarely sufficient to produce false belief in a savvy audience.

We might put the general point this way. There are minimal lies, and the set of competencies required to produce them, and there are mature minimal lies, which require additional competencies. Successful liars have as a constitutive part of their aim the production of two false beliefs: a false belief about some state of affairs and a false belief about their sincerity in portraying that state of affairs. Leekam, Bussey, and Tate and Warren have illuminating things to say about how the production of the impression of sincerity is produced.[14]

A minimal lie requires seeing others as intentional systems,[15] interpretable in terms of belief-desire psychology. Unlike misleading, a minimal lie requires understanding the complex relation between misleading actions (pointing in the wrong direction, speaking falsely) and the production of false beliefs in one's audience. When do children achieve the competence to tell minimal lies?

Children begin to use words such as "think," "know," "remember," "mean," and "guess" soon after their second birthday.[16] But the evidence is pretty convincing that they lack mastery of the concept of false belief until they are three and a half or four. Because linguistic competence can lag behind conceptual competence, the evidence for this comes from imaginative experiments that ask children to predict where an individual who wants the candy, and who believes it is still in the kitchen, will look, given that, unbeknownst to that individual, it has been moved to the living room. Children under four consistently predict that the individual will look where the candy *really* is, rather than where she would naturally (but mistakenly) believe it is, whereas children over four correctly predict that the individual's misrepresentation will guide his or her action.[17]

It is somewhat obscure why the concept of *false belief* is so hard for children to master. Children engage in imaginary and pretend play at very young ages. Such play would seem to involve holding false beliefs, and treating one's playmate as going along with these false beliefs. So what is missing and why? One possibility is that children do not conceive of imaginary thought or pretending as involving false beliefs at all, but simply as imagining and pretending—activities with their own internal nontruth functional logic. The idea is not incredible. Indeed, it is not obvious that adults think of imagination and pretense as involving falsehood in any straightforward sense. Imaginative fiction expresses deep truth, despite the fact that each sentence of a work of fiction is false, strictly speaking.

One theory is that when it comes to belief (but not imagination) children think that the mind is a mirror of nature, and therefore hold a "direct copy understanding of reality-oriented representations."[18] Minds mirror the way the world is through beliefs. Therefore, as just indicated, when asked to track the beliefs of a puppet or a friend who has been intentionally deceived about the whereabouts of some candy or a pencil, children under four will ascribe to a puppet or friend a belief that corresponds to where the candy or pencil actually is, rather than one that misrepresents, no matter how clear (to us) that is the right surmise, given the evidence available to that puppet or friend. It is as if it is part of the essential nature of beliefs that they represent reality. This is the default theory. It only gradually yields in the face of mountains of anomalies.

Children master the problem of other minds to a considerable extent during the third and fourth years of life. They deploy belief-desire psychology, and the mental verbs that are its stock, with increasing sophistication between their second and fourth birthdays. But mastery of the concept of false belief is a consistent laggard. Perhaps the explanation just offered is the right one for why this is so.

But false belief is not the only piece of the puzzle of other minds still not in place in children between three and four. Children are seriously deficient in the use of trait ascriptions, in deploying the vocabulary of lay personality theory.[19] Adults read other minds in part by ascribing stable character traits to individuals. Indeed, one of the main ways we assign initial probabilities to the utterances of others involves bringing complex characterological frames to these utterances.

Children understand minimal lies when they have mastered the concept of false belief, that is, around age four. But they are not very good at lying until age seven or so.[20] One plausible inference is that success at lying comes later than lying because it requires that children can think reliably about the effects of what they say and do on others, and, in particular, that they can think about what their occurrent actions and patterns of action cause others to think about them. Sophistication in thinking about what another thinks about oneself (one's intentions, motives, and character) requires skills of character appraisal, so one can judge the other, and an understanding of the logic of character inference, so one can judge how the other is appraising oneself (see Tate and Warren on the difficulty of coaching youngsters to display successfully the requisite skills).[21] If I am completely unreliable, realize this, and know that my audience knows that I am unreliable, then speaking the truth (for once) will produce the desired self-serving effect much better than stating yet another intentional falsehood. I tell a minimal lie because I believe that X and intend to make my audience believe "not X." But because my audience puts "not" before everything I say, I can best produce the desired effect by saying "X"!

Socialization for Honesty

The semantics of "lie," what *lie* means, depends on the network of semantic connections the concept has. One important set of connections involves the other moral terms one uses, the interpretation of these terms being fixed in complicated ways by the moral conception one abides. Relatedly, the epistemology of lying, what a child needs to know in order to tell a genuine lie, involves having solved the problem of other minds and knowing that lying is wrong. In this section I bring these connections to morality into clearer view.

When is an individual capable of telling a lie for which he or she is legitimately held morally responsible? Earlier I characterized a moral lie as involving the intention to cause harm. One might naturally think that culpability follows on the capacity to tell an intentional falsehood with the intention to cause harm. I think this is almost right. The child who knows full well that he or she harms a friend by denying knowledge of the whereabouts of the friend's toy, which he or she intends to keep for himself or herself, does what is morally wrong. We hold a child morally responsible when he or she understands the nature of harms and intends to produce one. However, it is not always easy to know when a child possesses this knowledge. The very same act may *cause* harm without involving the *intention* to cause harm. Imagine the child who lies to a friend simply in order to keep the friend's toy for himself, but who doesn't really understand that this harms the friend. This child, unlike the first child we imagined, causes harm to a friend but does not intend to do so. To make matters even more complicated, one might intend to cause harm without possessing a full understanding of the nature of harms, or even of the particular kind of harm one intends to produce. One might not completely understand, as we say, exactly what is wrong with the act in question or how it injures the other. The point is that our judgments of a child's culpability for a lie are tricky. Many more factors are considered mitigating for children than are considered mitigating for adults, and it is often unclear when a child possesses all the competencies required to be truly diabolical.

The competencies required for moral responsibility depend, in part, on an understanding of why lying is wrong and of the kinds of harms produced by lies. So we need to ask what children are taught about the immorality of lying. What exactly do we teach about the morality and immorality of lying? What do we teach about the different kinds of lies? How wrong do we teach that lying is? I cannot give a full answer to these questions here. But I can provide a sense for how complicated the full answers will be.

The answer to this cluster of questions is extremely important in the context of the present discussion because children's competence to testify in courts is standardly characterized as requiring evidence of two competencies: the epistemic competence to distinguish truth from falsehood, and the moral competence to understand the wrongness of lying. Apparently, the courts frame the second competence here as involving knowledge that one is obligated to speak the truth as a witness or "being sensitive

to the obligations of the oath."[22] The competent witness is one who understands the "duty" to tell the truth.[23]

There are three points that will help get at some of the complexities
involved in the socialization for honesty. First, there is the issue of when
children begin to receive instruction about the morality of lying, and what
sort of prominence it is given in the overall structure of the morality that is
being constructed in the mind of the child. Observations of normative
interactions between mothers and children in their second year indicate
that transgressions discussed in order of frequency involve issues of
destruction/dirt, place/order, teasing/hurting others, politeness, and shar-
ing.[24]

Lying itself is not a major issue before the second birthday. It is unlikely
that parents engage in instruction about the wrongness of lying before
children begin trying to lie. When does this occur? I'm not sure. But it
seems plausible that the first "ecologically valid" lies are ones about misdeeds,[25] and that they start to occur with enough frequency to be noticed
after the second birthday. We can presume then that children who already
understand that certain actions constitute misdeeds, and who know that
misdeeds are disapproved of, begin to be taught that lying about misdeeds
is also disapproved of.

How disapproved of is it? There is, I think, no simple and clear-cut
answer to this question. We teach children that it is wrong to lie about a
misdeed. But we understand—and convey this understanding—that it is
among the most natural things to try to cover up a misdeed. Furthermore,
even as children are learning that lying about misdeeds is wrong, they are
still in the process of learning what misdeeds are. Bunglings and accidents
are sometimes discounted by adults. But they are not always discounted—
at least not in the rush to anger. Thus children are rightfully wary about
underestimating what the adult theory of misdeeds includes and does not
include. Overgeneralizing is not a bad strategy.

Although many parents try to teach that lying is worse than the misdeed, children also realize that certain misdeeds are bad enough to be
worth a try at covering up. The added marginal cost of being caught in the
lie, as well as in the misdeed, is not so significant as to constitute a genuine
disincentive to lying.

The first set of points can be summarized this way. Initial learning about
the wrongness of lying is almost certainly tied to a certain class of lies—lies
about misdeeds. Children are not exposed, at least at first, to anything like
a general theory of lies and lying. Learning about the wrongness of lies
about misdeeds comes after there has been prior instruction in the wrongness of certain characteristic misdeeds. How wrong the child thinks lying
about misdeeds is, depends on how wrong adults convey that it is. But this

is variable. It depends on how parents, caretakers, and preschool teachers treat lies. Do children learn that they are under an obligation or have a duty to tell the truth at this stage? I doubt it. Certainly talk of "duty" and "obligation" is not normally introduced to youngsters. Do children learn that it is unconditionally wrong to lie about misdeeds? Again, I think not. Sensitive adults convey to the child an understanding of why she has lied. In this way they convey the impression that they understand that there are certain conditions that make it hard not to lie, and that moderate, possibly even dissolve, judgments of wrongness.

The second point relates to the question of the development of the child's general understanding of the virtue of honesty and the vice of dishonesty. Most lies involve speech acts. It follows according to the network theory of meaning that both the nature and wrongness of lies need to be considered in relation to the norms governing speech acts more generally. Thinking of lies in this way imperils thinking about lies as a simple class to pick out, or as a class with simple norms governing wrongness. The philosopher Annette Baier put the central point eloquently when she wrote:

> Talk, as we teach and learn it, has many uses. It is not unrelievedly serious—it is often an extension of play and fun, of games of hide and seek, of peekaboo, where deceit is expected and enjoyed, of games of Simon says, where orders are given to be disobeyed, of games of tag, where words have magic power, of skipping games, where words are an incantation. Speech, as we teach and learn it is not just the vehicle of cool rational thought, and practical reason but also of fun and games of anger, mutual attack, domination, coercion, and bullying. It gives us a voice for our many moods, for deceit and sly strategy, as well as for love and tenderness, humor, play and frolic, mystery and magic. The child is initiated into all of this and gradually learns all the arts and moods of speech. Among these are the arts of misleading others, either briefly and with intent soon to put them straight ("I fooled you, didn't I!") or more lastingly to keep deceit going for more questionably acceptable purposes.[26]

Exaggeration, politeness, tact, reserve in self-expression, omitting to say certain things, joking, and so on, all have to do with honest expression. Children are decidedly not taught that it is right, or even good, to be honest in the expression of all the matters that one could be honest about. The main point is that, insofar as children are taught that there is an obligation to be honest and thus not to lie, it is a complex, conditional, and culturally circumscribed obligation.

Consider in this regard the norms governing answers to polite queries about one's well-being. "If you ask me 'How are you?' and I reply 'Fine thanks, and you?' although I take myself to be far from fine, I have not lied."[27] Such speech acts are "a form of consideration for others, a protection of them from undue embarrassment, boredom, or occasion for pity. Truth, let alone 'the whole truth,' is something we very rarely want told to us. . . . Veracity is knowing *when* one is bound to speak one's mind and then speaking it as best one can."[28]

The third and final point relates to the implications of our style of socialization for honesty for the understanding of the special requirements of forensic contexts. In a culture of pure Kantians, children might learn that there is a categorical obligation to tell the truth (when the truth should be told, that is). In such a society, courts could count straightforwardly on children comprehending the obligation to tell the truth in a court of law. But, most children in this culture at least, are not raised to think of the obligation to tell the truth as a duty (notice the word itself has an almost archaic quality to it), or as a categorical obligation. This is not necessarily due to defects in our moral educational practices. It may as well be thought of, given what has just been said, as an accession to the complexity of moral life, and as based on the recognition that it is sometimes good, and not merely permissible, not to tell the whole truth.

But what this means is that children need to be taught explicitly that there are certain contexts in which the obligation to tell the truth is an unconditional duty, for example, when one is under oath in a court of law. This, no doubt, can be taught. I recall learning about this unconditional obligation watching *Perry Mason,* while at the same time being exposed to the constant perjury the show's plot line required. But it is worth noting that the lesson of the solemnity of oath taking is harder now to learn and take seriously than it once was. This may have implications for the ease with which competing motives might lead a child to wonder whether it might be permissible to lie in court, say, to protect an abusive parent whom she, nonetheless, loves.

The point can be brought out this way. The raised right hand signifying oath taking, followed by the words "I solemnly swear to tell the truth, the whole truth, and nothing but the truth," used to be followed by the phrase "so help me God," while the left hand was placed on the Bible. In most states the Bible is gone, as is the phrase "so help me God." But the concept of a "solemn swear" is a religious one, and the removal of the religious underpinnings (in a very literal sense) makes our solemn swears different from traditional solemn swears with the original underpinnings. Within an orthodox setting in which the Bible and the phrase "so help me God" meant, among other things, that this was a context in which the demand to speak the truth could not be overridden by any other consideration, the expectation of complete veracity (especially if a child was socialized to fear hellfire and brimstone) might be reasonable. But in a more secular context, in which the practice lacks these underpinnings, the worry that loyalty to an abusive parent or fear of parental punishment might exert greater motivational force than a "solemn swear" is a legitimate one.

Hopefully, there are ways to create secular equivalents of solemn contexts in which truth telling is understood as an unconditional obligation. It would be a great cultural loss, a loss in our capacities to trust each other in close relations, and a loss in the ability of our social and political institutions to adjudicate certain conflicts, if we cannot reconstitute grounds for individuals, young and old, to feel the moral pull of such obligations.

Culture and Honesty

Socialization for honesty is complex and culture-dependent. Children display honesty and dishonesty long before they are competent users of the relevant terms. Correct ascription, however, requires semantic competence. Proper use of the concept "lie" requires comprehension of a wide array of other concepts. These concepts include both the epistemic notions of belief, intent, and misrepresentation, as well as moral notions that specify, among other things, the sort of intent that counts as morally wrong and the sorts of situations in which dishonesty is wrong. The semantic task is not a simple one of learning, say, a dictionary definition. It involves the acquisition of an epistemic theory of other minds, as well as a moral theory. Because different moral conceptions construe the nature of lies, the kinds of lies, and the demands of honest expression in different ways, individuals will differ both in their ascriptions of lies and in their ascriptions of (degrees of) wrongness to different kinds of lies. In the end, the semantic problem of the meaning of "lie," the epistemic problem of coming to understand other minds as representational systems capable of containing misrepresentations, and the ethical task of coming to see oneself as a moral agent capable of doing good and harm (including the harms associated with creating misrepresentations in others) are inextricably intertwined. The sort of person that can be counted on to be honest will have had to learn many things, almost none of which is simple to teach. An honest character requires learning both our intricate theory of honest expression and caring that one exemplify that theory in one's life. Understanding other minds and comprehending the subtleties of our theory of honest expression is something the most manipulative cad needs to know as well as the saint. It is caring that one exemplifies this theory, that one be a person of a certain sort that makes all the difference. It is to this task of character formation and concern for one's own character that our moral community pays insufficient attention.

Notes

Acknowledgment—I am grateful to Debbie Zaitchik for helpful conversations on the issues discussed in this chapter. This chapter originally appeared in S. Ceci, M. Leichtman and M. Putnik (eds.), *Cognitive and Social Factors in Early Deception* (Hillsdale, N.J.: Lawrence Erlbaum Associates, 1992).

1. Sissela Bok, *Lying: Moral Choice in Public and Private Life* (New York: Random House, 1978), 15.

2. R. Burton and A. Strichartz, "Liar! Liar! Pants Afire!", in Ceci, Leitchman, and Putnik, *Cognitive and Social Factors in Early Deception* (Hillsdale, N.J.: Lawrence Erlbaum Associates, 1992), 11–28.

3. See C. Peterson, J. Peterson, and D. Seeto, "Developmental Changes in Ideas about Lying," *Child Development* 54 (1983): 1529–35; J. Piaget, *The Moral Judgement of the Child* (London: Kegan Paul, 1932); H. Wimmer, S. Gruber, and J. Perner, "Young Children's Conception of Lying: Lexical Realism–Moral Subjectivism," *Journal of Experimental Child Psychology* 37 (1984): 1–30.

4. K. Bussey, "Children's Lying and Truthfulness: Implications for Children's Testimony," in Ceci, Leitchman, and Putnik, *Cognitive and Social Factors* 89–110.

5. L. Coleman and P. Kay, "Prototype Semantics: The English Verb 'Lie,'" *Language* 57 (1981): 26–44.

6. G. Lakoff, *Women, Fire, and Dangerous Things: What Categories Reveal about the Mind* (Chicago: Chicago University Press, 1987), 72.

7. J. Haugaard and N. D. Reppucci, in Ceci, Leitchman, and Putnik, *Cognitive and Social Factors* 29–46.

8. M. Lewis, C. Stranger, and M. Sullivan, "Deception in Three-Year-Olds," *Developmental Psychology* 25 (1989): 439–43.

9. L. Coleman and P. Kay, "Prototype Semantics."

10. R. Burton and A. Strichartz, "Liar! Liar! Pants Afire!"

11. M. Chandler, A. Fritz, and S. Hala, "Small-Scale Deceit: Deception as a Marker of Two-, Three-, and Four-Year-Olds' Early Theories in Mind," *Child Development* 60 (1989): 1263–77; B. Sodian, "The Development of Deception in Young Children," *British Journal of Developmental Psychology* 9 (1991): 173–88.

12. S. Leekam, "Believing and Deceiving: Steps to Becoming a Good Liar," in Ceci, Leitchman, and Putnik, *Cognitive and Social Factors* 47–62.

13. Ibid., 50.

14. Ibid,; Bussey, "Children's Lying and Truthfulness"; C. Tate, A. Warren and T. Hess, "Adults' Liability for Childrens' 'Lie Ability': Can Adults Coach Children to Lie Successfully?" in Ceci, Leitchman, and Putnik, *Cognitive and Social Factors* 69–88.

15. D. Dennett, "Intentional Systems," *Journal of Philosophy* 8 (1971): 87–106.

16. H. M. Wellman, *The Child's Theory of Mind* (Cambridge: MIT Press, 1990).

17. Ibid., 63.

18. Ibid., 263.

19. Ibid., 119.

20. Leekam, "Believing and Deceiving."

21. Tate, Warren, and Hess, "Adults' Liability for Childrens' 'Lie Ability.'"

22. J. Haugaard and N. D. Reppucci, "Children and the Truth."

23. K. Bussey, "Children's Lying and Truthfulness."

24. J. Dunn, "The Beginnings of Moral Understanding: Development in the Second Year," in *The Emergence of Morality in Young Children*, ed. J. Kagan and S. Lamb (Chicago: Chicago University Press, 1987), 91–112.

25. See Bussey, "Children's Lying and Truthfulness."

26. A. C. Baier, "Why Honesty is a Hard Virtue," in *Identity, Character, and Morality: Essays in Moral Psychology*, ed. O. Flanagan and A. O. Rorty (Cambridge: MIT Press, 1990), 259–82.

27. Ibid., 268.

28. Ibid.

8

Ethics Naturalized: Ethics as Human Ecology

Why Ethics Naturalized Is Not Ethics Psychologized

In "Epistemology Naturalized," Quine[1] suggested that epistemology be assimilated to psychology. The trouble with this idea is apparent. Psychology is not in general concerned with *norms* of rational belief, but with the description and explanation of mental performance and mentally mediated performance and capacities.

The right way to think of epistemology naturalized is not, therefore, one in which epistemology is a "chapter of psychology," but rather to think of naturalized epistemology as having two components: a *descriptive-genealogical-nomological* component *and* a *normative* component.[2] Furthermore, not even the descriptive-genealogical-nomological component will consist of purely psychological generalizations, for much of the information about actual epistemic practices will come from biology, cognitive neuroscience, sociology, anthropology, and history—from the human sciences broadly construed. More obviously, *normative epistemology* will not be part of psychology, for it involves the gathering together of norms of inference, belief, and knowing that lead to success in ordinary reasoning, expert practical reasoning of the sort exhibited by good cooks and auto mechanics, and in science. And the evolved canons of inductive and deductive logic, statistics and probability theory, most certainly do not describe actual human reasoning practices. These canons—take, for example, principles governing representative sampling and warnings about affirming the consequent—come from abstracting successful epistemic practices from unsuccessful ones. The database is, as it were, provided by observation of humanity, but the human sciences do not (at least as standardly practiced) involve extraction of the norms. So epistemology naturalized is not epistemology psychologized.[3] But since successful practice—both mental and physical—is the standard by which norms are sorted and raised or lowered in epistemic status, pragmatism reigns.

I want to say that the same sort of story holds for a naturalistic ethics. Naturalistic ethics, too, will contain a descriptive-genealogical-nomological component that will specify certain basic capacities and propensities of *Homo sapiens*—sympathy, empathy, egoism, and so on—that are relevant to moral life. It will explain how people come to feel, think, and act about moral matters in the way(s) they do. It will explain how and in what ways moral learning, engagement, and response involve the emotions. It will explain what moral disagreement consists in and why it occurs; and it will explain why people sometimes resolve disagreement by recourse to agreements to tolerate each other without however approving of each other's beliefs, actions, practices, and institutions. It will tell us what people are doing when they make normative judgments. And finally, or as a consequence of all this, it will try to explain what goes on when people try to educate the young, improve the moral climate, propose moral theories, and so on.

It should be pointed out that every great moral philosopher has put forward certain descriptive-genealogical-nomological claims in arguing for substantive normative proposals, and although most off these claims suffer from sampling problems and were proposed in a time when the human sciences did not exist to test them, they are almost all testable—indeed some have been tested.[4] For example here are four claims familiar from the history of ethics that fit the bill of testable hypotheses relevant to normative ethics: He who knows the good does it; If you (really) have one virtue, you have the rest; Morality breaks down in a roughly linear fashion with breakdowns in the strength and visibility of social constraints; In a situation of profuse abundance, innate sympathy and benevolence will "increase tenfold" and the "cautious jealous virtue of justice will never be thought of."[5]

Presumably, how the descriptive-genealogical-nomological claims fare matters to the normative theories, and would have mattered to their proposers. Nonetheless no important moral philosopher, naturalist or non-naturalist, has ever thought that merely gathering together all relevant descriptive truths would yield a full normative ethical theory. Morals are radically underdetermined by the merely descriptive, the observational, but so too of course are science and normative epistemology. All three are domains of inquiry where ampliative generalizations and underdetermined norms abound.

The distinctively normative ethical component extends the last aspect of the descriptive-genealogical-nomological agenda: it will explain why some norms—including norms governing choosing norms—values, or virtues are good or better than others. One common rationale for favoring a norm or set of norms is that it is suited to modify, suppress, transform, or amplify some characteristic or capacity belonging to our nature—either our animal nature or our nature as socially situated beings. The normative component may try to systematize at some abstract level the ways of feeling, living, and being that we, as moral creatures, should aspire to. But whether such systematizing is a good idea will itself be evaluated pragmatically.

Overall, the normative component involves the imaginative deployment of information from *any* source useful to criticism, self/social examination, formation of new or improved norms, and values and from improvements in moral educational practices, training of moral sensibilities, and so on. These sources include psychology, cognitive science, all the human sciences, especially history and anthropology, as well as literature, the arts,[6] and ordinary conversation based on ordinary everyday observations about how individuals, groups, communities, nation states, the community of persons or sentient beings are faring.[7]

The standard view is that descriptive-genealogical ethics can be naturalized, but that normative ethics cannot. One alleged obstacle is that nothing normative *follows* from any set of descriptive-genealogical-nomological generalizations. Another alleged obstacle is that naturalism typically leads to relativism, is deflationary and/or morally naive. It makes normativity a matter of power: either the power of benign but less than enlightened socialization forces, or the power of those in charge of the normative order, possibly fascists or Nazis or moral dunces.

Both the standard view, and the complaint about naturalistic normative ethics, turn on certain genuine difficulties with discovering how to live well, and with a certain fantastical way of conceiving of what's *"really* right" or *"really* good." But these difficulties have everything to do with the complexities of moral life—of life, period—and have *no* bearing whatsoever on the truth of ethical naturalism as a metaphysical thesis *nor* on our capacity to pursue genuinely normative and critical ethical inquiry.

A Minimalist Credo for the Ethical Naturalist

It will be useful to provide a *minimalist credo* for the ethical naturalist. First, ethical naturalism is nontranscendental in the following respect: it will not locate the rationale for moral claims in the a priori dictates of a faculty of pure reason—there is no such thing—nor in divine design. Because it is nontranscendental, ethical naturalism will need to provide an "error theory" that explains the appeal of transcendental rationales and explains why they are less credible than pragmatic rationales, possibly because they are disguised forms of pragmatic rationales. Second, ethical naturalism will not be the slightest bit unnerved by open-question arguments or by allegations of fallacious inferences from *is* to *ought*. With regard to "open-question" problems, ethics naturalized need not be reductive, so there need be no attempt to define "the good" in some unitary way such that one can ask the allegedly devastating question, "But is that which is said to be 'good,' good?" To be sure, some of the great naturalists, most utilitarians, for example, did try to define the good in a unitary way. This turned out not to work well—in part because the goods at which we aim are plural and resist a unifying analysis. But also, the force of open-question arguments fizzled with discoveries about failures of synonymy across the board—with discoveries about the lack of reductive definitions for most interesting terms.

With regard to the alleged is-ought problem, the smart naturalist makes no claims to establish demonstratively moral norms—he or she points to certain practices, values, virtues, and principles as reasonable based on inductive and abductive reasoning.

Third, ethical naturalism implies no position on the question of whether there really are, or are not, moral properties in the universe in the sense debated by moral realists, antirealists, and quasi realists. The important thing is that moral claims can be rationally supported, not that all the constituents of such claims refer or fail to refer to "real" things. Fourth ethical naturalism is compatible a priori, as it were, with cognitivism or noncognitivism. Naturalism is neutral between the view that "gut reactions" or, alternatively, deep and cautious reflection, are the best guide in moral life. Indeed, ethical naturalism can give different answers at the descriptive level and the normative level. Emotivism might be true as a descriptive psychosocial generalization, while a more cognitivist view might be favored normatively.[8]

Progress, Convergence, and Local Knowledge

So far I've done two things. I've argued that neither epistemology naturalized nor ethics naturalized will be a psychologized discipline *simpliciter*—neither will be a "chapter of psychology." Both will make use of information from all the human sciences and, in the case of ethics, from the arts as well, for the arts are a way we have of expressing insights about our nature and about matters of value and worth. They are also—indeed at the same time and for the same reasons—ways of knowing, forms of knowledge. Norms will be generated by examining this information in the light of standards we have evolved about what guides or constitutes successful practice.

Second, I've sketched a brief credo for the ethical naturalist—one that captures what at a minimum you need to be committed to to count as one—a credo that leaves open the possibility of different answers to questions about moral realism and antirealism and about cognitivism and noncognitivism.[9]

So far I've been working with the proposal that ethics naturalized can go the very same route as epistemology naturalized. But things that are alike in many respects are not alike in all respects. Indeed, Quine himself is skeptical of a robust naturalized ethics, arguing instead that ethics is "methodologically infirm" compared to science[10] and that both naturalized epistemology and science, unlike ethics, have an unproblematic, uncontroversial end, truth and prediction—a goal which is, as it were, simply "descriptive." Quine writes: "A word now about the status, for me, of epistemic values. Naturalization of epistemology does not jettison the normative and settle for the indiscriminate description of ongoing procedures. For me normative epistemology is a branch of engineering. It is the technology of truth seeking, or, in a more cautiously epistemological term, prediction. Like any technology, it makes free use of whatever scientific findings may suit its purpose. It draws upon mathematics in computing standard deviation and probable error and in scouting the gambler's fallacy. It draws upon experimental psychology in exposing perceptual illusions, and upon cognitive psychology in scouting wishful thinking. It draws upon neurology and physics, in a general way, in discounting testimony from occult or parapsychological sources. There is no question here of ultimate value, as in morals; it is a matter of efficacy for an ulterior end, truth or prediction. The normative here, as elsewhere in engineering, becomes descriptive when the terminal parameter is expressed. We could say the same of morality if we could view it as aimed at reward in heaven."[11]

I don't see how the argument can be made to work. To be sure, any socially enriched theory of what happiness or welfare or flourishing consists in will be irreducible to observation or, what is different, to basic facts about human nature. But it is hard to see how this constitutes a significant objection since, according to Quine, the slide from unreduced to unjustified is illegitimate. "There are electrons" is, after all, irreducible, but not thereby unjustified. Furthermore, it is not as if our noninstrumental socially enriched moral conceptions are picked from thin air. In the first place, they invariably have some, possibly very remote, links to certain basic appetites and aversions. Second, even if we cannot reduce our ultimate values to something else, we can often say nontrivial things about them which have justificatory bearing. For example, we can sometimes say things about the ways in which some newly discovered good is good. This need not involve instrumental reduction as much as feature specification of the nature of the particular good. Third, even if we find that there are certain things, pain, for example, about which we have little more to say than allowing one part of our ethical conception to bottom out in such a bald fact engenders lack of justification—especially since science's bottoming out in similarly bald facts is taken by Quine to ground it. It is simply stipulative to suggest that the values that guide science and normative epistemology, as we know them, are unproblematic "ulterior ends"—some sort of "descriptive terminal parameter" specified by nature in the way our values would be specified by God if there was a God. We do science and epistemology in ways that show every sign of being driven by socially specific values. Furthermore, insofar as we can ground some sort of minimal transcultural "need to know" it will be grounded in certain basic features of persons as epistemically capable biological organisms as well as in certain basic desires to live well—characteristics that may also drive our ethical constructions across social worlds. The attempt to draw a distinction between the unproblematic ulterior ends of truth and prediction that guide science and epistemology and our ultimate ethical values that sit "unreduced and so unjustified" tries to mark a distinction where there is none and represents yet another remnant of positivistic dogma.

My conclusion then is that these ways of characterizing the situation of ethics, on the one side, and epistemology and science, on the other, are off-target. Doing science at all *and* then doing it the ways we do it, and for the reasons we do it, involve a host of normative commitments. Nonetheless, I do think we need an account for the often observed fact that ethical wisdom, insofar as there is such a thing, fails to reach convergence in the way epistemic norms and scientific knowledge do—where by "science" I mean, for ease of argument, to restrict myself to areas like anatomy, physiology, inorganic and organic chemistry, and physics without general relativity or quantum physics. Convergence in epistemology and science is, over long periods of time, thought to be correlated with, tracking ever more closely "the right ways to collect and utilize evidence" and "the truth about the way things are." So there is *both* convergence and progress.

For the rest of this chapter I want to explain why the lack of convergence about ethical matters, insofar as there is such lack, and the difficulty with applying the concept of progress to moral knowledge are things we ought to accept, and that they harm neither the naturalistic project nor the idea that there is, or can be, ethical knowledge. In effect, I'll argue for a certain asymmetry between epistemology naturalized and science, on the one side, and ethics, on the other, even though, up until now, I have been emphasizing some of their similarities.

A way to state my general idea is this: The links between any inquiry and the convergence and/or progress such inquiry yields is, assuming the domain is open to creatures with our kinds of minds, determined in large part by the degree of contingency and context dependency the target domain exhibits and the way the end or ends of inquiry are framed. The basic sciences, due to the univocality and consistency of their ends and to the nonlocal nature of the wisdom they typically seek, converge more and give evidence of being progressive in ways that ethics does not. The explanation has to do with the fact that the ends of ethics are multiple, often in tension with each other, and the wisdom we seek in ethics is often local knowledge—both *geographically local,* as it were, and *temporally local*—and thus convergence is ruled out from the start. Indeed, even in one and the same geographical and temporal location, different groups occupying that location might hold different norms and values.[12]

Some naturalists take the refinement and growth of moral knowledge over time—for the individual and the culture—too much for granted. For example, most neo-Piagetian models emphasize the invisible hand of some sort of sociomoral assimilation-accommodation mechanism in accounting for the refinement of moral knowledge over time. Others emphasize the visible processes of aggregation of precedent, constraint by precedents, and collective discussion and argument that mark sociomoral life. One can believe that moral knowledge exists without thinking that it grows naturally over time, that it has increased in quality and quantity in the course of human history.

Moral Network Theory

The best way to explain these points is by discussing a specific account of moral learning recently proposed by a fellow pragmatist and naturalist, Paul Churchland.[13] I call Churchland's view "moral network theory."[14] I'm attracted to the theory in certain ways, ways I will explain as I proceed. But I want to be clear that I am using the model as illustrative of a naturalistic model of moral learning, not as one I have decided to advocate yet. First, I'll offer a brief reconstruction of the descriptive-genealogical-nomological component of moral network theory. Then I'll address the tricky problem of extrapolating from moral network theory as a credible model of moral learning, habit and perception formation, moral imagination, and reasoning to the conclusion that the process yields convergence, leads to progress, and yields objective knowledge, now pragmatically understood. Still I'll insist that the worries I raise offer no solace to those who think that the naturalist has no resources, no perspective, from which to make judgments about what is good and right.

Acquiring knowledge, according to moral network theory is primarily a process of learning *how:* how to recognize a wide variety of complex situations and how to respond to them appropriately. Through exposure to situations—situations that include talk—moral perception, cognition, and response develop and are refined. According to moral network theory, there is a straightforward analogy between the way a submarine sonar device that needs to learn to distinguish rocks from mines might acquire the competence to do so and the way a human might acquire moral sensitivities and sensibilities.

One way to teach the mine-rock device would be simply to state the rule specifying the necessary and sufficient characteristics of rocks and mines. The trouble is that these are not known (indeed it is part of the mine producers job to make them as physically nondistinct as possible). Despite these efforts at disguise there are bound to be (or so we hope) subtle features that distinguish mines from rocks. So it would be good if the device could be trained in a situation where it starts by guessing mine or rock and then, by being clued into the accuracy of its guesses, develops a profile for recognizing rocks from mines. Indeed, this can be done with computers that learn from experience. A suitably designed computer given feedback from a trainer about whether its mine-rock guesses are right or wrong will figure out for itself how to improve its performance. Eventually the mine-rock detector which, of course, never becomes perfect at its job, comes to be able to make judgments of kind very quickly and reliably.

According to moral network theory, the fundamental process is the same in the case of moral learning. Children learn to recognize certain prototypical kinds of social situations, and they learn to produce or avoid the behaviors prototypically required or prohibited in each:

> Children come to *see* certain distributions of goodies as a *fair* or *unfair distribution*. They learn to recognize that a found object may be *someone's property*, and that access is limited as a result. They learn to discriminate *unprovoked cruelty*, and to demand or expect punishment for the transgressor and comfort for the victim. They learn to recognize a *breach of promise*, and to howl in protest. They learn to recognize these and a hundred other prototypical social/moral situations, and the ways in which the embedding society generally reacts to those situations and expects them to react.[15]

The observations here are no more or less ampliative (although they are possibly more complex) than judging that "it looks like rain," that "the peach is not ripe yet," that "the air conditioning doesn't sound right," that "Jane is shy," that "the fans are in a frenzy," that "Bob is impatient."

These are the sorts of discriminative judgments we learn to make with ease, but not one of them is an observation sentence.

To indicate how complex the learning problem the child faces in just one domain, consider learning to tell the truth—learning, as we say, that honesty is the best policy. One thing we know for sure is that we do not teach, nor do we want to teach, the child that he has a categorical obligation to "tell the truth whenever the truth can be told."

With respect to *truth telling* the child needs to learn

a. What truth telling is (why jokes and fairy tales aren't lies)
b. What situations call for truth telling
c. How to tell the truth.

Perhaps this sounds simple: it is a nice short list after all. But consider the fact that we consider it important that novices learn to distinguish among situations that seem to call for truth telling, not all of which do—or which do, but not in the same way. Consider just four kinds of situations and what they require in terms of discrimination and response:

Situations that call for straightforward truth telling
"The cookies were for dessert; did you eat them all, Ben?"

Situations that call for tact
"So, Ben, you are enjoying school, aren't you?" (Said by teacher to child in front of parents)

Situations that call for kind falsehoods/white lies
"Kate, I got my hair cut a new way for the party tonight; how do you like it?" (One preteen to another)

"Kate, don't you think I'm getting better at soccer?" (Said by one teammate to another—and supposing Kate does not think Emily has improved one bit over the season)

Situations that call for lying/misinformation depending on who is asking
"Little boy—what is your address?" (Asked by stranger)

How exactly a child or an adult responds to a novel moral situation "will be a function of which of her many prototypes that situation activates, and this will be a matter of the relative similarity of the new situation to the various prototypes on which she was trained." Situations will occasionally be ambiguous and there will be disagreements about what is occurring. *"What seems a case of unprovoked cruelty to one child can seem a case of just retribution to another."*[16] Moral ambiguity creates mental cramps of various sorts, which lead to reflection, discussion, and argument, as does disagreement among persons about how to describe a certain act or situation. These in turn lead to prototype adjustment.

Two comments are in order before we proceed further. First, it should be emphasized, in case it is not obvious, that the moral network theorist is using the concept of a "prototype" in a very broad but principled sense. Indeed, Churchland argues that the *"prototype activation model"* is general enough to account for perceptual recognition *and* scientific explanation, for example, inference to the best explanation is (roughly) activation of "the most appropriate prototype vector" given the evidence.[17] So prototypes cover both *knowing how* and *knowing that*. This point is crucial. For it is an obvious objection to the model if it is just a model of *knowing how* that it is too crude. For the moral community engages in talk, often theoretical talk, designed to get at underlying regularities that ought to govern moral perception and response. Thus, what Churchland calls *"social-interaction* prototypes" "underwrite *ethical, legal,* and *social-etiquette* explanations." And despite the emphasis on informational pick-up based on right and wrong, approved- and disapproved-of responses, as when the mine-rock detector gets simple yes's and no's, we know that there are linguistic practices that both reflect, and can be used to refine, the practices.[18] So, for example, we explain why the Czech driver stops to help the man with the flat tire by explaining that there are "Good Samaritan" laws—rules to be applied in certain situations—in the Czech Republic. Conversely, the existence of the relevant social expectations expressed in such laws explains why the Czech driver *sees* a person with a flat as a person in need of his help and sees helping as something he ought to do—perhaps for prudential reasons, perhaps because Samaritanism is deeply engrained. The sort of sociomoral learning that takes place in the Czech Republic, but not in (most parts of) America, means that Czech drivers just stop to help people stuck on the side of the road, and that seeing drivers stuck on the side of the road engages certain feelings, either fear of the law if one is observed not stopping or a moral pull to help if the ingrained disposition involves some sort of genuine compassion or fellow-feeling.

The second comment is that the prototype activation model designed to explain moral learning must explain our notion of *morality* itself. Morality does not pick out a natural kind. What is considered moral, conventional, personal, and so on, depends on the complex set of practices, including practices involving the use of certain terms, that have evolved over time in different communities. If one asks for a *definition* of "moral" in our culture, it will be framed initially in terms of rules designed to keep humans from harming other humans—in terms of conflict avoidance and resolution. If, however, one looks to the meanings that reveal themselves in ascriptive practices, and in response to verbal probes of a more complex sort, one will also find that we think of the moral as having an intrapersonal component. That is, there are norms governing personal goodness, improvement, and perfection, as well as norms governing self-respect and self-esteem that are not reducible to conformity to interpersonal moral norms.[19] This point will matter for what I say later.[20]

So far I have sketched moral network theory as a descriptive-genealogical-nomological theory. It has some credibility, despite its sketchiness. Indeed, there are two aspects of the view that I find particularly compelling and fecund. The first is the idea that moral responsiveness does not (normally) involve deployment of a set of special-purpose rules or algorithms that are individually applied to all, and only, the problems for which they are designed specifically. Nor does moral responsiveness normally involve deployment of a single general-purpose rule or algorithm, such as the principle of utility or the categorical imperative, designed to deal with each and every moral problem. Moral issues are heterogeneous in kind, and the moral community wisely trains us to possess a vast array of moral competencies suited—often in complex combinations and configurations—to multifarious domains.

It is a controversial fact, but one that I believe to be a fact, that morality resists theoretical unification under either a set of special-purpose rules or a single general-purpose rule or principle, such as the categorical imperative or the principle of utility. If this is right, and if it is right because the ends of moral life are plural and heterogeneous in kind and because our practices of moral education rightly reflect this, then we have some greater purchase on why the project of finding a single theoretically satisfying moral theory has failed.

The second feature of the view that I like is this: The theory is, as I call it, a moral network theory. But the total network is comprised of more than the neural nets that contain the moral knowledge a particular individual possesses. Whatever brain state instantiates (or is disposed to express) some segment of moral knowledge, either in the form of "know-how" or in propositional form, it does so only because it is "trained" by a community. The community itself is a network providing constant feedback to the human agent.

The neural network that underpins moral perception, thought, and action is created, maintained, and modified in relation to a particular natural and social environment. The moral network includes but is not exhausted by the dispositional states laid down in the brains of particular individuals.

Normativity

It is time to see how moral network theory—as an example of one sort of descriptive-genealogical-nomological theory likely to be offered up by the naturalist—handles the normative issue. Churchland himself raises the worry in vivid terms:

> What is problematic is whether this process amounts to the learning of genuine Moral Truth, or to mere socialization. We can hardly collapse the distinction, lest we make moral criticism of diverse forms of social organization impossible. We want to defend this possibility, since . . . the socialization described above can occasionally amount to a cowardly acquiescence in an arbitrary and stultifying form of life. Can we specify under what circumstances it will amount to something more than this?[21]

Churchland claims that "an exactly parallel problem arises with regard to the learning of Scientific Truth," since almost no scientific learning is first-hand, and even that which is, occurs within a research tradition with a particular orientation, sets of methods, and so on. Nonetheless, despite overblown views of *Scientific Truth* and the *Correspondence to the Real* held by certain scientistic thinkers and hard-core metaphysical realists, Churchland insists that "there remains every reason to think that the normal learning process, as instanced both in individuals and in the collective enterprise of institutional science, involves a reliable and dramatic increase in the amount and the quality of the information we have about the world."[22] And, he claims, the same is true of moral knowledge:

> When such powerful learning networks as humans are confronted with the problem of how best to perceive the social world, and how best to conduct one's affairs within it, we have equally good reason to expect that the learning process will show an integrity comparable to that shown on other learning tasks, and will produce cognitive achievements as robust as those produced anywhere else. This expectation will be especially apt if, as in the case of "scientific" knowledge, the learning process is collective and the results are transmitted from generation to generation. In that case we have a continuing society under constant pressure to refine its categories of social and moral perception, and to modify its typical responses and expectations. Successful societies do this on a systematic basis.[23]

Churchland then asks:

Just what are the members of the society learning? They are learning how best to organize and administer their collective and individual affairs. What factors provoke change and improvement in their typical categories of moral perception and their typical forms of behavioral response? That is, what factors drive moral learning? They are many and various, but in general they arise from the continuing social experience of conducting a life under the existing moral framework. That is, moral learning is driven by social experience, often a long and painful social experience, just as theoretical science is driven by experiment. Moral knowledge thus has just as genuine a claim to objectivity as any other kind of empirical knowledge. What are the principles by which rational people adjust their moral conceptions in the face of unwelcome social experience? They are likely to be exactly the same "principles" that drive conceptual readjustment in science or anywhere else, and they are likely to be revealed as we come to understand how empirical brains actually do learn.[24]

The core argument is this: Moral knowledge is the result of complex socialization processes. What keeps moral socialization from being "mere" socialization has to do with several features of sociomoral (and scientific) life. "Mere" socialization is socialization toward which no critical attitude is taken, for which there are no rational mechanisms that drive adjustment, modification, and refinement. The reason moral socialization is not (or need not be) "mere" socialization has to do with the fact that there are constraints that govern the assessment and adjustment of moral learning. We are trying to learn assessment and adjustment of moral learning. We are trying to learn "how best to organize and administer [our] collective and individual affairs." Social experience provides feedback about how we are doing, and reliable cognitive mechanisms come into play in evaluating and assessing this feedback. So there are aims, activities to achieve these aims, feedback about success in achieving the aims, and reliable cognitive mechanisms designed to assess the meaning of the feedback and to make modifications to the activities.

What are these reliable cognitive mechanisms? They include individual reflection and collective reflection and conversation. Now it is important to understand what our reflective practices are ontologically. They do not involve the deployment of some rarefied culture-free faculty of Reason. Dewey puts it best: "The reflective disposition is not self-made nor a gift of the gods. It arises in some exceptional circumstances out of social customs. . . . [W]hen it has been generated it establishes a new custom."[25] We need to recognize that our practices of reflection are themselves natural developments that emerged in large measure because they were useful.[26] Our reflective practices, from individual reflection to collective conversation and debate, are themselves customs that permit "experimental initiative and creative invention in remaking custom."[27] The choice "is not between a moral authority outside custom and one within it. It is between adopting more or less intelligent and significant customs."[28]

I think of these Deweyan points as extensions of moral network theory's general line about moral knowledge.[29] But this idea that to be rational,[30] self-conscious, and critical are developments of natural capacities, that they are things we learn to be and to do, not transcendental capacities we simply have, is still not well understood, nor is it widely accepted. But it is true. Critical rationality is a perfectly natural capacity displayed by *Homo sapiens* socialized in certain ways. Fancy, yes. But nothing mysterious metaphysically.

So far I have tried to extend and develop the picture of moral learning favored by moral network theory—indicating how it might account for complex prototype activation, how it can account for our rational practices, ethical theory included, as themselves socially acquired and communally circumscribed in structure and content.

Moral Progress and Moral Convergence

I now want to speak about *two* concerns with the picture of normativity Churchland paints in the name of moral network theory. The first concern has to do with the strong similarity alleged to obtain between scientific and ethical knowledge; the second with the problematic view of moral objectivity, convergence, and progress that the too-tidy analogy supports. My main reservation has to do with Churchland's overly optimistic attitude about the capacities of the moral community to arrive at high-quality moral knowledge[31] *and* with the failure to emphasize sufficiently the local nature of much moral knowledge.

First, there is the overoptimistic attitude about moral progress. Now both Paul Churchland and I are pragmatists. So I agree with him completely when he says that "the quality of one's knowledge is measured not by any uniform correspondence between internal sentences and external facts, but by the quality of one's continuing performance."[32] I also agree with him when he writes of sociomoral knowledge acquisition that "[w]hat the child is learning in this process is the *structure of social space* and *how best to navigate one's way through it.* What the child is learning is practical wisdom: the wise administration of her practical affairs in a complex social environment. This is as genuine a case of learning about objective reality as one finds anywhere. It is also of fundamental importance for the character and quality of any individual's life, and not everyone succeeds equally in mastering the relevant intricacies."[33]

Here's the rub: What the child learns about "the wise administration of her practical affairs" is a complex mix of moral knowledge, social savvy, and prudential wisdom. These things overlap in important ways, but they don't overlap in all respects, and they are worth distinguishing. Once they are distinguished, it is easy to see that these things are typically in some tension with each other. The demands of social success and prudence can compete with each other and with the demands of morality. If most knowing is knowing "how," then what the sociomoral community must do is teach people how to resolve such conflicts. Communities of possessive individualists learn one form of resolution, Mother Teresa's nuns learn a different one. Practical success may come to both communities *as they see it,* but one might argue that moral considerations are hardly improved or developed equally in both communities. This may be fine, the way things should go, all things considered. But it is important not to think that when Churchland writes that "we have a continuing society under constant pressure to refine its categories of social and moral perception, and to modify its typical responses and expectations" that the "constant pressure to refine" is primarily working on the moral climate. The reason we shouldn't think this is simply because there are too many competing interests besides moral ones vying for control of our sociomoral responses: there is simple self-interest, prudence, concern with economic, social, and sexual success, and much else besides.[34]

A different but related point comes from reflecting on the ends of ethics. I certainly don't think that the ends of science are simple or unambiguous, but I suspect that they do not display the inherent tension that the ends of ethics do. What I have in mind here goes back to what I said earlier about the two sides of ethics: on the one side, the interpersonal, concerned with social stability, coordination, prevention of harms, and so on; and, on the other side, the intrapersonal, concerned with individual flourishing, personal goodness, and the like. The tension between impartial moral demands and what conduces to individual flourishing is ubiquitous. Moral ambiguity is endemic to the first steps of ordinary moral life. We wonder how spending so much on luxuries could possibly be justified, given the absolute poverty that exists in many places in the world. Much recent philosophical attention has been given to this tension between the more impartial demands of morality as we are exposed to it, and the goods of personal freedom, choice, and integrity that we also learn.[35] There are conceivable ways to remove the tension: just remove one of the dual ends of moral life from the way we construct our conception of it. But this seems an unappealing idea. It seems best to leave the tension as is. It is real, and more good comes from having to confront it again and again than could come from simply stipulating it away. But one consequence of leaving the causes of moral ambiguity in place is that we will often rightly feel a certain lack of confidence that we have done the right thing. This suggests that we are often, at least in the moral sphere, in situations where we have no firm knowledge to go on.

A related consequence of the fact that the very aims of ethics are in tension is this: The requirements of interpersonal ethics require that we cast the normative net widely and seek agreement about mechanisms of coordination and about what constitutes harm. The requirements of intrapersonal ethics create pressures to cast the net narrowly. It is good that some communities think that benevolence is the most important individual virtue, while others think that humility or peace of mind are. And we think it is good that different individuals find their good in different ways. So long as a life satisfies certain minimal conditions of ethical goodness, we relish differences in artistic, musical, aesthetic, spiritual, and intellectual self-expression. And, of course, some (but not all) ways of living we disapprove of we may nonetheless tolerate even while speaking up about the wastefulness or degeneracy involved.[36] The interpersonal side, in casting its nets more widely, may well yield relatively global moral knowledge: it just is wrong to kill someone except in self-defense.[37] But the idea that different persons find their good in different ways will require acknowledgment that much, possibly most, ethical knowledge is local knowledge. It is knowledge possessed by a particular group, Catholics, the Amish, secular humanists, Hindus, Muslims, and it is hugely relevant to the quality of the lives of the members of the group that they live virtuously as they see it.[38] This is not to suggest that there are not aspects of these forms of life worth objecting to. It is, however, to say that some of the objectionable aspects will be meaning-conferring. Whatever moral objections are made to such aspects by insiders or outsiders will need to come to terms with the fact that the critique of some interpersonal aspect, say, patriarchy, may be difficult to rationally assimilate because the critique sits, for the time being at least, in tension with some meaning-conferring, intrapersonal component of the group's life. It is also to say that we should beware moral nosiness and moral zealotry; there simply will be things that members of certain groups believe that will be odd but unobjectionable by our lights—for example, the Hindu belief that it is very bad for a son to have his hair cut and eat a chicken the day after his father's death.

Moral network theory, indeed all moral learning theories I know of, save Kohlberg's stage theory, which is no longer taken seriously as a theory of moral development—goes badly with naive enlightenment optimism about moral progress and convergence. Progress and convergence *might* come our way. But they won't come by way of some natural dialectic of reason (conceived again in the enlightenment sense) and experience. The moral community will no doubt yield some workable ways to "organize and administer" our "collective and individual affairs." But, for reasons I have suggested there is no remotely reliable guarantee that these "workable ways" will be morally workable. The pragmatist needs to be sensitive to different and conflicting senses of "what works."

In closing, I comment on Dewey's insight that "[m]oral science is not something with a separate province. It is physical, biological, and historic knowledge placed in a humane context where it will illuminate and guide the activities of men."[39] What is relevant to ethical reflection is everything we know, everything we can bring to ethical conversation that merits attention—data from the human sciences, from history, and literature, and the other arts, from playing with possible worlds in imagination, and from everyday commentary on everyday events. Critique is perspectival not transcultural or neutral—it originates in reflection from the point of view of this historical place and time.[40]

One lesson such reflection teaches, it seems to me, is that if ethics is like any science or is part of any science, it is part of *human ecology* concerned with saying what contributes to the well-being of humans, human groups, and human individuals in particular natural and social environments.[41]

Critique, on the view I am defending, can be as radical as one wishes.[42] It is just that it will be *perspectival.* It will originate from here and now, and not from some neutral, transcultural, or transcendental perspective. When we engage in the projects of self-understanding and self-criticism by looking to other moral sources—within our tradition or from another culture—we obviously challenge our own modes of self-understanding. Less obviously, but no less truly, when we criticize an alternative way of being or acting, our own ways of being and acting are changed in the dialectic of critique. But all critique is immanent. *Its meaning and outcome is source-dependent.*[43]

Thinking of normative ethical knowledge as something to be gleaned from thinking about human good relative to particular ecological niches will, it seems to me, make it easier for us to see that there are forces of many kinds, operating at many levels as humans seek their good; that individual human good can compete with the good of human groups and of nonhuman systems; and finally, that only some ethical knowledge is global, most is local, and appropriately so. It might also make it seem less compelling to find ethical agreement where none is needed.

Of course, saying what I have said is tantamount to affirming some form of moderate relativism. I intend and welcome this consequence.

Epilogue

Defending ethics naturalized, a pragmatic ethic conceived as part of human ecology, originally seemed enough for this essay. However, I have been continually questioned about this—an issue I have tried to hold off to another time and place—in Los Angeles, St. Louis, and Ithaca. So for the sake of the reader who wonders how the argument for moderate relativism would go on from here, I provide this sketch. The question that invariably arises is, How can a relativist make any credible value judgments? A relativist might try to *influence* others to adopt certain norms, values, and attitudes but this couldn't be done *rationally,* since the relativist doesn't believe in rationality.

This is old debate, one the antirelativist cannot win. The charges against the relativist are indefensible and invariably unimaginative. We are to imagine that the relativist could have nothing to say about evil, about Hitler, for example. Here I can only gesture toward a two-pronged argument that would need to be spelled out in detail. The first prong emphasizes that relativism is the position that certain things are relative to other things. So "being a tall person" is relative. Relative to what? Certainly not to everything. It is relative to the average height of persons. It is not relative to the price of tea in China, or to the number of rats in Paris, or to the temperature at the center of the earth, or to the laws regarding abortion, or to zillions of other things. The relativist is attuned to relations that matter, to relations that have relevance to the matter at hand. Even if there is no such thing as "transcendent rationality" as some philosophers conceive it, there are perfectly reasonable ways of analyzing problems, proposing solutions, and recommending attitudes. This is the essence of pragmatism. Pragmatism is a theory of rationality.

The second prong of the argument involves moving from defense to offense. Here the tactic is to emphasize the contingency of the values we hold dear, while at the same time emphasizing that this contingency is no reason for not holding them dear and meaning-constitutive. If it is true, as I think it is, that whether consciousness of the contingency of life undermines confidence, self-respect, and their suite, depends on what attitudes one takes toward contingency, then there are some new things to be said in favor of emphasizing "consciousness of contingency." Recognition of contingency has the advantage of being historically, sociologically, anthropologically, and psychologically realistic. Realism is a form of authenticity, and authenticity has much to be said in its favor. Furthermore, recognition of contingency engenders respect for human diversity, which engenders tolerant attitudes. This has generally positive political consequences. Furthermore, respect for human diversity and tolerant attitudes are fully compatible with deploying our critical capacities in judging the quality and worth of alternative ways of being. There are judgments to be made of quality and worth for those who are living a certain way, and there are assessments about whether we should try to adopt certain ways of being that are not at present our own. Attunement to contingency, plural values, and the vast array of possible human personalities, opens the way for use of important and underutilized human capacities: capacities for critical reflection, for seeking deep understanding of alternative ways of being and living, and for deploying our agentic capacities to modify our selves, engage in identity experimentation, and meaning location within the vast space of possibilities that have been and are being tried by our fellows. It is a futile but apparently well-entrenched attitude that one ought to try to discover the single right way to think, live, and be. But there is a great experiment going on. It involves the exploration of multiple alternative possibilities, multifarious ways of living, some better than others and some positively awful from any reasonable perspective. The main point is that the relativist has an attitude conducive to an appreciation of alternative ways of life and to the patient exploration of how to use this exposure in the distinctively human project of reflective work on the self, on self-improvement. The reflective relativist, the pragmatic pluralist, has the right attitude—right for a world in which profitable communication and politics demand respect and tolerance, but in which no one expects a respectful, tolerant person or polity to lose the capacity to identify and resist evil where it exists; and right in terms of the development of our capacities of sympathetic understanding, acuity in judgment, and self-modification, and on occasion, radical transformation.

Notes

Acknowledgments—Earlier versions of this paper were given at the APA meetings in Los Angeles, and at the Mind and Morals Conference at Washington University in March and April 1994, in June 1994 at Monash University, Australia, and in October 1994 at Cornell University. I am grateful to many individuals for helpful comments and criticisms.

1. W. V. O. Quine, "Epistemology Naturalized," in *Ontological Relativity and Other Essays* (New York: Columbia University Press, 1969), 69–90.

2. I'm not sure whether there are laws of the human mind that are relevant to ethics, but the "nomological" holds a place for them should some turn up.

3. To my mind the best work in naturalized epistemology is that of Alvin Goldman; see *Epistemology and Cognition* (Cambridge: Harvard University Press, 1986), and *Liaisons: Philosophy Meets the Cognitive and Social Sciences* (Cambridge: MIT Press, 1992). Goldman never tries to derive normative conclusions from descrip-

tive premises, although he rightly thinks the descriptive is relevant to the norma-tive. Furthermore, he continually emphasizes the historical and social dimensions of epistemology in a way that Quine does not.

4. See Owen Flanagan, *Varieties of Moral Personality: Ethics and Psychological Realism* (Cambridge, Mass.: Harvard University Press, 1991).

5. David Hume, *An Enquiry Concerning the Principles of Morals*, (edited with Introduction, by J. B. Schneewind, Indianapolis: Hackett Publishing Company, 1983, originally published 1751), 21.

6. Richard Rorty convincingly suggests that the "formulation of general moral principles has been less useful to the development of liberal institutions than has the gradual expansion of the imagination" through works like those of Engels, Harriet Taylor, and J. S. Mill, Harriet Beecher Stowe, Malinowski, Martin Luther King Jr., Alexis de Tocqueville, and Catherine MacKinnon ("On Ethnocentrism," in R. Rorty, *Philosophical Papers* 1, [Cambridge: Cambridge University Press, 1991], 207).

7. Critics of naturalized ethics are quick to point out that notions like "flourish-ing," "how people are faring," "what works for individuals, groups, nation states, the world," etc., are vague, virtually impossible to fix in a noncontroversial way. This is true. The pragmatist is committed to the requirement that normative judgments get filled out in conversation and debate. Criteria of flourishing, what works, and so on, will be as open to criticism as the initial judgments themselves. It is hard, therefore, to see how the criticism *is* a criticism. The naturalist is open to conversational vindication of normative claims, she admits that her background criteria, cashed out, are open to criticism and reformulation, and she admits that words like "what works," "what conduces to flourishing," are superordinate terms. Specificity is gained in more fine-grained discussion of particular issues. But in any case there is no ethical theory ever known, naturalist or nonnaturalist, that has not depended on abstract concepts. Thin concepts sometimes yield to thick concepts—"That's bad." "Why?" "Because it is immodest." Now one can and often does stop here. But one can go on in any number of directions. "Why is it immodest?" "Why should I care about immodesty?"

8. Bernard Williams, like myself, thinks that the descriptive underdetermines the normative. But there is a relevance relation. See his *Shame and Necessity* (Berke-ley: University of California Press, 1993) for an evaluation of the positives and negatives associated with shame versus guilt cultures. This is work that has, indeed, that requires as its database, sophisticated psycho-social-historical knowledge. Allan Gibbard's book, *Wise Choices, Apt Feelings: A Theory of Normative Judgment* (Cambridge, Mass.: Harvard University Press, 1990), is another one that links the descriptive and normative. Gibbard describes his "expressivist view" as noncogniti-vist, but I find it more useful to think of it as cognitivist, as a rational reconstruction of what is involved in moral competence, where what is involved is expressing our allegiance to norms that have been vindicated by assessments in terms of aptness, in terms of what it makes sense to think, feel, believe, and so on.

9. In both the realism/antirealism cases and the cognitivist/noncognitivist case, different answers might be given at the descriptive and normative levels.

J. L. Mackie, author of *Ethics: Inventing Right and Wrong* (New York: Penguin, 1977), is an example of a philosopher who thought that ordinary people were committed to a form of realism about values but were wrong. In spite of this, Mackie saw no problem with advocating utilitarianism as the best moral theory and in that sense was a cognitivist—a cognitivist antirealist, as it were.

10. W. V. O. Quine, "On the Natural of Moral Values," *Critical Inquiry* 5 (1979): 471–480.

11. W. V. O. Quine, "Reply to Morton White," in *The Philosophy of W. V. Quine,* ed. L. E. Hahn and P. A. Schilpp (La Salle, Ill.: Open Court, 1986), 664–65.

12. And, even if there are shared values in this locale, moral knowledge might be *domain-specific.* This is an idea that has been pressed in different ways by Virginia Held, *Rights and Goods* (Minneapolis: University of Minnesota Press, 1984); Michael Walzer, *Spheres of Justice* (New York: Basic Books, 1983); and Flanagan, *Varieties.*

13. Paul M. Churchland, *A Neurocomputational Perspective: The Nature of Mind and the Structure of Science* (Cambridge: MIT Press, 1989). See also Mark Johnson, *Moral Imagination: Implications of Cognitive Science for Ethics* (Chicago: Chicago University Press, 1993).

14. Owen Flanagan, "The Moral Network," in *The Churchlands and Their Critics,* ed. R. McCauley (London: Basil Blackwell, 1996).

15. Churchland, *Neurocomputational Perspective,* 299.

16. Ibid., 300.

17. Ibid., 218.

18. Ibid., 216.

19. Flanagan, *Varieties.*

20. One issue I haven't emphasized here, but discuss at length in *Varieties of Moral Personality,* is the way personality develops. One might think that it is a problem for a network theory that it will explain the acquisition of moral proto- types in such a way that character is just a hodgepodge of prototypes. I don't think this is a consequence of moral network theory. One idea is to emphasize the fact that the human organism is having its natural sense of its own continuity and connectedness reinforced by the social community. A self, a person, is being built. The community counts on the individual developing a sense of his own integrity, of seeing himself as an originator of agency, capable of carrying through on intentions and plans, and of being held accountable for his actions. The commu- nity, in effect, encourages a certain complex picture of what it means to be a person, and it typically ties satisfaction of moral norms to this picture. Identity involves norms, and the self is oriented toward satisfying these norms. This helps explain the powerful connections that shame, guilt, self-esteem, and self-respect have to morality. Morality is acquired by a person with a continuing identity who cares about norm satisfaction and about living well and good.

21. Churchland, *Neurocomputational Perspective,* 300.

22. Ibid., 301.

23. Ibid., 301–2. Churchland continues the quoted passage this way: "A body of legislation accumulates, with successive additions, deletions, and modifications. A

body of case law accumulates, and the technique of finding and citing relevant precedents (which are, of course, *prototypes*) becomes a central feature of adjudicating legal disputes." The law is a good example of a well-controlled normative domain where previous decisions produce weighty constraints and norms accumulate. But it is not obvious that the law and morality, despite both being normative, are alike in these respects. In the law, publicity, precedent, and stability are highly valued—indeed they are partly constitutive of the law. Public, stable norms, with precedents, are thought to be good, and essential to successful and reliable negotiation of the parts of life covered by the law. But it is also recognized that the goods of stability, publicity, and so on, are perfectly compatible with irrational or immoral laws. So one point is that the aims of the law are not the same as that of ethics (ignorance of the law is no defense; ethical ignorance can be). Another issue arises in the first part of the quoted passage where Churchland frames the issue as one of humans confronting "the problem of how best to perceive the social world, and how best to conduct one's affairs within it." This is, I think, just the right way to see the problem. But I want to insist that there is a telling difference between, for example, learning about legal reality or how best to perceive the causal, temporal, spatial structure of the world, and how to conduct one's affairs in this (these) world(s). The difference is simply this: These latter structures are relatively more stable and relatively more global than the moral structure of the world is. This is one reason why Piagetian developmental stage theories have had some success with space, time, causality, conservation, and number, while Kohlberg's extension of Piaget's model to the moral sphere has turned out to be a dismal failure, an utterly degenerate research program despite many true believers.

24. Ibid., 302.

25. John Dewey, *Human Nature and Conduct* (1922; reprint, Carbondale: Southern Illinois University Press, 1988), 56.

26. In all likelihood, the capacities for reflection are rooted in the architecture of a system attuned both to similarities and differences, the latter producing cognitive adjustment of various sorts, including protoreflection.

27. Dewey, *Human Nature,* 56.

28. Ibid., 58. It is an illusion to which the moral theorist is historically but, perhaps not inevitably, prone that his pronouncements can move outside the space of human nature, conduct, and history and judge from the *point of view of reason alone* what is right and good. This is a silly idea. The key to a successful normative naturalism is to conceive of "reasoning" in the cognitive loop, as a natural capacity of a socially situated mind/brain, and to argue for the superiority of certain methods of achieving moral knowledge and improving the moral climate. Arguments for the superiority of certain methods and certain norms need to be based on evidence from any source that has relevance to claims about human flourishing.

29. We might also compare the view being floated to Allan Gibbard's norm-expressivist view in *Wise Choices.* For Gibbard, norms express judgments about *what it makes sense to feel, think, and do.* Norm expression involves endorsement, as it does in classical emotivism. But it is endorsement that can be rationally discussed among conversants—endorsement that can be "discursively redeemed" to give it

its Habermasian twist (195). Setting talk of the literal truth or falsehood of normative utterances generally—and normative moral utterances specifically—to one
side, there is still plenty to be said on behalf of the rationality or sensibility of
particular normative claims. There are conversational challenges to meet, facts to
call attention to, consistency and relevance to display, and higher-level norms that
govern the acceptance of other norms to bring on the scene. We will need to
explain whether the norms we endorse forbid a particular act, require it, or simply
allow it. And we may be called upon to explain the point behind any of our norms.

For Gibbard, morality is first and foremost concerned with interpersonal *coordination* and *social stability*. Given linguistic capacity, it is natural that the need for
coordination will lead eventually to norms of conversation that govern normative
influence, to the vindication of specific normative judgments, and so on. It makes
sense to develop such norms if our aim is coordination. We expect our fellow
discussants to be consistent in their beliefs and attitudes and thus we can ask them
reasonably to show us how it is that their normative system is consistent. We can ask
them to say more about some normative judgment to help us to see its rationale.
We can ask them to provide a deeper rationale or to provide us with reason for
taking them seriously as reliable normative judges, and so on. A "reason" is
anything that can be said in favor of some belief, value, or norm, any consideration
that weighs in favor of it. Since the things that can be said on behalf of most
anything constitute an indefinitely large class, reasons abound in normative life.
No set of reasons may yield conviction in the skeptic or in someone whose life form
lies too far from our own. But this in no way distinguishes normative life from the
rest of life.

30. I'm using "rational," "rationality," and their suite without capitals or raised-
eyebrow quotes to indicate that I am speaking of natural not transcendental human capacities.

31. This attitude continues to reveal itself in Churchland's *The Engine of Reason,
The Seat of the Soul* (Cambridge: MIT Press, 1995).

32. Churchland, *Neurocomputational Perspective.* See also Owen Flanagan,
"Quinean Ethics," *Ethics* 93 (1982): 56–74.

33. Churchland, *Neurocomputational Perspective,* 300.

34. Furthermore, it really is in the interest of different individuals and social
groups to train others to believe (and even to make it true up to a point) that their
being well and doing well involves conforming to norms that produce dispropor-
tionate good for the trainers.

35. Rawls, *Political Liberalism* (New York: Columbia University Press, 1993),
sees the tension as one between the ends of politics and ethics, but the basic point is
the same.

36. One problem that often occurs, and that this picture helps us understand, is
that wide-net policies, e.g., U.S. abortion laws, can not only conflict with the ways
some individuals and groups find ethical meaning but also undermine their sense
of their own integrity by virtue of their complex commitment to both the larger
culture *and* the values of their group.

37. Stanley Hauerwas has pointed out to me that my example is less plausible

empirically than this one: It is wrong to kill someone except when they are being sacrificed for the sake of the gods.

38. Of course, much of science, even chemistry, biology, physics, is local. Ecology itself is local with a vengeance. The generalizations true in tropical and Arctic zones may have no interesting commonalities. The point is that the first few of these aspire to nonlocal generalizations that will be true locally, so if there is any light around, it is traveling at *the* speed of light. Ecology aspires to local knowledge that conforms, of course, to whatever general laws of nature there are.

39. Dewey, *Human Nature,* 204–5.

40. "We postmodern bourgeois liberals no longer tag our central beliefs and desires as "necessary" or "natural" and our peripheral ones as "contingent" or "cultural." This is partly because *anthropologists, novelists, and historians* have done such a good job of exhibiting the contingency of various putative necessities . . . [and] philosophers like Quine, Wittgenstein and Derrida have made us wary of the very idea of a necessary-contingent distinction. . . . [T]hese philosophers describe human life by the metaphor of a continual reweaving of a web of beliefs and desires" (R. Rorty, "On Ethnocentrism," 208).

41. Why think of ethics naturalized as a branch of human ecology? Well, as I insist in *Varieties of Moral Personality,* the principle of minimal psychological realism is not sufficient to fix correct theory because many more theories and person types are realizable than are good, *and* because many good ones have yet to be realized. Moral theories and moral personalities are fixed (and largely assessed) in relation to *particular environments* and *ecological niches* which change, overlap, etc. Therefore, it is best to think of ethics as part of human ecology, i.e., neither as a special philosophical discipline nor as a part of any *particular* human science. Are all ways of life OK? Are the only legitimate standards of criticism "internal" ones? The answer is no. What is good depends a great deal on what is good for a particular community, but when that community interacts with other communities then these get a say. Furthermore, what can *seem* like a good practice or ideal can, when all the information from history, anthropology, psychology, philosophy, literature is brought in, turn out to have been tried, tested, and turned out not to be such a good idea. So if ethics is part human ecology, and I think that it is, the norms governing the evaluation of practices and ideals will have to be as broad as possible. To judge ideals it will not do simply to look and see whether healthy persons and healthy communities are subserved by them in the here and now, but that this "health" is bought without incorporating practices, slavery, racism, sexism, and the like, which we know can go unnoticed for some time, but that can keep persons from flourishing, and eventually poison human relations, if not in the present, at least in nearby generations.

42. It seems to me that a common worry about naturalism is that it will be conservative. One can see why excessive dependence on the notions of the self-correcting aspects of morality might fuel this worry. This is one reason why I recommend rejecting the self-correcting, progressive idea. It is naively Panglossian.

43. This point about the perspectival nature of moral critique is widely granted

across philosophical space. See, e.g., all of Alasdair MacIntyre's and Richard Rorty's recent work; C. Taylor "Understanding and Ethnocentrism," in C. Taylor *Philosophical Papers* 2, (Cambridge: Cambridge University Press, 1985); Hilary Putnam writes, "We can only hope to produce a better conception of morality if we operate from within our own tradition" (*Reason Truth and History* [Cambridge: Cambridge University Press, 1981], 216). The point is that there is no other tradition to operate from, no other perspective to take, as one begins and engages in the project of moral critique. Of course, the moral source one starts from changes as critique proceeds, and one can modify one's source by adopting the convictions of other individuals or groups.

9

Identity and Reflection

What is the connection between identity and reflection, between possession of an integrated, motivationally effective self and articulate self-comprehension? To what extent is ethical self-evaluation necessary for personhood and for ethical goodness itself? I want to discuss these fundamental questions of philosophical psychology by exploring a provocative and influential attempt to answer them. This influential answer goes wrong in certain subtle but consistent ways. It overstates the degree to which rich and effective identity, as well as moral decency, are tied to articulate self-comprehension and evaluation. And it overstates the centrality of ethical identifications in human life.

Reflection is a good. But it is a relative, contingent good. Identity and goodness do not require reflectiveness to any significant degree, nor is distinctively ethical identification the indispensable font of all modern identity.

Moral Self Examination

In several important papers[1] and in his book *Sources of the Self: The Making of Modern Identity,*[2] Charles Taylor argues that the capacity for what he calls strong evaluation is a necessary feature of persons. He writes that "the capacity for strong evaluation in particular is essential to our notion of the human subject. . . . Without it an agent would lack a kind of depth we consider essential to humanity."[3] "The capacity for . . . strong evaluation is an essential feature of a person."[4] More recently, Taylor insists that strong evaluation is an inescapable feature of "undamaged" personhood. Strong evaluation involves "discrimination of right and wrong, better or worse, higher or lower, which are not rendered valid by our own desires, inclinations, or choices, but rather stand independent of these and offer standards by which they can be judged."[5] It is clear that Taylor conceives of the relevant capacity as one that is realized. It is an actualized potentiality not a bare potentiality. An individual is a person if and only if she is a strong evaluator.

In his more recent work, Taylor makes a number of significant modifications in the original picture of strong evaluation as it is used and described in *Sources of the Self*. He does not remark on any of these changes. But since these modifications involve both improvements in the view, some of which blunt the force of certain criticisms I make, and certain new problematic twists in the characterization of strong evaluation, I will be careful to call attention to them as the discussion proceeds.

Taylor employs Harry Frankfurt's well-known distinction between first- and second-order desires[6] as a basis for drawing the distinction between strong and weak evaluation. Here are several passes at an interpretation, each more refined than its predecessor, of the distinction Taylor wants to make.

1. In weak evaluation we are concerned ultimately only with how, given our circumstances, we can most effectively satisfy our first-order desires. Our second-order desires, insofar as we have any, are concerned with scheduling and ordering consummations, possibly within an overall hedonistic plan. In strong evaluation, on the other hand, we are concerned with the "qualitative *worth*" of different desires, values, and action tendencies.[7] The strong evaluator, unlike the weak evaluator, may "be called deep because what weighs with him are not only the consummations desired but also what kind of life, what quality of agent, they are to be."[8]

2. This way of contrasting weak and strong evaluators turns out not to work exactly, since the weak evaluator need not weigh things in simple quantitative terms, in terms of what is more pleasure-producing along some single dimension. The weak evaluator might think a southern vacation better than a northern one along an axis, or along various axes, of qualitative distinctions—it is more beautiful in the south than in the north, the environment is more serene in the south than in the north, the diet more spare and elegant in the south, and so on.

3. The weak and the strong evaluator cannot be distinguished, then, simply in terms that the latter judges things qualitatively whereas the former does not, or that the latter is reflective while the latter is not.[9] The difference lies more precisely in the fact that the strong evalua-

tor characterizes his "desires and inclinations as worthier, or nobler, or more integrated."[10] The weak evaluator's qualitative assessments either do not involve her own motives, desires, and inclinations, or if they do, involve only nonethical assessment of these motives, desires, and inclinations. The desire for the spare southern diet fits better than the northern diet with the plan of keeping her weight down, or the choice of a southern diet will be perceived as classier by those whose impression of her she fancies most.

4. It might seem that what distinguishes the weak from the strong evaluator is that the strong evaluator has the ability to condemn and override some of her own desires as unworthy, despite her powerful motivation to act in accordance with them. But the weak evaluator can do this, too. She can decide that a northern vacation is unworthy of a person as refined as herself, even though she would actually prefer to be in the north. If she is trying to live her life oriented around a ground project in which refinement, sophistication, and savoir faire are the central goals, she may well choose against what she prefers in this way. This shows that it is not the case that the weak evaluator's second-order evaluations are all instrumental, concerned only with how well her second-order plans and motives are suited to realizing her first-order desires. She may care about the quality of her sophisticated life in its own right. Furthermore, the standards of sophistication she abides by may exist independently of her own inclinations and desires. Strong evaluators cannot be distinguished, therefore, from weak evaluators in terms of the independence or objectivity of the standards they abide by.[11]

5. Insofar as the contrast between strong and weak evaluators has to do with capacities to overrule one's own motives, it has to do not with the capacity itself but with the reasons behind such overriding. When the strong evaluator overrules her own desires, she does so on the basis of some sort of ethical assessment. The weak evaluator, if she evaluates and overrides at all, does so on the basis of other kinds of assessment—kinds that need not be purely instrumental, however.

Sometimes Taylor paints the weak evaluator as a simple wanton who blows whichever way the winds of his own motivational economy blow. But the overall picture is best understood as one in which weak evaluators range from the simple wanton who makes no motivational assessments at all to persons who do make motivational assessments along a wide variety of dimensions, so long as these dimensions are not ethical. Groucho Marx, Truman Capote, Gore Vidal, Paul Gauguin, Lucille Ball, and Mick Jagger might fit the bill of persons, even decent persons, whose lives are not, or were not, guided in any central way by ethical commitments or distinctively ethical evaluation.

It seems best to think of weak evaluators as comprising an extraordinary variety of types. We might think of these types as sorted along a continuum that plots degree of reflectiveness. Or we might think of them as sorted along various continua individuated by motivational content, with each continuum plotting degree of reflectiveness within a content type. The aimless youths who "wild" in Central Park and the savvy, single-minded head of a drug cartel might both be seen as weak evaluators of a single-content type. Aesthetic types—think, for example, of Kierkegaard's character A. in *Either/Or* or of a Gauguin who does not see or otherwise experience the moral relevance of his prior commitments to Madame Gauguin and his children as he plans to pursue his artistic project in Tahiti—would form a different type. Within each type, self-comprehension might range from the virtually vacant to continuous, highly refined, and well-focused assessment of how well one is doing what one is trying to do or being what one is trying to be.

6. There is an ambiguity, however, in the concept of the ethical. This ambiguity is due in the first instance to the fact that the concept can be understood broadly or narrowly. In his book, Taylor is explicit that he intends the broad conception of the ethical as including not simply obligations, respect for rights, and conflict avoidance but also a wide range of intrapersonal concerns as well—concerns with how one should live, what one should care about, and so on. Whereas Williams draws the distinction between the narrow and wide conceptions in terms of the "moral" on the one hand and the "ethical" on the other[12] Taylor draws it as one between the "moral" and the "spiritual."[13] A life can be spiritually unworthy even if it is not, strictly speaking, immoral. Strong evaluators judge their lives in such broad ethical terms in a way that is "a bit broader than what is normally described as the moral."[14]

The conclusion we are drawn to is this: Strong evaluation is distinguished from weak evaluation not because only it involves second-order desires, not because only it involves qualitative assessment from the second level, nor because only it involves assessment from the perspective of a long-standing life plan or in terms of objective social standards, nor even because only it involves depth—although it is sometimes marked from weak evaluation in these ways—but because of the kind of evaluation involved. The strong evaluator assesses his or her motives and life in specifically ethical terms, "ethical" now broadly understood.

Implicit in this strong evaluation is thus placing our different motivation relative to each other, the drawing, as it were, of *a moral map of ourselves;* we contrast a higher, more clairvoyant, more serene motivation, with a baser, more self-enclosed and troubled one, which we can see ourselves as potentially growing beyond, if and when we come to experience things from the higher standpoint.[15]

Distinguishing the Strong from the Weak

Taylor wants there to be a distinction between weak and strong evaluators. From what I have said so far, one might reasonably suspect that the distinction between weak and strong evaluators will be hard to draw in any unequivocal terms. This is a reasonable suspicion. Five reasons weigh in its favor. First, the ethical is not neatly cordoned off from other domains of life, especially once one opts, as Taylor now does, for a broad conception of the ethical. Second, the domain of the ethical and thus what counts as ethical assessment is notoriously observer-relative. What looks like non-ethical assessment from an outsider's perspective may be ethical from an insider's perspective (Taylor himself makes this sort of point in his 1982 essay).[16] Third, evaluation can be nonethical without being counterethical. Imagine a person who lives a life built around love of baseball or the person Rawls imagines, who lives a life absorbed in the fate of blades of grass. Presumably even if we construe the ethical in broad terms, it will not include everything. Strong "spiritual" evaluation will still need to involve "discriminations of right or wrong, better or worse, higher or lower, which are not rendered valid by our own desires, inclinations, or choices."[17] The trouble is that we can imagine complex disagreements about whether the lives I have imagined fit the bill. And we can easily imagine that the persons who live lives built around baseball or the fate of grass or sophistication might fully abide what morality, commonsensically construed, demands. Fourth, there simply is no such thing as a pure strong evaluator (whether there can be a pure weak evaluator is a separate question). Normal persons sometimes behave wantonly; for example, we scratch where it itches. And even when we assess and evaluate our motives, we often do so in nonethical terms. Persons who go in for strong ethical evaluation often make vacation plans on the same bases as savvy weak evaluators. It would be unrealistic as well as excessively moralistic to think that they should do otherwise. Fifth and relatedly, insofar as there are strong evaluators, they, like weak evaluators, reflect to various degrees of depth and breadth, and they deploy vocabularies whose primary saliencies are not only Taylor's Nietzschean parade of nobility, worth, and their suite but also concepts of justice, love, humility, and many others besides (this point is quietly conceded in *Sources of the Self*).

My proposal that we think of weak evaluation as involving any kind of nonethical assessment, with the caveat that what counts as ethical assessment is a matter of social construction and thus a matter of interpretation and relativity, fits with most of what Taylor says, but not with everything. Usually he grounds strong evaluation in ethical evaluation, but sometimes he grounds it in any evaluation that is Nietzschean in the sense that it deploys a vocabulary of nobility and worth, but not necessarily a vocabulary of ethical nobility and worth, even broadly construed. Taylor rightly points out that such evaluative categories are sometimes used to make assessments of one's own and other's bearing, style, and demeanor.[18] This is because "the languages of qualitative contrast embrace more than the ethical."[19] Furthermore, in such cases, both insiders and outsiders would agree that such assessments are not intended as ethical ones.

The contrast between strong and weak evaluation will be much less useful (see Slote[20] for an argument to the effect that it already is useless), as well as internally inconsistent with the dominant line of analysis in Taylor's writings, if we make formal linguistic properties—the mere use of certain evaluative terminology—criterial for it. If we understand the ethical so broadly that anyone who evaluates her desires in terms of "better" and "worse" is a strong evaluator, then the person convinced of the superiority of her style, fashion, or social class will turn out to be a strong evaluator. I conclude that the best way to understand the contrast between strong and weak evaluation is as one involving ethical assessment, on the one hand, and any kind of nonethical assessment, on the other hand. Counting the sophisticate as a strong evaluator cuts too much against Taylor's dominant line that it is definitive of modern identity that we are strong evaluators who are concerned with the quality of our lives in broad ethical terms. The downside for Taylor of thinking of the contrast in the way I recommend, and thus not counting all qualitative assessment as ethical, is that it means that not everyone is a strong evaluator.

The Importance of Being Articulate

We now have a firm interpretation of how the contrast between weak and strong evaluation is supposed to work. The next step is to examine two different sorts of claims that Taylor makes about strong evaluation. One set of claims is descriptive or empirical; the other set is normative. There are two main descriptive claims. First, "the human beings we are and live with are all strong evaluators." Second, "our identity is defined by our fundamental [strong] evaluations."[21] Taylor elaborates on the second claim in this way:

> The notion of identity refers to certain [strong] evaluations which are essential because they are the indispensable horizon or foundation out of which we reflect and evaluate as persons. To lose this horizon, or not to have found it, is indeed a terrifying experience of disaggregation and loss. This is why we speak of an "identity crisis" when we have lost our grip on who we are. A self decides and acts out of certain fundamental [strong] evaluations.[22]

Because the two claims are broadly empirical—that all contemporary persons *are* strong evaluators and that only strong evaluations, not weak evaluations, can constitute identity—they can be assessed as such.

These empirical claims are distinct, however, from the normative claims that strong evaluation is necessary for ethical goodness, for ethical excellence, or for gaining, in the deepest possible ways, nonatomic self-understanding, autonomy, a sense of communal obligation, and so on. Fortunately for the defender of strong evaluation, the falsity of the empirical claims is compatible with the truth of the normative claims.

Is Taylor right that a realized capacity for strong evaluation is critical for personhood in these two senses—the first empirical, the other normative? I think not. In order to make out this case, it will be useful to set out three theses about persons that I claim should be accepted by any credible philosopohical psychology. These three claims are prior to and less controversial than the claims in question. They will help us understand better where and how the strong evaluative picture goes wrong.

First, there is the claim for the *intersubjective conception of the self*, the claim that identity is invariably created in the context of some social relation or other and is formed or constituted from the cloth of prior social forms and the possibilities available therein. Prior social forms enter into our formation as persons through the activity of previously socialized caretakers, and we are trained and sustained as persons with certain kinds of structured identities in social relations that we help change and modify but do not in the first instance create. We are neither creators nor sole guardians of our identities. The intersubjective conception of the self is something every moral or political conception should accept. It is a fundamental truth of philosophical psychology that we are intersubjective selves.

The second fundamental truth is that we are *self-comprehending creatures*. Some minimal form of self-awareness is critical for being a person. According to child psychologists, a sense of self is pretty firm by age two.[23] However, one needs to be careful not to pack too much into this fact. Compatible with the bare-bones truth that all normal *Homo sapiens* develop self-awareness and are self-comprehending in some minimal sense is the fact that normal persons often lack a deep reflective appreciation of who they are. The sort of self-awareness required for personhood can be extremely dim and inchoate. Furthermore, it can fail to track the truth.

It is important to keep these two things separate: dim and inchoate self-comprehension, on the one hand, and epistemically misguided self-comprehension, on the other hand. A person would be making a mistake if she were actually to deny the truth of the intersubjective conception—if she saw herself as a pure self-creation, if she denied her dependence on prior social structures and relations, and if she saw her identity as in no way sustained by certain ongoing social relations. It would be good, because true, to comprehend one's life in intersubjective terms.

However, it does not follow from this that every individual person must comprehend herself in terms expressed by the intersubjective conception of the self. That is, although it would be a mistake for any individual to deny the truth of the intersubjective conception and it applicability to herself, it is not so obviously an error not to have articulated this truth and incorporated it into one's reflectively held self-conception. One might simply not have a very reflectively held self-conception. One might even lack the ability to understand and thus to assent to (or dissent from) the appropriately formulated sentences when they are expressed in abstract philosophical terms. Both possibilities are compatible with one's being a self-comprehending and self-interpreting creature. The characters of many of Tolstoy's stories are unreflective and inarticulate in something like the relevant senses. I am thinking, for example, of Simon, the cobbler, and his wife, Matrena, in "What Men Live By," Efim and Elisha in "Two Old Men," and Nikita, the servant to Vasali Andreevich Brekunov, in "Master and Men." Most of Tolstoy's characters comprehend themselves to some degree and care that their lives express certain values: compassion and love, on the one hand, and a certain calm resignation to God's will, on the other hand. The intersubjective conception is true of the lives of the characters in Tolstoy's stories because it is true of every life. Furthermore, his noble peasants typically express a humble comprehension of their role in carrying out certain communal projects whose origins are antecedent to their own births and that will continue long after they die. But it is not clear that their intersubjectivity is very reflectively held or that it is subject to articulate containment by them in the form of some abstract philosophical truth.

Tolstoy's peasants serve as reminders that we must distinguish between the truths of philosophical psychology or anthropology that any acceptable moral or political theory must give articulate expression to, and the requirements we place on individual persons to know and articulate these same truths.[24]

Tolstoy's peasants (occasionally his characters are noble inarticulate merchants, for example, Ivan Dmitrich Aksenov in "God Sees the Truth, but Waits") allow a further distinction. There is as I've said the ubiquitous truth of philosophical psychology or anthropology expressed by the intersubjective conception. There is in addition to empirical intersubjectivity what I will call "normative intersubjectivity." *Normative intersubjectivity* comes in multifarious forms. Roughly, a life (or an ethical conception) expresses normative intersubjectivity if it treats it as good or worthy to partake of social union and if it treats the worth of social union as more than merely instrumental. I say "treats" rather than "sees" or "understands" because I want to allow for comprehension of the good of social union of the dim and inchoate sort that I have been emphasizing and I want to allow for a life that expresses the truth of normative intersubjectivity in the activities of living rather than, in the first instance, in how one linguistically conceives of things.

I cannot argue for normative intersubjectivity here. But it seems fair to say that especially in the bare-bones terms just expressed, it constitutes a third truth that, like the intersubjective conception itself and the idea that we are self-aware, self-comprehending creatures, is part of any credible philosophical psychology.

The analysis so far suggests this much: the three core truths of philosophical psychology express certain necessary conditions of distinctively human lives. But satisfying these conditions is compatible with not being a strong evaluator. Persons can satisfy these three truths and live morally good lives without satisfying the further conditions of strong evaluation.

Tolstoy's peasants are a case in point. Taylor stresses that the strong evaluator evaluates within some sort of contrastive space, and—at least in his original formulations—he seems to think that such contrasts can only be drawn within linguistic space. "The strong evaluator can articulate superiority just because he has a language of contrastive characterization."[25] Most of Tolstoy's noble peasants are inarticulate. Indeed, Tolstoy often uses articulateness as a dimension along which peasants are contrasted with persons of means, education, and refinement. In stories like "Master and Man" and the earlier "Three Deaths," the person of means, education, and refinement uses language to express querulousness, elitism, acquisitiveness, self-absorption, self-righteousness, and a rageful inability to accept the contingencies and vagaries of human experience, especially human finitude. This is contrasted with the goodness and calm resignation of the uneducated and inarticulate peasant.

Tolstoy's characters typically comprehend the contrast between a Christian life of love and compassion and its alternatives. If an agent can contrast her life or the values it expresses with alternatives, even if the alternative is only that of not living the life she knows in her sinews and bones to be good, then perhaps she can be said to possess a minimal language, or better, a minimal sense, of contrastive characterization. But Tolstoy's peasants cannot be very articulate about this contrast.

If comprehension of some contrastive space and motivation and evaluation that originate from some morally informed location within that contrastive space are sufficient for strong evaluation, then Tolstoy's peasants are strong evaluators. But if articulateness is taken as necessary as well (as it is by Taylor, but see the change in *Sources of the Self* discussed below), then they will not fit the bill. In either case, the alleged link between strong evaluation and moral personhood is weakened. This means that there is no easy route to the claim for the normative necessity of strong evaluation by way of an argument for its necessity for moral agency. Tolstoy's peasants are good, and they are good because their lives exemplify what they value and because what they value is good. That much seems firm.

We might question even the idea that comprehension of contrastive ethical space is necessary for being counted among the strong evaluators, or if it is necessary for being counted among them (because Taylor stipulates that it is), we might question whether contrastive comprehension is partly constitutive of being a good person with a rich identity, ethical motivation, and agency. There seems to be no impossibility in the idea that a particular individual, perhaps a whole social group, might see no other way to be. Not living as they do is not seen or otherwise experienced as a genuine possibility. Occasional temptations not to muster the effort to live their life as it should be lived provide at most a "notional" sense of contrast, not a "real" sense of contrast. Such persons could easily be imagined to gather motivational strength from their life form, and their integrity and self-worth might be totally tied up with living the life they live. If such persons are possible, then it is not a truth of any acceptable philosophical psychology that evaluating one's life contrastively in any very robust sense is necessary for being a person.[26] If firm, self-respecting identity is possible for persons who are both inarticulate and (let us suppose) unaware of contrastive possibilities, and if both these things are necessary for strong evaluation, then it follows that strong evaluation is not a necessary foundation and indispensable font of identity and motivation. And if some such persons are appropriately judged as good, strong evaluation is not necessary for moral goodness.[27]

Tolstoy's peasants have identities, as do the persons I have just been imagining, yet they do not fit the original characterizations of strong evaluation. But surely Tolstoy's peasants are not properly characterized as weak evaluators. They are not simple weighers of desires. They have rich identities that they express in action. Their identities are morally informed and express good, possibly excellent, values. This suggests that Taylor's distinction does not usefully capture many types of persons. For one thing, it is too intellectualist.

The analysis also implausibly projects a realized capacity for ethical self-appraisal onto the minds or consciousness of all our contemporaries. The idea that all contemporary persons are strong evaluators who cast their lives in terms of nobility, integration, and worth seems patently false. It conceals not only the good and unreflective types depicted by Tolstoy, but the hedonist, the amoralist, and the immoralist as well. One response is that all immoralists are strong evaluators with bad standards. Some are, but many are not. Furthermore, this move does nothing whatsoever to account for the hedonist, the rich, conspicuously consuming modern character who is committed to being a savvy weak evaluator, or for the amoralist, the aesthete of Kierkegaard's *Either/Or,* who does not care about or go in for ethical evaluation. Further evidence that there is something wrong with Taylor's picture comes from the psychological sources on which he claims to depend.

There is nothing in the canonical descriptions of persons who are suffering identity crises, and who are thereby immobilized and alienated from their own lives, that requires that we think of them as former virtuosos at strong evaluation or alternatively as persons who have never discovered the good of strong evaluation and have thereby come undone.[28] Even among those who suffer identity crises and were formerly strong evaluators, there is no necessity in thinking of their loss of identity as rooted primarily or exclusively in the loss of their capacities for strong evaluation. It seems plausible to think that in such cases the loss of strong evaluative identity is sometimes—perhaps often or usually—the effect of some awful process that makes all aspects of identity come undone, rather than its cause. Erik Erikson writes,

> The term "identity crisis" was first used, if I remember correctly, for a specific clinical purpose in the Mt. Zion Veterans' Rehabilitation Clinic during the Second World War. . . . Most of our patients, so we concluded at the time, had neither been "shellshocked" nor become malingerers, but had through the exigencies of war lost a sense of personal sameness and historical continuity. They were impaired in that central control over themselves for which, in the psychoanalytic scheme, only the "inner agency" of the ego could be held responsible. Therefore I spoke of loss of "ego identity."[29]

Individuals in identity crisis, of the sort Erikson describes, possess a sense of "mere" identity. That is, they normally experience themselves as the locus of a set of subjectively linked events, as a sort of conduit in which a certain bland and low-level sameness and continuity subsists. What they lack, and what horrifies us and immobilizes them, is any sense of coherent and authoritative "me-ness," of personal sameness—any sense that these subjectively linked events occurring to and in them constitute a person, a self, a life. Erikson asks what "identity feels like when you become aware of the fact that you undoubtedly *have* one," and he answers that it consists of "a *subjective sense* of an *invigorating sameness* and *continuity.*"[30] Without the invigorating sense of self there is no person and thus no coherent cognitive and motivational core from which the individual can generate purposes or in which he could find the energy required to sustain them were he able to find any in the first place.

Taylor claims to depend on standard notions of identity and identity crises in framing the notion of strong evaluation. But there is nothing in the passage quoted from Erikson, nor in the text around it, that indicates that persons in identity crises are all former strong evaluators. Identifying powerfully with one's desires, whatever they are, or with a superficial scheme of evaluation, such as persons who are centrally absorbed with style or fashion do, is enough to stave off an identity crisis in Erikson's sense. The best analysis of what persons in identity crises have lost is what Wong calls "effective identity."[31] Persons in identity crises have a dim and inchoate self-awareness. But the self of which they are aware is ghostly. It lacks robustness and vivacity, and it fails to energize. Persons in identity crises are in some significant sense care-less. It is because they have lost the capacity to care or are numb to caring that they are unmoved, that their agency is immobilized.

It is unclear whether the loss of the capacity to find one's self and gain one's motivational bearings through the self is best conceptualized as a loss of some reflexive capacity, so that a self cannot be found although there is still, so to speak, a self there, or whether the problem should be seen as rooted in the dissolution of the self, so that although one still has capacities for self-comprehension, self-control, and so on, there is no longer any robust self—no set of cares and identifications—to provide motivation, to be comprehended, controlled, and so on. The first problem would involve an access problem; the second a wipeout. But in neither case need the "lost self" be thought of as one (formerly) essentially constituted by ethical aims and purposes, and even less plausibly as a self whose whole horizon of being and motivational power was grounded in ethical aims and purposes.

Weak evaluators possess actual identities, which engender some subjective sense of who they are, and which they can lose touch with or which can become extremely disintegrated or dissolute. Recall that weak evaluators (if there are any) range from those types of persons who have only a dim and inchoate sense of who they are to persons who possess a perfectly clear and firm awareness of themselves as systems constituted by aims of a certain kind. The weak evaluator's life is built around nonethical aims but is not, I emphasize again, necessarily counterethical. It is easy enough, I think, to imagine Groucho Marx in an identity crisis. Indeed, the picture I am drawn to is one in which most weak evaluators will possess ethical standards and have the capacity to see their lives in ethical terms—it is just that doing so will not be central for them. A weak evaluator's loss of his sense of himself—of his sense of where his "center of narrative gravity" lies and in what it consists[32]—can be sufficient to cause an identity crisis in Erikson's sense, and it can lead to the immobilization of agency. Many professional athletes, whom we would not think of as particularly reflective or as centrally motivated by ethical concerns, fall prey to identity crises when they lose their central project, when the framework of their lives changes at the end of their playing career. Mental hospitals and therapists' offices are not disproportionately filled with formerly strongly reflective types.

As a consequence, it is not a simple truth of psychology that a "self decides and acts out of certain fundamental [strong] evaluations." Persons who don't go in for strong evaluation do not do so. Some such persons are familiar to most everyone, and some of them are pretty good (accidentally perhaps) and happy to boot. Being a weak evaluator is a necessary condition for being any person whatsoever. Nonetheless, being a strong evaluator, one who has well-developed capacities for specifically ethical evaluation and even, more implausibly, for whom such evaluation is the pivot on which her being turns, the basis on which all other motives are assessed, is neither a standard feature of all persons nor unambiguous and unproblematic as a moral ideal. Since the empirical claim is false, the unabashedly essentialist claim Taylor makes in *Sources of the Self* is false as well. He puts the essentialist claim this way: "I want to defend the strong thesis that . . . the horizons within which we live our lives and which make sense of them have to include these strong qualitative discriminations. Moreover this is not meant just as a contingently true psychological fact about human beings."[33] Indeed, it is extremely puzzling that such a historicist as Taylor is tempted to make such essentialist claims at all. I suspect that the cause lies in the theism that lurks ever more prominently in his writing.

Furthermore, the fact that every conceptual scheme leaves certain things unseen and characterizes some things it sees in self-serving, ethically, or epistemically dubious ways means that nothing guarantees that a person who engaged in strong evaluation sees herself clearly, makes the right qualitative assessments, has the power to make the needed character adjustments in light of these assessments, or actually decides and acts on the basis of the considerations she thinks she decides and acts on. Taylor stresses that strong evaluation is essentially linked to articulateness. This is true. Articulateness is necessary for strong evaluation as he describes it.[34]

But it is not sufficient for it.[35] Weak evaluators can be articulate. Furthermore, articulateness can be the able servant of self-deception and manipulative and mendacious self-presentation, as well as of accurate self-interpretation and honest and sincere self-presentation. One can have strong evaluative identity in Taylor's sense and have everything wrong.

Of course, Taylor never claims that articulateness or strong evaluation is sufficient for moral goodness, only that articulateness is necessary for strong evaluation, which is in turn necessary for personhood in general, and moral personhood in particular. I have called these last two necessary-condition claims into question. Once these claims are called into question and the compatibility of strong evaluation with severe self-deception, immorality, and neurosis are highlighted, one might wonder whether it is even true that strong evaluation is a friend to the ethical life by way of certain characteristic relations it allegedly has to it. I will come back to this issue shortly. But first I want to diagnose why the strong evaluative picture goes wrong in the ways I have isolated so far.

The Importance of Importance

The mistake in Taylor's original picture of personhood has, I think, two main sources. First, he ties the sort of self-comprehension that is necessary for personhood too closely to linguistic competence. Second, he ties motivation too closely to judgment, or better, to judgment of a heavily cognitive sort. These two problems are closely related, but let me develop each in turn.

Taylor rightly points out that we are language-using creatures and that the sort of self-interpretation that is constitutive of being a person is typically linguistically informed. The strong evaluator differs from the weak evaluator because he possesses a vocabulary of ethical evaluation and because he frames his self-interpretation in terms of this vocabulary. The strong evaluator possesses a "vocabulary of worth."[36] "The strong evaluator envisages his alternatives through a richer language."[37] "The strong evaluator can articulate superiority just because he has a language of contrastive characterization."[38] The strong evaluator has "articulacy about depth."[39]

Although it is true that we are essentially language-using animals and that identity and self-comprehension are in large part linguistically created, sustained, and informed, it is a mistake to think that all self-comprehension, all self-interpretation, is linguistic. Piaget's psychology provides the relevant theoretical alternative.[40] Piaget's genetic epistemology is a well-respected theory in which the picture is one in which the child develops various competencies, with conservation, space, number, even morality over time,[41] and engages in reflexive comprehension and deployment of these competencies prior to the emergence of the capacity to formulate linguistically what he or she is doing. Children understand conservation and solve conservation problems long before they can linguistically formulate their comprehension or solution strategies.[42]

To be sure, our emotions, the imports they have for us, and the standards associated with them are gathered together for us, and accrue the meanings they have, by being given various culturally specific significances. And these significances are typically attached in part by linguistic means—minimally by way of some linguistically mediated reinforcement provided by primary socializers. Selves are constituted within "webs of interlocution."[43] Furthermore, a linguistic map of the network of signification can invariably be drawn. But, and this is one point I want to stress, the map of signification cannot always be drawn by the agent for whom the significances obtain. To be sure, Taylor is right that even our "prearticulate sense of our feelings is *not* language independent. For they are the feelings of a language being, who therefore can and does say something about them, for example, that he feels something disturbing and perplexing, which baffles him, and to which he cannot give a name. *We* experience our pre-articulate emotions as perplexing, as raising a question. And *this* is an experience that no non-language animal can have."[44] And he is right to emphasize that "our sense of dignity, and shame, and moral remorse, and so on" are very different from the experience of a baboon (assuming he can experience relatives of these emotions), since our sense of these things "are all shaped by language."[45] But to accept that nothing in our experience is *language-independent* does not remotely entail that all self-comprehension requires that the self so comprehended be linguistically corralled. Taylor often speaks as if it does.[46] But there is no incoherence whatsoever in thinking that identity and self-comprehension can accrue in environments that are relatively impoverished linguistically and by means of all manner of intrapersonal and extrapersonal feedback mechanisms: by way of feelings of coordination, integration, and integrity, of fit with the social world mediated by the body language of others, and so on. Such self-comprehension might involve an evolving sense of who one is, of what is important to oneself, and of how one wants to live one's life. But the evolution of this sense might proceed relatively unreflectively, possibly for the most part unconsciously. It might be conceived of along the lines of the acquisition of athletic know-how and savvy by way of continuous practice.

Great athletes often cannot coach, because they cannot say how they do what they do. It is not that they linguistically know how they do what they do but simply cannot get at the module that contains the relevant linguistic description. Often, if they were not themselves coached in certain ways, there was never cause to formulate the relevant skills linguistically. But surely what such athletes are able to do involves highly developed know-how, reflexive comprehension, and self-control.

Taylor now concedes this point that moral comprehension can be "pre-articulate,"[47] In discussing the ancient warrior ethic, he writes that "the framework within which we act and judge doesn't need to be articulated theoretically. It isn't usually by those who live the warrior ethic."[48] But this reasonable retraction of the articulacy requirement is, I want to insist, a genuine change in his view, and it is in tension with the emphasis Taylor continues to place on the powerful connection between identity, meaning, and articulation. For example, Taylor writes that we "find the sense of life through articulating it."[49] But if my argument is right and if Taylor's recent retraction of the articulation requirement is motivated by considerations of the sort I have raised, then finding "the sense of life" cannot be so closely linked to articulating what that sense consists in.

The implausible idea that all self-comprehension is linguistic is related to a second implausibility. This is the mistake of thinking that "our identity is defined by our fundamental [strong] evaluations"[50] and that "a self decides and acts out of certain fundamental [strong] evaluations."[51] Taylor gets things right, I think, when he says that "what is crucial about agents is that things matter to them."[52] And he is right when he says that to "be a moral agent is to be sensitive to certain standards." He is right still when he adds, "But 'sensitive' here must have a strong sense: not just that one's behavior follow a certain standard, but also that one in some sense recognize or acknowledge the standard."[53] But the point that needs to be stressed and that is in tension with Taylor's heavily linguistic picture is that one can be sensitive to a standard and "in some sense recognize or acknowledge" it without ever having linguistically formulated that standard and without even possessing the ability to do so when pressed.[54]

The idea that identity is defined by our strong evaluations is Taylor's way of trying to express the idea that identity is constituted by what is important to us, by what we care (most) about. Frankfurt puts the relevant idea this way: "A person who cares about something, is, as it were, invested in it. He *identifies* himself with what he cares about in the sense that he makes himself vulnerable to losses and susceptible to benefits depending upon whether what he cares about is diminished or enhanced."[55]

It seems to me that this way of thinking about identity, like the picture of identity as constituted by the plans, projects, and commitments in accordance with which a particular individual lives, are better ways than Taylor's of getting at what is essential about identity. The advantages of the latter sorts of characterizations over Taylor's heavily intellectualist picture are twofold: First, they allow for identity in people whose lives are guided by cares, concerns, imports, and commitments, but who are, for whatever reason and to whatever degree, inarticulate about them. Second, these ways of characterizing identity are nonmoralistic in a way the strong evaluative picture is not. For better or worse, what a particular human individual cares about can involve all manner of nonethical concerns (not all of which are thereby loony and low-minded, although they might be) and involve almost nothing in the way of ethical valuation.

There is an idea recently floated in the literature that might seem to help Taylor here but that actually works against him. This is Dennett's idea that the self is the "center of narrative gravity."[56] Dennett's fruitful metaphor is an attempt to point to the fact that what we call the "self" is a construction that involves locating what in one's motivational economy one perceives as most important, what one cares most about. But Dennett's picture of the self is wisely neutral on the question of whose narrative web the self is captured in. A particular self might be self-comprehended without being subject to elegant narrative construction by the self who so comprehends it. A third party might be better at spinning out the relevant narrative. The only constraint, except in cases of self-deception, is that the narrative told from the third-person, heterophenomenological point of view resonates with autophenomenological, first-person comprehension, insofar as there is any, and with the cares, concerns, and projects as revealed in how the person lives.

Fragile Foundations

In *Sources of the Self*, Taylor introduces an interesting equivocation in the way he describes strong evaluation, an equivocation that ironically moves the idea in a more plausible direction. Taylor writes that for us, strong evaluative identity involves some "strongly valued good."[57] It involves finding a framework that renders life meaningful. This way of putting things is more consonant with the Frankfurt-Williams-Dennett formulation and with the conception of identity I argued for earlier. It does not require that identity be grounded in an articulate sense that one lives an ethically noble life. Identity in the first instance requires that there be something or someone—baseball, sophistication, concern for the fate of grass or one's teammates—with which one strongly identifies. The original and less plausible formulation focuses on the link between identity and reflection and evaluation of a certain distinctivey ethical kind. The new, equivocal, and more plausible formulation links identity to the strength of one's identifications—to absorption in some end or ends, whatever that end or those ends might be.

There is another important change marked in *Sources of the Self*. Originally, the idea of strong evaluation was linked, as I have argued, to locating and orienting one's life from the perspective of some ethical, meaning-grounding framework. This framework was to provide the grounds for both identity and agency. But one of the main themes of this book is "that frameworks today are problematic."[58] We moderns find no framework immune to skeptical doubts. We find no rational grounds sufficient to warrant our adherence to the ethical values we avow. We have high ethical standards—powerful commitments, for example, to justice and benevolence—but we cannot, upon reflection, find sources strong enough to support these values.

The point about the fragility of frameworks seems right, as does the point that, to the degree that one lacks confidence in one's framework and cares that one possesses such confidence, problems of meaning can arise and identity crises may ensue. But this point leads to an interesting problem for Taylor. According to the original view, all contemporary persons are strong evaluators. Most strong evaluators are reflective and possess identities constituted by frameworks that have passed scrutiny. Normally, the scrutinizing of the framework engenders confidence in the framework. Strong evaluation legitimizes a framework. It is only when reflective evaluation fails to engender such confidence that the agent is prone to an identity crisis. But now we discover that *all* frameworks are problematic—none of the available ones can pass muster in the face of stringent reflective scrutiny. This would seem to imply that all strong evaluators, that is, all contemporary persons on Taylor's view, are either in identity crises or highly vulnerable to them. Indeed, the stronger and deeper the evaluation, the more likely will it be that the framework being scrutinized will be seen as unstable, and thus the more likely will it be that the person will succumb to a crisis of identity.[59]

But this doesn't quite seem to be an accurate picture of us—teetering so precariously on the edge of our own identities. Furthermore, if it is, then strong evaluation reveals a particularly disturbing downside—it makes identity and agency prone to coming undone by demanding that our frameworks pass tests they cannot pass. It is puzzling why we would want to recommend a way of being that is destined, at least in our time, to make demands that cannot be met. Third, and relatedly, a new implausibility begins to lurk—this is the implausible idea that frameworks need to be seen as extremely secure if they are to ground identity and agency. Taylor thinks that unless we can find some transcendent ground for our projects, commitments, and ethical frameworks, we will suffer losses in identity and agency (indeed, it is a consequence of his view that we already have).[60] But here, I think, he misses an important feature of the psychology of many contemporary persons. There are many people who have come to grips with the contingency of their selves, with their fallibility, and with their naturalness, in ways that do not throw them into existential turmoil when they experience their frameworks as lacking transcendent grounding. There is no incoherence in the idea of persons, be they strong or weak evaluators, operating effectively and happily within frameworks that they simply do not see or experience as final or foundational.[61]

Reflection and Community

So far I have called into question the idea that there are any essential empirical or normative connections between strong evaluation, possession of a rich and effective identity, personhood, and moral goodness. Rejection of these claims is compatible with thinking that it is a worthy ideal to possess an identity that involves an accurate evaluative conception of where one stands, that has withstood deep critical reflection, and in accordance with which one assesses one's motives and guides one's activities.

In this final section I want to explore briefly some of the ways the idea of strong evaluation gets tied up with certain ideas in political philosophy, in particular with communitarianism. Taylor suggests an interesting connection between a certain kind of reflective evaluation (which need not, I think, be identified with distinctively strong evaluation) and recognition of communal duties.[62] Sandel links strong evaluation to what he calls "expansive self-understanding,"[63] which he in turn links to fraternal motivation, to a desire to nourish and sustain one's community partly out of a sense that by so doing one is nourishing and sustaining one's own identity.

I admit to having been initially puzzled in seeing the use both Taylor and Sandel make of the idea of strong evaluation in their defenses of communitarianism.[64] Strong evaluation involves a depth of criticism, reflection, and evaluation that seems, at least at first, in tension (for reasons just mentioned in the previous section) with the emphases on shared values, strong group identification, likemindedness, homogeneity, and the stability of character and identity strongly associated with communitarian thinking. Most communitarians abhor the idea that, in theory, all one's ends might become an object of critical scrutiny, and they disdain communities in which the contrastive possibilities are so multifarious that every single thing—individual selves, interpersonal relations, social practices, and political structures—can be made to look deficient against some other socially available option or ideal.

This ambivalence about critical reflection is rooted partly in the correct perception that reflection has the capacity to reduce confidence in and admiration of the object reflected upon—be that object a set of social arrangements, particular others, or even the self. In cases where alternatives are available to improve upon or to replace those that lose some status to reflective scrutiny, the grounds are ripe for a certain amount of social or personal upheaval. For reasons such as these, many of the more Aristotelian communitarians, especially those who stress the good of unreflective lives rooted in habitual responses that are learned and sustained within good communities, would not, I think, find much attractive in the suggestion that strong evaluation is necessary for certain traits dear to their hearts: nonatomistic self-comprehension, a firm sense of identity suited to the narrative ideal of life, comprehension of communal obligations, and moral goodness.

If sound, the argument linking ethical reflection to communitarian ideals is important, however. Indeed, if Taylor is right about these links, then some of the distance between communitarian and liberal conceptions is closed. Reflectiveness of something like the strong evaluative variety will be a virtue on both views, although, for reasons already suggested, not necessarily a mandatory virtue.

One possible route to the desired conclusion might deploy the barebones truths of philosophical psychology discussed earlier. A person can comprehend herself only in social terms, as one whose abilities, plans, projects, and self-respect are rooted in past and present social relations and in preexisting social and institutional structures (the intersubjective conception of the self). And one can grasp the good of social union (normative intersubjectivity) only if one is a strong evaluator.

But this argument is unsound. I showed earlier that unless we require self-comprehension to have a highly articulated structure and in this way beg the interesting question, certain relatively unreflective persons can be said to comprehend both these truths.

The argument fails on another basis as well. Even if we demand reflective articulation, there is no incoherence in the idea that a reflective and articulate social psychologist, for example, might know that both truths obtain. Furthermore, he might consciously infer that both apply to his own case. This would involve, at a minimum, a recognition of the fact that he finds noninstrumental good in certain human relations and that his identity, interests, abilities, self-esteem, and so on, have sources in the activities of past and present others. This might even lead him to appreciate more than he did before the contributions that others made and continue to make to his flourishing. But such a person might not be a strong evaluator. There is nothing in the picture I have drawn so far that would require deployment of a vocabulary of ethical assessment, and in particular one in which the central concepts are those of nobility, worth, and so on. Being the sort of social psychologist I have imagined, who knows that the intersubjective conception is true, who finds good in social union, and who consciously appreciates such union, is compatible with being largely (but probably not completely) ethically indifferent.

However, a different and better case for the normative superiority of a high degree of reflectiveness involving the deployment of an array of ethically sensitive standards can be made, although, for reasons that have emerged, I do not think such reflectiveness needs to be identified with strong evaluation in Taylor's sense. Here is the argument: Although a weak evaluator may in some sense know her center and fully identify with her constitutive ends and be moved by them, she is not in a position, since she hasn't engaged in the requisite reflection, to try to recognize, change, or modify possibly problematic features of her moral personality. The problematic features may be problematic only in unlikely counterfactual situations. But as the case of the Holocaust shows, such features can cause untold moral harm if the unlikely and unanticipated possibilities do arise, and thus there is much to be said for modifying problematic dispositions in anticipation of the counterfactuals. Call this "the counterfactual advantage." The argument linking reflectiveness to the counterfactual advantage can be bolstered by noting that there is almost always room for ethical improvement. So unreflective persons can be good, as can reflective persons who do not normally conceive of their lives in ethical terms. But all things equal, an ethically reflective person has more resources at her disposal for ethical improvement, for satisfactorily meeting unusual and unanticipated ethical situations, and so on.

Securing this argument is more difficult than it might at first seem, for among other reasons, reflectiveness can have, as we have seen, a confidence-undermining downside. Furthermore, many morally vicious persons, many Nazis for example, were articulate, reflective, and self-scrutinizing. The problem was that they scrutinized and reflected with vicious values. We must keep constantly in mind that reflectiveness is a virtue of form,[65] not of substance. Reflectiveness is good if and only if it is carried out with decent ethical standards.

But let us assume, what seems generally true, that the capacity for reflectiveness is a necessary condition for *efficiently* criticizing one's ends, and that criticizing one's ends is in many cases essential to recognizing one's deficiencies, to ethical improvement, and so on. I don't want to say that it is absolutely necessary for the refinement and adjustment of ends, for seeing one's deficiencies and seeing how one can improve, because I think these sorts of things are done all the time by relatively unreflective and inarticulate persons. The connection is between reflection and articulateness, on the one hand, and *efficient* criticism, not between reflection, articulateness, and criticism as such.

There is a third argument that might be mustered to bolster the reasons for succumbing to the belief in the great worth of reflective criticism of wide scope and depth. This third argument is similar in certain respects to the first argument considered above, which I claimed failed. This one, however, works. How can this be? The argument works, so to speak, for pragmatic reasons rather than for purely logical reasons. It provides a rationale for reflectiveness of a certain sort for those with a prior commitment to reflectiveness but who reflect with too narrow a conception of personhood and who, because of this narrow picture, are unable to see any firm ground for communal obligations and responsibilities. The argument works to move persons who are already reflective but who have what Taylor calls "ultra-liberal" sensibilities and who conceive of persons "atomically" in strongly possessive, individualist terms. The argument works in effect because it is well designed for a certain audience. It is designed both to persuade this audience of the truth of the intersubjective conception of the self and of normative intersubjectivity, to enable them to see more clearly what these truths mean and to move them to see the links between these truths about our social natures and our possession of certain communal obligations.[66]

The conclusion the communitarian wants the ultraliberal—the atomistic philosophical psychologist—to draw is that in virtue of being socially formed and in virtue of being constituted, encumbered, and implicated in a certain way of being, we incur certain responsibilities and obligations to particular others, as well as to the form of life itself, within which we are formed.

On one standard analysis of responsibility and obligation, call it the "explicit contract analysis," the very idea of responsibilities and obligations one simply has or acquires by virtue of having a certain history, by being a certain kind of person, or by way of one's nonverbal behavior will seem incoherent. On such an analysis, P has an obligation to do q for S if P has reached a voluntary agreement with S to do q.

This notion of responsibility is in the end too narrow. It fails to make room for "tacit" agreements of the sort a citizen has with her state or for the responsibilities we rightly think parents bear toward their children. Furthermore, even for persons who find such a strong analysis appealing, the voluntary-agreement condition must be interpreted as only providing grounds of prima facie obligation. The reason is simple: if one agrees to perform some morally heinous action, one is *not*—on any credible account of obligation—obligated to do that act.

It is important to see that this sort of objection is an objection not only to an unconditional, explicit contract analysis. It is a legitimate objection to *any* view that grounds obligations on purely formal grounds and pays insufficient attention to their ethical content. As such it is an objection that can be brought against certain kinds of role moralities, as well as against all notions of responsibility and obligation that turn too unconditionally on one's encumbrances or on the conditions for maintaining an integrated unalienated identity.[67] It is a plausible constraint on any acceptable theory of obligation that prima facie obligations become bona fide ones only after there has been (or could be) a passable qualitative assessment of the promises, activities, traditions, or kinds of persons one is helping to sustain by being or behaving in the prescribed way.

This means that on all accounts, we do best if we reflectively examine the encumbrances we have and judge what kinds of goods, if they are goods at all, these encumbrances are (or at least if we are disposed to do so and capable of so doing when the need arises). The operative notion of obligation is one in which the existence of an obligation is linked to passing such inspection, or to the ability to do so if scrutinized. One plausible and suitably weak analysis of the underlying idea is that respect and gratitude and a certain amount of reciprocity are appropriate when one is given something of worth (libertarians might object that nothing is owed even in such cases if the benefits were not specifically requested).

Taylor eloquently expresses the relevant set of ideas in the specific context of the modern ideal of the autonomous agent. He writes,

> The free individual or autonomous moral agent can only achieve and maintain his identity in a certain type of culture . . . [the relevant facets of which] do not come into existence spontaneously each successive instant. They are carried on in institutions and associations which require stability and continuity and frequently also support from society as a whole. . . . [I] am arguing that the free individual of the West is only what he is by virtue of the whole society and civilization which brought him to be and which nourishes him; that our families can only form us up to this capacity and these aspirations because they are set in this civilization. . . . And I want to claim finally that all this creates a significant obligation to belong for whoever would affirm the value of this freedom.[68]

Although Taylor is skeptical of the objection that claims that past gifts do not necessitate ongoing gratitude or obligation, he suggests a reply that might persuade even someone who is tempted by such an objection.

Future generations will need this civilization to reach these aspirations; and if we affirm their worth, we have an obligation to make them available to others. This obligation is only increased if we ourselves have benefited from this civilization and have been enabled to become free agents ourselves.[69]

In these passages, obligation to one's society is tied in the first instance to both gratitude and a kind of self-consistency. If "we ourselves have benefited from this civilization" and if "we affirm the value" of its institutions in forming us the way they have, then there are credible grounds on the basis of which we can be said to have obligations toward those institutions. The postulation of motivational concern for the good of future generations provides further reason for sustaining a life form one thinks is good.

The question remains, of course, as to whether one has been given something of worth, or more probably, what aspects of the traditions and persons to whom one rightly owes one's identity formation are most worth sustaining, respecting, and shoring up. In order to answer such questions, it follows that an acceptable communitarian account of obligation to one's tradition(s) will need to be content-sensitive. But such content sensitivity requires possession of a sophisticated set of reflective tools (whether it requires these to be applied consciously and with analytic acuity is something I am more skeptical of). The communitarian proposal, then, is best read as involving the following plausible claim: If one's life form passes reflective scrutiny and is judged as good, or at least above a certain acceptable threshold of decency, then claiming and perpetuating this life form is in part a way of staking and discovering the good of one's own identity and it is ethically acceptable as well. The overall conclusion, then, is this: Reflection is good in two respects: first, it can help ultraliberals to understand themselves in less atomic terms and thereby to see the grounds on which they incur communal obligations; second, reflectivneness is good because it provides one with the critical tools needed to assess the content of one's life form so that one can judge the *ethical* bases for such communal obligations.

I close by pointing to a paradoxical feature of this last argument. I have claimed that the argument is effective against a certain liberal, individualistic way of thinking about things. The argument shows that for persons socialized within a certain liberal life form that (over)emphasizes personal autonomy, individual projects, self-actualization, and so on, it has become hard to see why we should care about others. The argument I have just rehearsed provides an argument for those who need it. It is a good argument relative to a certain audience. The fact that certain contemporary ultraliberals need to hear this argument, that they can understand it only if they are reflective, sensitive to reason and argument, and so on, does not show that having these last attributes is a necessary condition for possessing the desired communitarian sensibilities. These highly reflective attributes are necessary for those who do not possess the relevant communal sensibilities and have beliefs and desires that militate against developing them. But one can imagine that persons socialized within a different life form that imbues neophytes with less individualist sensibilities might already express in their personal lives and political structures the relevant sensibilities and thus might have no overwhelming need for the sort of deep reflection on their social natures designed to make them open to communitarian sentiments.

However, the fact would remain that human life is subject to great contingency, including the possibility of being formed within ethically problematic social systems. Having communitarian sentiments is good if one's community is good, but it is obviously not good if one's community has bad values, values that one is motivated to sustain and maintain because of these sentiments. This is where the second, content-sensitive aspect of reflectiveness becomes important. The realistic possibility that one will live in a community with some or many ethically problematic features means that it is probably never bad in and of itself to have realized reflective capacities and to be open to rational argument. But, and this is the conclusion I am drawn to at every turn, such reflectiveness is not necessary for identity, personhood, or moral goodness. It is an intellectualist projection to think otherwise. Deep critical reflection is a good, and it rightly has a valued place in our conception of the good life. But it is not a truth of philosophical psychology that all persons, even all ethical persons, are reflective.

Notes

Acknowledgments—I am grateful to David Wong for extremely helpful comments and criticisms and especially to Ken Winkler for his acute reading of both my paper and Charles Taylor's *Sources of the Self*.

1. C. Taylor, "What Is Human Agency?" in *The Self: Psychological and Philosophical Issues,* ed. T. Mischel (Oxford: Basil Blackwell, 1977); C. Taylor, "Self-Interpreting Animals," first published 1977, reprinted in C. Taylor, *Human Agency and Language: Philosophical Papers* I (Cambridge: Cambridge University Press, 1985); C. Taylor, "The Concept of a Person," first published 1981, reprinted in Taylor, *Human Agency*.

2. C. Taylor, *Sources of the Self: The Making of Modern Identity* (Cambridge, Mass.: Harvard University Press, 1989).

3. Taylor, "What Is Human Agency?"

4. Ibid., 43.

5. Taylor, *Sources of the Self*, 4.

6. H. Frankfurt, "Freedom of the Will and the Concept of a Person," *Journal of Philosophy*, 68, 1971, 5–20. Reprinted in *Philosophical Essays: The Importance of What We Care About* (Cambridge: Cambridge University Press, 1988). Page references are to the reprinted version.

7. Taylor, "What Is Human Agency?" 16; Taylor, "Self-Interpreting Animals," 65.

8. Taylor, "What Is Human Agency?" 34.

9. Ibid., 23.

10. Ibid., 25.

11. See Taylor, *Sources of the Self*, 20. Actually in Taylor there is no characterization of weak evaluation, while strong evaluation continues to figure prominently as a defining feature of modern identity. This may be because Taylor is convinced that there are no persons who fit the description and thus no such persons to draw our attention to. This fits with Taylor's claim that the characterization of personhood in terms of strong evaluation captures an essential truth, not a contingent psychological truth.

12. B. Williams, *Ethics and the Limits of Philosophy* (Cambridge: Harvard University Press, 1985.)

13. Taylor, *Sources of the Self*, 53.

14. Ibid., 4.

15. Taylor, *"Self-Interpreting Animals," 67*, my emphasis.

16. C. Taylor, "The Diversity of Good," first published in 1982. In Taylor, *"Human Agency,"* 67.

17. Taylor, *Sources of the Self*, The example of the person devoted to blades of grass is from John Rawls, *A Theory of Justice* (Cambridge: Harvard University Press, 1971), 432.

18. Taylor, "Self-Interpreting Animals," 68.

19. Taylor, "The Diversity of Good," 239.

20. M. Slote, Critical notice of C. Taylor, *Human Agency and Language: Philosophical Papers*, vol. 1, *Canadian Journal of Philosophy*, 18, 1988, 579–587.

21. Taylor, "What Is Human Agency?" 34.

22. Ibid., 35.

23. J. Kagan, *The Nature of the Child;* D. Stern, *The Interpersonal World of the Infant* (New York: Basic Books, 1985.)

24. See Taylor, *Sources of the Self*, chap. 4, for a general defense of the worth of articulating the good in some sort of "philosophical prose."

25. Taylor, "What Is Human Agency?" 24.

26. In "Atomism," first published in 1979 (In Taylor, *Human Agency*, 24), Taylor acknowledges the possibility of persons who can conceive of no other way to be. But he rightly denies that persons who live such lives have the kind of freedom made available within modern liberal democracies in which many of the possibilities revealed in our contrastive spaces present live social options (204).

27. There is a widespread belief in the idea that evaluative concepts can only be comprehended contrastively. I admit to being unable to see why this view seems so

obvious. First, we do not think that comprehension of most concepts in our language require contrast. "Table," "chair," "red," "electron," are all comprehensible in their own right without being contrasted with anything else. To be sure, in an actual world in which there is a perceived contrast between what is good and evil, what tastes good and bad, and what is beautiful and hideous, the contrastive space affects comprehension at both ends of the spectrum. But I have trouble seeing how it follows that comprehending what is morally good, what tastes good, or what is beautiful requires contrast, especially contrast with its opposite. One could understand how something that satisfied the description "moral," or "beautiful" could fail to satisfy that description, namely by failing to possess the relevant properties, without understanding the description in some sort of yin-yang space. Negation alone might be thought to be sufficient to establish the relevant contrast. But this cannot be right. First, if there are no things around deserving negation, it seems implausible to think that we will necessarily formulate the relevant negated thought. Second, even if we do formulate the negated thought, it is not clear that it will have determinate content in situations where it lacks clear referents, nor again is it clear why having the negated thought would be remotely necessary for clear comprehension of the affirmative referring term.

28. See Taylor, "What Is Human Agency?" 35.

29. E. Erickson, *Identity: Youth and Crisis* (New York: W. W. Norton, 1968), 16–17.

30. Ibid., 19.

31. D. Wong, "On Flourishing and Finding One's Identity in Community." In P. A. French, T. E. Uehling, and H. K. Wettstein (eds.), *Ethical Theory: Character and Virtue*, vol. 13 of Midwest Studies in Philosophy (Notre Dame: Notre Dame University Press, 1988.)

32. D. Dennett, "Why Everyone Is a Novelist," *Times Literary Supplement*, 4, no. 459, 1988.

33. Taylor, *Sources of the Self*, 27.

34. Taylor, "What Is Human Agency?" Taylor, "Self-Interpreting Animals; Taylor, "Concept of a Person."

35. In "What Is Human Agency?" (28) Taylor wonders perhaps whether Camus's Meursault in *L'Étranger* isn't perhaps the exception who proves the rule that all contemporary persons are strong evaluators. One interesting thing about Meursault is that he is very articulate; he simply does not use ethical categories to judge lives or motives as more or less worthy. One life, Meursault says, is "as good as another." And after he murders his Arab attacker, firing four gratuitous shots into his dead body, he acknowledges that regret is not an emotion that he is capable of experiencing. But if Meursault is an example of a weak evaluator, it is not because he is inarticulate or because he is unreflective, it is because he does not evaluate in ethical terms. Actually, he may be a good example of a person in an identity crisis, for on one reading, he fails to see worth along any dimensions whatsoever. He is articulate and reflective, but he evaluates neither weakly nor strongly, neither in moral terms nor in nonmoral ones. But he is not a wanton either.

36. Taylor, "What Is Human Agency?" 24.

37. Ibid., 23.

38. Ibid., 24.

39. Ibid., 26. It is this side of Taylor's view that has led Annette Baier to write that Taylor "takes men with their rational wills to be special, if not a Father God's favorites at least his speaking likenesses. This remarkable tradition, for which Taylor is an eloquent spokesman, is a cultural artifact of enormous expressive power. It fascinates, and will continue to fascinate more naturalist anthropologists, as they are fascinated by the mitres, head dresses, breastplates, mirrors and fetishes of less intellectual tribes" (A. Baier, Critical notive of C. Taylor, *Philosopohy and the Human Sciences: Philosophical Papers,* vol. 2. *Canadian Journal of Philosophy,* 18, 589–594.)

40. See Taylor "What Is Involved in a Genetic Psychology?" (first published in 1971. In Taylor, *Human Agency*) for a valuable assessment of Piaget that nonetheless fails to see clearly enough the implications of this aspect of his psychology.

41. J. Piaget, *The Moral Judgment of the Child* (New York: Free Press, 1932.)

42. See Van Gulick, ("A Functionalist Plea for Self-Consciousness, *Philosophical Review,* 92, 1988, 149–181) for another interesting analysis of self-comprehension, which wisely shies away from tying it too closely to linguistic competence.

43. Taylor, *Sources of the Self,* 36.

44. Taylor, "Self-Interpreting Animals," 74.

45. Ibid., 69.

46. Taylor, "What Is Human Agency?"; Taylor, "Self-Interpreting Animals"; Taylor, "The Concept of a Person," (first published 1983. In Taylor, *Human Agency,* 103).

47. Taylor, *Sources of the Self,* 77–78, 91–92.

48. Ibid., 20.

49. Ibid., 18.

50. Taylor, "What Is Human Agency?" 34.

51. Ibid., 35.

52. Taylor, 98.

53. Ibid., 102.

54. As I indicated above, Taylor in *Sources of the Self* now thinks that there is a "sense" of qualitative distinction that can be revealed in the lives of the inarticulate. indeed, it may be entirely up to third parties to articulate what the guiding frameworks of such lives are.

55. H. Frankfurt, "The Importance of What We Care About," *Synthese,* 53, 1982, 257–272. Reprinted in *Philosophical Essays,* 83.

56. Dennett, "Why Everyone is a Novelist."

57. Taylor, *Sources of the Self,* 29–30.

58. Ibid., 17.

59. The structure of modern identity actually consists of three levels: there are first-order desires, there are the second-order desires and valuations deployed in strong evaluation of the first-order desires, and there are (often) what Taylor calls "hypergoods." Hypergoods "provide the standpoint from which [strongly valued

goods] must be weighed, judged, decided about" (*Sources of the Self,* 63). The three-level picture is credible. But Ken Winkler has pointed out to me that it has the following consequence: Assuming that a hypergood is part of one's framework, it follows that frameworks can be self-undermining, since, as Taylor points out, a hypergood can lead to the rejection of goods that are valued at the second level (ibid., 65).

60. Ibid., 520–521. Taylor admits that he has no argument (yet) for this view.

61. See R. Rorty, *Contingency, Irony, and Solidarity* (Cambridge: Cambridge University Press, 1989). Taylor acknowledges that some persons identify their framework in a "tentative, semi-provisional way" (*Sources of the Self,* 17). But he seems to think that such persons need to be seen as on a "quest," as seeking some firmer ground. The possibility I am suggesting is that one can identify fully with one's framework while at the same time seeing it is imperfect, subject to revision, and as hardly the only or best framework. Or to put it another way, one can see one's framework as nonfinal in Richard Rorty's sense, without one's absorption in one's framework being half-hearted or tentative.

62. Taylor, "Atomism."

63. M. Sandel, *Liberalism and the Limits of Justice* (New York: Cambridge University Press, 1982), 143–144; 154–161.

64. It is a significant feature of Taylor (*Sources of the Self*) that communitarianism (with his liberal coloration) no longer appears to be able to function for him as the sort of framework that can unproblematically ground a meaningful life. The book ends with poignant hopes that we can once again find some sort of transcendent ground for meaning—larger and more significant than even deep and fulfilling social relations. One can only infer that reflection undermined Taylor's conviction that communitarian social ideals could play the role of a grounding framework for him. Atomism is still criticized for being too individualistic and for dividing us from each other (500–501). But Taylor is strangely silent—"inexplicit" is a better word—as to what aspects of communitarianism he has come to find wanting. The insufficiency has something to do with the failure of philosophical arguments for communitarian social arrangements to agree on what such arrangements would be like, and even where there is agreement on the right kind of arrangements, these arguments are insufficient to win the case for specifically communitarian ideals against rivals. It is Taylor's sense of the ubiquity of such underdetermination relative to all contending ethical ideals that seems to have headed him more firmly in a theistic direction.

65. J. Rawls, *A Theory of Justice.*

66. Wong, "On Flourishing and Finding One's Identity in Community."

67. O. Flanagan, *Varieties of Moral Personality: Ethics and Psychological Realism* (Cambridge: Harvard University Press, 1991).

68. Taylor, "Atomism."

69. Ibid., 206.

10

Virtue and Ignorance

In "The Virtues of Ignorance," Julia Driver discusses the important question of whether there exists some class of virtues that require as a necessary ingredient that she who possesses or displays any one of them lacks knowledge.[1] Driver thinks there is such a class. She calls the class of virtues that involve ignorance in an essential way "virtues of ignorance." The argument is important, if true. Many recent writers have pointed to an ineliminable tension between our ethical and personal ideals. If successful, Driver's argument would establish the existence of a different, but equally ineliminable tension: between our ethical and epistemic ideals. The argument for virtues of ignorance, however, goes wrong in several important places. Let me explain why.

Virtue and Knowledge

Driver claims first that it is a common assumption within virtue ethics, including on Aristotle's account, that

> (A′) the agent who possesses some virtue v "exercises it knowingly" (373).

(A′) is provided with a variety of interpretations. The one that Driver makes central use of is implausibly strong. We are told that (A′) is true because (a) the virtuous person acts with practical wisdom; (b) the virtuous person chooses the mean between excess and defect; (c) he performs the act that expresses the mean disposition; and (d) "in order for a person to act according to virtue, that person must know what he is doing under the description that makes the action characteristic of the virtue" (373).

Driver treats (a)–(d) as if they were more or less equivalent. But this is not true.

(A′) is a common assumption of virtue theories if the requirement of exercising virtue knowingly is interpreted as requiring a kind of *know-how*. The agent who possesses some virtue v must possess some sort of procedural knowledge and the relevant sort of knowledge can be cashed out perhaps in terms of (a)–(c). That is, the person who possesses some virtue v must have certain habits of perception, feeling, and action; she must be a good detector of the moral saliencies relevant to that virtue, of the mean action, and so on. But it is not a general requirement that to be ascribed some virtue v the agent must possess declarative or propositional knowledge. In particular, it is not a consequence of (A′), properly interpreted, that (d) *"in order for a person to act according to virtue, that person must know what he is doing under the description that makes the action characteristic of the virtue"* (373, my emphasis). Reason (d) requires a sort of linguistic sophistication, reflectiveness, taxonomic ability, and conscious awareness that virtue theorists have historically expressed is decidedly not necessary for virtue.

The first mistake then involves using (d) as the proper interpretation of (A′). The second mistake follows immediately when it is claimed that a "consequence of such a view of virtue" is

(A) No virtue is constituted by, or based upon ignorance" (373).

Initially, Driver unpacks (A) in terms compatible with a procedural, or know-how analysis. So the generous person must, in order to be properly ascribed the virtue of generosity, "pick up" on the needs of others and give aid. She writes: "(A) is necessary to most accounts of virtue, because on these accounts being virtuous is largely a matter of *knowing what to do*" (373, my emphasis). This way of putting things hardly entails that the generous agent needs to know what "he is doing under the description that makes the action" an act of generosity. But this is the interpretation Driver goes on to deploy. For the class of virtues she calls virtues of ignorance are virtues on her view because it is necessarily the case that the person who possesses or displays a virtue of ignorance does not comprehend it under the appropriate type description.[2] Driver sees the existence of virtues of ignorance as falsifying (A). It looks initially as if the argument is a very simple case of modus tollens:

1. If "(A) No virtue is constituted by, or based upon ignorance" (373), then there are no virtues of ignorance.
2. There are virtues of ignorance.

3. Therefore, some virtues are constituted by or based upon ignorance.

But actually it is a more complex case of the argument form:

1. If (A'), the agent who possesses some virtue v "exercises it knowingly," then (d), "that person must know what he is doing under the description that makes the action characteristic of the virtue" (373).
2. If (d) "in order for a person to act according to virtue, that person must know what he is doing under the description that makes the action characteristic of the virtue" (373), then (A) "No virtue is constituted by, or based upon ignorance" (373).
3. If "(A) No virtue is constituted by, or based upon ignorance" (373), then there are no virtues of ignorance.
4. There are virtues of ignorance.

---

5. Therefore, it is false that "(A) No virtue is constituted by, or based upon ignorance" (373); and it is false that (d) "in order for a person to act according to virtue, that person must know what he is doing under the description that makes the action characteristic of the virtue" (373); and it is false that (A') the agent who possesses some virtue v "exercises it knowingly" (373).

The point of emphasizing the argument's complexity is to make clear that the existence of a class of virtues of ignorance would not falsify either (A') or (A) so long as these are not interpreted in accordance with (d). No plausible form of virtue theory does so, so we should reject Driver's initial characterization. This defeats her claim that the existence of the virtues of ignorance, if it could be established, would show that virtue theory is deeply mistaken in its commitment to (A') or (A).

Knowing Modesty

This much seems firm. But the rejection of the interpretation of (A') and (A) in terms of (d) is compatible with the existence of a class of virtues of ignorance. Most everyone thinks that the virtues are heterogeneous in kind, so it is possible that Driver is correct that there is a type of virtue that is correctly characterized as essentially involving an epistemic deficit.

The person who possesses any virtue must, according to the analysis I have recommended so far, display (or be disposed to display) that virtue in appropriate situations, and thus she must possess whatever know-how such expression requires. But it is compatible with this that there is a class of virtues whose proper ascription requires that the agent who possesses a member of this class must be ignorant of certain things, possibly even that she possesses that very virtue. The generous person might not know that what she does falls under the description of generosity. But it would not disqualify an ascription of generosity if she did. Virtues of ignorance, however, are allegedly different in this respect. If the agent knows that she has the virtue, she does not; or so Driver argues. This is an interesting and important claim in its own right, so it is worth a closer look.

Driver carefully works out an argument for a paradigm-case virtue of ignorance: modesty. The sort of modesty she has in mind is not sexual modesty, but the sort of modesty "associated with self-deprecation, or an underestimation of one's self-worth" (374). The first question is, What is it of which the modest person must be ignorant? Sometimes, indeed usually, Driver claims that it is essential for a correct ascription of modesty that the modest person not know that she possesses the virtue of modesty itself. The modest person is not allowed, unlike the generous person, to know that she is modest. The second interpretation is that the modest person must be (generally) ignorant of, and thereby underestimate her worth, accomplishments, and so on. Call the first interpretation the *strong-ignorance claim*. It requires ignorance at the second level, at the level of the general virtue description that applies. Call the second interpretation, the *weak-ignorance claim*. It requires ignorance of certain facts or features of the self, others, or the world.

One might think that the modest person could satisfy the weak-ignorance claim without satisfying the strong-ignorance claim. That is, some person *P* might know that she typically underestimates her worth and accomplishments and thus know that she is modest. But Driver thinks that is not possible. She correctly points out that the statement "I am modest" is odd from a performative point of view. But it is important to emphasize that it is not nearly a contradiction, nor is it nearly as odd as G. E. Moore's paradox ("It's raining, but I don't believe it"). And it is not odd at all in certain contexts. For example, in a communicative situation with close friends or a therapist, a person might be brought to see that she is modest, and thus come to understand some of her behavior under that description. Such self-comprehension might even result from self-reflection in a savvy, strong evaluator in Charles Taylor's sense. It would be extremely odd, counterintuitive, and moralistic if it disqualified a person from being modest if she knew she was. To be sure, if she started to brag, "I am modest," she would generate her own disqualification. But this is for other reasons than that she possesses the reflexive knowledge that she possesses the virtue in question. I conclude that we have been given no reason to think that believing that one possesses some virtue *v* is ever sufficient by itself to disqualify the ascription of v. This undermines one interesting but excessively strong claim about the virtues of ignorance—what I have called the strong-ignorance claim. Driver is wrong to say that "I can be modest, but I cannot *know* it" (376). And she is wrong to claim that there is a self-other asymmetry in the case of the virtues of ignorance which takes this form: "I can ascribe the virtue to another, but I cannot coherently, and sincerely ascribe it to myself" (380).[3]

If it is not the virtue itself of which the person who possesses a virtue of ignorance must be ignorant, what is it of which she must be ignorant? Perhaps the weak-ignorance claim is true, even if the strong-ignorance claim is false.

Modesty and Self-Esteem

Driver favors what she calls an "underestimation" account of modesty over either a behavioral or an understatement account on grounds that a person can behave modestly without being modest and a person can understate her accomplishments knowingly and manipulatively. According to the underestimation account, the modest person:

> [i]f he speaks, then he underestimates the truth, but he does so unknowingly. This entails that the modest person is ignorant, to a certain degree, with regard to his own self-worth. He underrates himself, and therefore only takes part of the credit due him. (376)

> In order for a person to be modest, she must be ignorant with respect to her own self-worth. She must think herself less deserving, or less worthy, than she actually is. (377)

I have already argued that the modest person can know that she is modest. And although I think the underestimation account is wrong, this point is compatible with it. A person might know that she is modest in Driver's sense that she possesses "a dogmatic disposition to underestimation of self-worth" (378). That is, an individual might know that she possesses such a disposition, but be unaware in specific occurrent cases that she is engaging in underestimation or, even if she is aware that she is probably underestimating herself in some particular situation, she might be in the dark as to what exactly it is about her worth, accomplishments, and so on, which she is underestimating.

Even though the underestimation account is, or can be made, compatible with my claim that modesty can involve knowledge that one is modest, there is something wrong, I think, with the underestimation account.

Compare it to a fourth account, which Driver never considers, and which I call the *nonoverestimation account.*

According to the nonoverestimation account, the modest person may well have a perfectly accurate sense of her accomplishments and worth but she does not overestimate them. This account is better than the behavioral account, since nonoverestimation is more than behavioral. It involves the manner in which the modest person sees herself and experiences her worth and accomplishments. And it is better than the understatement account for the same reason: the state of mind presupposed rules out manipulative reserve in one's publicly expressed self-estimations.

Finally, it is better than Driver's underestimation account for four reasons. First, there is in the end something deeply problematic about a characterization of the virtue of modesty in terms of a "dogmatic disposition to underestimation of self-worth" (378). On Driver's view, there are no modest people who do not possess this dogmatic disposition. But this, it seems to me, is deeply counterintuitive. Perhaps there is a kind of modest person who fits her description. But I doubt it. I think we would be inclined to think that the epistemic deficit of systematic underestimation made such cases into cases of "false modesty." The truly modest person cannot be so systematically in the dark about her worth. In fact, in the sorts of cases Driver describes, I suspect that the question of modesty would not even enter into evaluative discussion. I think we would just say of her so-called modest person that she lacked appropriate self-esteem or self-respect.

In the second place, and relatedly, on Driver's view, the person who "has an accurate assessment of his accomplishments and character" can behave modestly, but cannot be modest. This, too, is paradoxical. Its only warrant, as far as I can see, is the strong-ignorance claim rejected above, which disqualifies ascription of virtues such as modesty to all persons who know they have it. The nonoverestimation account avoids this paradox. Modesty is compatible with accuracy of self-assessment. The modest person simply does not overestimate her worth.

It is easy to imagine that the world's fastest runner might be modest and know that he is (suppose that sports commentators are forever pointing it out to him because they are exasperated by his modesty). He is not ignorant either of his modesty or of his accomplishments. Perhaps he not only has no dispositions to immodesty, but also assesses his accomplishments as less significant than others do. He might think that being the world's fastest human is not so important *sub specie aeternitatis,* or he might think that his being the world's fastest human involves a significant amount of luck. It is easy to imagine that a person who thought this way might eventually come to think that he was not really modest at all, but rather that he appraises things realistically. He simply does not overestimate his accomplishments, as others do. This suggests that over- or underestimation involves a significant amount of observer relativity.[4]

Third, Driver's underestimation account has the further paradoxical consequence that, "[s]ince modesty necessarily involves ignorance, it is also necessarily involuntary in nature" (381). Indeed, Driver is attracted to the view that only modesty that arises spontaneously, from a person's temperament, is true modesty. This is because working at being modest would require that one "would need to practice self-deception" (382). Driver is led to this conclusion because of two mistakes. There is the mistake of thinking that the cultivation of modesty would need to aim at the cultivation of the "dogmatic disposition to underestimation of self-worth" (378). For the person who is not now modest, this would require practice and eventual success in the acquisition of a vice, the vice of not seeing the self accurately. Apparently, it is Driver's view that, if one is naturally disposed to dogmatic self-delusion, this has no bearing on our ascriptions of true modesty. Whereas if this delusion is the product of work on one's character, it is a total disqualifier. The second mistake arises from thinking that learning to underestimate self-worth in the way required would have to eventuate, in its last step, with the person's somehow making herself ignorant of the fact that she had made herself modest. Otherwise, she would be modest occurrently, so to speak, in all episodes requiring underestimation, but she would know the general truth that she was modest. This is not permitted according to the requirement of strong ignorance. To me, the twin ideas that the virtues of ignorance are essentially characterized by ignorance at both levels, as well as closed, in principle, to self-cultivation, are extremely implausible consequences of the underestimation account. Indeed, I take them to be a reductio of the account.

The nonoverestimation account avoids all such trouble. Working at becoming modest is possible because one does not need to acquire any dogmatic disposition of underestimation. One simply needs to learn not to overestimate one's accomplishment and worth. Furthermore, there is no deep paradox in knowing that one is modest on the nonoverestimation account. The modest person, of course, does not, as Bernard Williams says, act "under the title of modesty." She does not overestimate simply because she wants to be modest. But that is a different issue.

The fourth point in favor of the nonoverestimation account is that it fits nicely with findings in cognitive social psychology regarding self-serving attributional biases. Shelley Taylor and Jonathan Brown[5] have provided evidence, based on a meta-analysis of a large array of experiments, that most people dramatically overestimate themselves across a wide variety of situations. The evidence suggests that most people are prone to unrealistically positive self-evaluations. Here are some of the relevant findings: Given a list of trait names, subjects judge positive traits to be overwhelmingly more characteristic of self and intimates than negative traits; subjects rate self and self-performance more positively than observers do; persons score themselves and their intimates better than all others on all measures; they judge the group(s) to which they belong as better than other groups; they have more trouble recalling failure than success; recollection of task performance is exaggerated in recollection; favored abilities are seen as rare, disabilities are seen as common; favored abilities are seen as important, disabilities as unimportant; improvement is exaggerated on tasks that are considered important; initially modest attributions of success or failure become more self-serving over time, for example, on a joint performance, credit given to one's partner shifts to oneself over time.

The strength and pervasiveness of these self-serving attributional biases support the intuition that what we need is not more people who underestimate their self-worth, but more people who do not overestimate their worth and accomplishments. Most of us are immodest overestimators. Modesty is the best policy, but it need not involve, ideally it should not involve, the relatively rare defect of underestimation. There is no need for the modest person to be ignorant of her worth and accomplishments. The modest person simply sees more clearly than most how the base rates work; she understands, perhaps, and thereby avoids, certain natural tendencies to frame things in self-serving ways, and she does not need to perceive her self-worth as so much better than average. Modesty and realism in self-appraisal are perfectly compatible.

Dumb Virtues

Driver gives two other examples of virtues of ignorance: blind charity, charity that involves seeing the good in others but not the bad; and the refusal to hold a grudge. Neither of these fits the desired characterization of virtues of ignorance. But they fail to do so for somewhat different reasons. One common feature is that neither remotely requires strong ignorance. It is easy to imagine persons who possess the relevant dispositions—to overlook the bad in people and to forgive and forget quickly, respectively—and who know that they do. Furthermore, with respect to blind charity, it is hardly uncontroversial as a virtue. Charity of thought, characterized essentially in terms of an epistemic defect of never seeing the bad in others, might well lead the blindly charitable person to support and sustain all sorts of bad habits in others. Even if this did not happen, we would think of such a person as sweet and dear perhaps, but also as naive and blindsighted.

The third example, that of refusal to hold a grudge, is supposed to involve a person with a general disposition to forgive and forget. It is often good to forgive and forget. If the disposition to do so is indiscriminate, however, it, like the disposition to blind charity, will be taken rightly to involve a defect—to be applied without practical wisdom or without a measured disposition. Furthermore, it is hard to see, even in a best-case scenario, how this disposition would really count as a virtue of ignorance. The person who forgives and forgets hardly *really* forgets in the epistemic sense that she does not remember, or cannot remember, the insult or injury. She does not become amnesiac with respect to the relevant hurt. It is just that she is able to put the insult or injury out of mind on an ongoing occurrent basis. In this way, the memory is kept from poisoning ongoing relations.

There are ignorant people who are virtuous.[6] Tolstoy has written about them. But nothing in the argument of "The Virtues of Ignorance" convinces me that there is a class of virtues that require essentially a kind of ignorance. In each of Driver's cases, there are grounds for doubting that the alleged virtue is a bona fide one. But even if one accepts that she has isolated a virtue in each case, there is no essential link between possession of any of her alleged virtues and ignorance that one possesses the virtue itself (the strong-ignorance claim), or of ignorance of some particular feature of the self or world (the weak-ignorance claim).

Notes

Acknowledgment—This essay first appeared in the *Journal of Philosophy* 87, no. 8 (August 1990): 420–28.

1. J. Driver, "The Virtues of Ignorance," *Journal of Philosophy* 86, no. 3 (July 1989): 373–84. The page numbers cited in parentheses in the text are all to this article by Driver.

2. Strictly speaking, there is the superordinate-type: virtue of ignorance. This type consists of the subordinate virtue of ignorance types; for example, modesty, blind charity, the refusal to hold a grudge, and so on. Finally, there are the tokens of these subordinate types, e.g., particular instances of modesty or blind charity.

3. It is a general feature of virtue ascription—indeed, according to attribution theorists, it is a general feature of trait ascription, period—that we are less disposed to ascribe general traits to ourselves than to others. But this is an altogether different point.

4. Discussion of this paper with Amélie O. Rorty, David Wong, and Ken Winkler was helpful on this point.

5. "Illusion and Well-Being: A Social Psychological Perspective on Mental Health," *Psychological Bulletin* 103 no. 2 (February 1988): 193–210. I discuss this research at greater length in *Varieties of Moral Personality: Ethics and Psychological Realism* (Cambridge, Mass.: Harvard University Press, 1991).

6. The relation between reflectiveness and goodness is discussed in chapter 9.

11

Admirable Immorality and Admirable Imperfection

The belief that moral considerations override all other considerations is a central assumption of secular, post-Enlightenment moral theory. Recently, several widely respected philosophers have questioned this assumption of the sovereignty of the moral good. One of the more interesting recent arguments in this regard involves the attempt to tap intuitions that support the existence of the phenomena of *admirable immorality* and *admirable moral imperfection*. Bernard Williams, Susan Wolf, and Michael Slote are all, to varying degrees, sympathetically disposed toward the alleged phenomena.[1]

My purpose in taking up the issues of admirable immorality and admirable imperfection is to force further reflection on this issue of the sovereignty of the moral good. Whereas I am skeptical of some of the arguments put forward for admirable immorality and sympathetic with those put forward for admirable imperfection, I think that reflection on both alleged phenomena is important. Such reflection, it seems to me, undermines the contentfulness, and therefore the interestingness, of the thesis that morality is supreme.

Admirable Immorality

I begin with the case for admirable immorality. Slote distinguishes between a strong thesis and a weak thesis, neither of which he intends to defend:

Strong thesis: immoral behavior *as such* is sometimes admirable.

Weak thesis: sometimes certain nonmoral features of immoral actions are admirable, as are some features of persons which are contingently associated with the commission of immoral acts.[2]

The *strong thesis* is that some behavior is admirable precisely because it is immoral. Whereas this thesis is not worth defending because it is patently false, the *weak thesis* is not worth defending because it is so obviously true. The courage involved in stealing the crown jewels may well arouse our admiration, but courage has an utterly contingent relation to jewel heists. It is part of the folk psychology of courage, after all, that courage is neither necessary nor sufficient for criminality, even though in combination with certain other traits and temptations, courage might increase the probability of criminal activity.

Slote's aim is to argue for an *intermediate thesis.*

Intermediate thesis: sometimes certain admirable features of persons are "intrinsically connected" with immorality. Such features cannot be understood as merely contingently related to the immorality, and therefore cannot be admired without that admiration also accruing to or carrying over to the immorality.

The strategy is to find "cases that do *not* permit such a neat separation between what we admire and what is immoral"[3]—cases in which our admiration is caused by some feature of the persons involved, where the feature in question cannot be coherently admired independently of the immorality it gives rise to. Such cases, if they exist, are cases in which the immorality is implicated in our admiration because the admired feature is "intrinsically connected" to the immorality.[4]

In some such cases our admiration may be strong enough to generate the conviction that the action that is "intrinsically connected" to the admired trait is acceptable, all things considered, even though the demands of morality have not been met. By implicating our reflective admiration in the immorality in this way, such cases, if they exist, help undermine the overridingness thesis.

I'll first describe the cases Slote thinks fit the bill and then explain why I think there are no cases that satisfy the *intermediate thesis.* My criticisms of the *intermediate thesis* are not intended, as will become clear, as a defense of the overridingness thesis. I too think that thesis is problematic.

Case 1: Gauguin, in deep anguish, nonetheless decides to leave his family in order to pursue his artistic project in the South Pacific. (The example of course is Bernard Williams's.)

Case 2: A father who believes that it is his duty to turn in criminals, nonetheless misleads the police as to the whereabouts of his criminal son.

Case 3: Churchill, single-mindedly devoted to Nazi defeat, approves the fire bombing of Dresden (contrary to the conventions of war protecting civilian targets) in order to bring Germany to its knees.

Case 4: A reformist political leader, who believes that torture for political ends is categorically wrong, nonetheless tortures the ringleader of a terrorist group in order to get information about the location of a series of time-bombs that are set to go off around the capital. (The example is Michael Walzer's.)

In order to satisfy the *intermediate thesis* three things need to be established about each case: first, that immorality has occurred, second, that there is some trait of the agents that we admire, and third, that this trait is "intrinsically connected" to the immorality.

The first problem is that it is easy to imagine complex disagreements in all four cases about the admirability of the traits and about the immorality of the action. There will be some people who feel no admiration in any of these cases, for example, those who are incapable of admiration where they believe there is immorality. Furthermore, among those who do feel admiration there will be a variety of causes and a variety of foci. For example, there will be those who see the cases of Gauguin and the reformist as cases of moral conflict, or just plain conflict between incompatible goods, and who see the decisions as admirable because they are heroic, given the binds the agents are in. And there will be those who have a certain positive feeling regarding the outcomes of the stories, but whose positive feeling has nothing to do with admiration for Gauguin or the reformist. Such people are simply glad that paintings like "D'où venons nous? Que sommes nous? Où allons nous?" exist and that the bombs have not gone off. But these individuals would be just as glad if Gauguin's oeuvre had been produced by an artist who had never married and if the terrorists had been thwarted by a leader with a less rigid sense of what was permissible in situations were evil was unavoidable.[5]

But the most important point regarding admiration is that admiration for particular character traits is invariably conditional. We admire traits, such as artistic passion, patriotism, and parental devotion on the assumption that they are not excessive, on the assumption that they are moderated by other devotions and sensitivities within the psychological economy of a whole character. This means that it is always open to us to admire some trait in the abstract—on the assumption that it occurs to the right degree in a morally and otherwise well-modulated

personality—but to find its particular instantiation in some person problematic.

Furthermore, even if we agree that there is something (conditionally) admirable in these cases, similar complexities will arise in trying to establish that immorality has occurred. Moral theorists of a variety of denominations will be able to save all four situations from the immorality charge. Gauguin can be defended from perspectives that count self-realization as a centrally important moral goal. Most (but not all) consequentialists will find the story of the reformist heartwarming; and many virtue theorists will be able to accommodate the father straightforwardly—he has proper sensitivities to the domain-specificity of moral rules and to the particular domain of the particular virtue. The Churchill case is slightly tougher, but the situation still is ripe for some kind of utilitarian analysis. Churchill is, after all, trying to maximize narrow, that is, Allied, utility. Alternatively, we can imagine a defense of both Churchill and the reformist that turns on the responsibility of government leaders to do everything in their power to protect the lives of their citizens. Such a defense will be open to contract theorists as well as to certain types of consequentialists (e.g., rule and motive utilitarians) and virtue theorists. The point is that there is an almost inexhaustible number of strategies on the basis of which to defend these cases from the immorality charge.

Troublesome Traits

Keeping in mind that all four cases will evoke multifarious intuitions regrading both admirability and immorality, let us concentrate on the Gauguin case and assume what is surely correct, namely that some, perhaps many, will see Gauguin's desertion as immoral and his passionate devotion to his art as admirable.

What needs to be done in order to establish that the case so understood satisfies the intermediate thesis is to show that Gauguin's passionate devotion to his art is "intrinsically connected" to this act of desertion. My view is that even if there are cases that pass the admirability and the immorality parts of the test there are no cases where the admired trait is "intrinsically connected" to the immorality—at least not on any interesting interpretation of "intrinsic connection."

Slote is clear that something stronger is needed than cases where we admire people for "traits whose possession makes them *more likely* to act wrongly."[6] There are three senses of "intrinsic connection" which might capture the sort of nonprobabilistic relation he is after. First, some particular trait (or motive or belief) might be necessary for some immoral action in the sense that the action would not have been the immoral action it was if that particular trait (or motive or belief) had not entered into its production. Call this *token necessity*. The basic idea is the familiar one that the nature of a particular action is uniquely determined by the cluster of mental events that brings it about; and that, therefore, these mental events are necessarily constitutive of what action it is. Second, some trait might be necessary for some action not only in the sense that the trait was implicated in the actual causal etiology of that action, but in the sense that no token action of that type could occur without a token of that trait figuring in its production. Call this *type necessity*. Third, possession of some trait might be *sufficient* for immorality.

It should be obvious that the last kind of "intrinsic connection" is a nonstarter. There simply are no character traits that, according to either folk psychology or scientific psychology, are sufficient to produce some specific type of immorality, say, family desertion, nor, for that matter, immorality of any, even unspecified, type. To be sure, there may be all sorts of interesting probabilistic connections among various traits and kinds of actions—generalizations about how complex interactions among systems of character traits, talents, beliefs, desires, and all sorts of features of the external world make immorality more or less probable. And there are undoubtedly some constellations of character traits, some person-alities, that dramatically increase, in the ordinary run of things, the proba-bility that a person with that constellation of traits will engage in immo-rality. But admiration for any specific character trait that figures in such generalizations will always be admiration for a trait, none of whose tokens is sufficient for immorality. This means that the trait, if it is worth admir-ing at all, can be prized independently of whatever immorality it is causally connected to. The required sense of "intrinsic connection" therefore can-not be sufficiency.

Token necessity looks like a more plausible candidate explication of "intrinsic connection" since there are obvious examples of the relation. The trouble is that there are too many examples of it. Token necessity is ubiquitous; some form of it is true of all actual(ized) actions. Every charac-ter trait or motive or belief that is causally important in bringing about a particular action is plausibly thought of as necessarily linked to that action and as partly constitutive of the kind of action it is. Token necessity, therefore, cannot be the kind of "intrinsic connection" we are after. After all, the required relation is supposed to enable us to distinguish the con-nection between Gauguin's artistic passion and his desertion from the relation between the robber's daring and his crime. But Gauguin's passion has the same kind of actual causal connection to his desertion as the robber's daring has to his brazen jewel heist in broad daylight. If we look only at the actual causal relations that obtain, it is impossible to see any grounds for maintaining that the robber's daring can be conceived independently of his immorality, whereas, Gauguin's passion cannot be conceived independently of his.

The claim therefore must be that the connection between Gauguin's passion and his immorality is one of type necessity; that is, that Gauguin's passion (but not the robber's daring) belongs to a kind whose members have some necessary, lawlike link to immorality. It is important to pay attention to the way the types are individuated on both the trait and action side of the equation in order to evaluate this claim. But it seems to me that no mode of individuation will yield interesting type-necessary links. In the first place it is manifestly false that artistic passion is necessary for immorality as such. So the claim must be that artistic passion (of the right kind) is necessary for some particular kind of immorality, say, family desertion. But this too is manifestly false. Maybe the claim is that artistic passion is necessary for a particular kind of family desertion. But what kind? The only kind that comes to mind is the kind where the artist leaves his family because of his artistic passion. We are led to some such banal and unlawlike generalization as "Artistic passion is necessary for the kinds of immorality caused by artistic passion."

Furthermore, identical logic applies to the allegedly distinct case of daring. Daring has no necessary link to immorality as such; nor does it have necessary relations to the type "daring crime," broadly construed. It is easy to imagine some such crimes being perpetrated by cowardly religious fanatics. The only cases where type necessity obtains is where the crimes in question are those in which daring is actually causally implicated. Again the only remotely plausible type necessity claim is dismally uninformative.

The same sort of argument applies to the other cases. The traits of parental devotion and single-minded devotion to a political cause do not, to the best of my knowledge, have any interesting type-necessary connections to action. Nor can I think of any traits (outside of very general traits like rationality) that do. However, even if it could be shown that some admirable character trait had some interesting necessary connection to immorality, we would still not have a case that satisfies the intermediate thesis as originally formulated. The reason is this: although type-necessary connections can be stated in nonstatistical form (no action of type A without a token of trait t), the actual causal relations between the trait and action type will be probabilistic through and through. Indeed the probabilistic causal picture will, I suspect, invariably reveal two things: first, that the trait occurs a certain percentage of the time (typically high) without the immorality; second, that it is only in combination with lots of other traits, beliefs, desires, and real-world circumstances that immorality is highly probable. But these facts mean that the trait can always be "conceptually prised" from immorality—especially if we imagine it not interacting with these other variables that make the immorality likely.

In several places Slote suggests a somewhat different understanding of "intrinsic connection"—one that links certain traits to a tendency to immorality rather than to immorality itself. At one point, in speaking of Gauguin's passionate devotion to his art, he says that "it is criterial of having a passion that incompatible impulses, concerns, desires *tend* to give way to it."[7] In another place he claims that the trait of artistic passion, unlike traits such as daring, intelligence, and physical strength, is "inconceivable apart from the *tendency* to wrongdoing."[8] This claim is best interpreted as follows: some traits, for example, artistic passion, great parental devotion, and political ambition, are sufficient for a tendency to immorality; other traits, for example, daring, passion for horticulture, and athletic prowess, are not sufficient for such a tendency.

I'm not completely sure what to make of this move. It seems to me that whether a particular trait is sensibly thought of as grounding a tendency to wrongdoing will depend in large part on how it is described. Nevertheless, it seems implausible to think of garden-variety artistic passion, or, for that matter, passion for philosophy or science, as grounding a tendency for wrongdoing. If there is a temptation to think this way it may originate in a sense that there are interesting probabilistic connections between these passions and immorality. But if such connections do in fact exist (which I doubt), it seems more reasonable to think of them as due to the complex way the demands of artistic, philosophical, or scientific life typically interact with real-world moral demands, than to think of these garden-variety passions as sufficient for, or partly constituted by, a tendency to wrongdoing. Furthermore, even if there is a kind of artistic passion that can be thought of as grounding a tendency to wrongdoing, for example, passion that is partly constituted by a conscious commitment not to let morality or anything else stand in one's way, its existence will not help win the intermediate thesis. The reason is simple: the ascription of admirability to this kind of passion will not be easily secured, and, even if it is, the fact remains that such tendencies are neither necessary nor sufficient for the kinds of immoral action we have been imagining.

In correspondence, Slote makes two interesting points. First, he suggests that if we focus less on the connection between character traits and action and more on the morality/immorality and admirability/unadmirability of the traits themselves, we will discover traits that are considered both admirable and morally objectionable quite independently of any connections they have to action. Second, and relatedly, he suggests that a trait can be morally objectionable even if it never in fact leads to any wrong-doing.

Neither point helps the intermediate thesis. Although it is true that we apply the predicate pairs moral/immoral and admirable/unadmirable to traits considered in isolation, such ascriptions are best read as based on views we have about the typical causal relations the traits have with action and overall personal bearing. This means that the claim that some trait is both admirable and immoral always needs to be analyzed in terms of its wider causal relations. To be sure, there will be traits—perhaps artistic passion is one of them—that will be implicated with some frequency both in activities we admire and in immoral activities (according to the lights of some moral conception or other). The wily spy has an admirable trait relative to his job description, but this very same trait, if it carries over to his family life and friendships, will quite possibly end up implicated in immorality. What is doubtful, however, is that the wider causal picture will reveal any traits that are "intrinsically connected" in any interesting way both to vicious activity and to admired activity.

With regard to the second point the same sort of response applies. There are, no doubt, some traits, just as Slote maintains, that are deemed morally objectionable but that never lead to immorality for some particular person. Because traits are a kind of disposition they will enter into interesting counterfactual generalizations of the following form: If an agent has traits $t_1 \ldots t_n$ and beliefs $b_1 \ldots b_n$ and desires $d_1 \ldots d_n$ and circumstances c obtain, then the probability of immorality will be high. Trait tokens achieve the status of being considered morally problematic when they are insufficiently tempered by other traits and when the activating conditions in the belief-desire system and in the environment are easily and commonly satisfied. But such relations are irrevocably probabilistic and therefore can't help win the intermediate thesis. The important point remains. There are no examples of traits that cannot be admired independently of the specific immoral episodes in which one of their tokens is implicated.[9]

The Sovereignty of Morality

Defense of admirable immorality, then, is not the way to undermine the thesis that morality is supreme. This does not mean, however, that the overridingness thesis emerges unscathed. Our discussion thus far provides some reason to wonder independently about that thesis. First, the intuition pumping required to engage in such reflection as we have been engaged in reminds us just how much disagreement there is about the

domain of the moral and about the order of goods and obligations, especially when we confront complex cases. Even when there is agreement that
moral considerations reign supreme there may not be agreement about
what the moral considerations are or how they are to be weighted, and this
suggests that the overridingness thesis is not particularly contentful,
action-guiding, or dispute-resolving. Second, even if Slote's cases are not
cases that satisfy the intermediate thesis, they are cases in which a person's
commitment to a particular project or goal leads him to reject the demands of morality as he or his community construes them. They are cases
where, at least from the subjective point of view, the action was seen as
immoral but as what had to be done. What should we say about cases
where some agent or some community deems an action acceptable, all
things considered, but acknowledges that the demands of morality have
not been met? The fact remains that whether we admire Gauguin or not,
many of us understand and accept him and his action.

This problem may be even clearer if we consider Gauguin's more ordinary contemporary counterpart. Most people believe in both marriage *and*
in divorce. We believe both in publicly promising "to have and to hold
from this day forward 'til death do us part," and in the acceptability of
sometimes breaking these very promises. One might think that we believe
in marital promise breaking only when one party has already violated the
marriage contract. But this isn't quite right. We also understand why
people split up just because love is gone and boredom has taken hold.

Suppose that both members of a couple realize that they are in a situation like this, and that both parties think rightly that hard work won't get
them back to the place they both wish they were at. Suppose further that
one party finds the situation more intolerable than the other and initiates
divorce. What are we to think of this individual?

My impression (based on a small sample of philosophers' reactions)
is that, regardless of whether one's sympathies are Kantian, utilitarian,
contractarian, or virtue-theoretical, moral philosophers understand, tolerate, and appreciate that such an action might be necessary all things
considered—not simply excusable, but acceptable.[10] If this is right, it is
important. The reason is this: Every contemporary moral theory will see
some salient moral considerations on the side of the individual bearing up
and abiding by his or her vows, and almost no moral theory will assign
overriding weight to his or her boredom or misery. But if it is true that we
will nonetheless accept, tolerate, and understand the decision to leave,
despite the failure to meet the demands of morality, we have some prima
facie evidence that the thesis of the sovereignty of the moral good is not as
gripping as has been traditionally alleged. Some might think that this is
not a moral issue at all. But that thoroughly modern move, although it is

compatible with preserving the thesis of the sovereignty of the moral good, does so only at the price of dramatically restricting its range of applicability and thereby undermining it as well.

Admirable Imperfection

Some of the problems with the thesis of the sovereignty of the moral good can be brought out more clearly by examining a different thesis from the thesis that there is admirable immorality. This thesis is put forward by Susan Wolf in "Moral Saints." Wolf's argument proceeds as follows. First, she defines a "moral saint" as a "person whose every action is as morally good as possible." Second, she argues that both Kantian and utilitarian theories project ideals of such saints—respectively, the ideals of the rational and the loving saint. Third, she has us imagine the demands of a life of moral sainthood:

> [A]bove all, a moral saint must have and cultivate those qualities which are apt to allow him to treat others as justly and kindly as possible. He will have the standard moral virtues to a nonstandard degree. He will be patient, considerate, even-tempered, hospitable, charitable in thought as well as deed. He will be very reluctant to make negative judgments of other people. He will be careful not to favor some people over others on the basis of properties they could not help but have.[11]

Wolf thinks that for such an individual the moral virtues "are apt to crowd out the nonmoral virtues, as well as many of the interests and personal charcteristics that we generally think contribute to a healthy, well-rounded, richly developed character."[12] The claim is that the ideal of moral sainthood is, upon reflection, incompatible with our ideals of desirable personal lives. We admire, indeed we aspire to, the less than morally perfect. Wolf puts it this way: "[A] person may be *perfectly wonderful* without being *perfectly moral.*"[13] Call this *admirable imperfection.*

The important idea is not merely that the ideals of morality cannot provide a comprehensive guide to the conduct of life, but that nonmoral ideals and projects may be in conflict with—and not just additional to—our moral ideals. We admire lives constituted by traits—loving to cook, study chemistry, or to play and follow sports—that are developed for nonmoral reasons and that obstruct satisfying the ideal(s) of moral sainthood. The obstructions can be temporal or conceptual. Someone with a passion for solving problems in neuroscience will, by virtue of pursuing that passion, have less time than she otherwise would have for "doing good." Someone with a deep-seated love and concern for his children will have conceptual trouble taking seriously the demands of impersonal morality when they conflict with his particular loyalties. He will have trouble, for example, appreciating the (alleged) moral weightiness of his decision to invest in his children's education rather than in some other activity that will make the worst-off marginally better off.[14] If one thinks that every situation is ripe for the production of moral good and if one views the production of moral good as an unconditional and overriding demand, then passions for neuroscience, sports, fine wine, music, and philosophy will be more than arguably frivolous. They will be positively pernicious.[15]

It is important for analytic purposes to distinguish between two possible overridingness theses: (1) the thesis of the overridingness of the *morally ideal* and (2) the thesis of overridingness of the *morally required.* The standard way around the view that there is something morally deficient about persons who do not seek to maximize the moral good in each and every act, and the way to avoid the otherwise inevitable conflicts that would result from adherence to both overridingness theses, is to create a concept of supererogation and make the production of the morally ideal an optional rather than an overriding demand.

The very idea of supererogation is predicated on the assumption that the moral good can almost always be advanced if we pay attention and care to make the effort. Having admitted this much, the trick is to provide a principled rationale for making the production of certain kinds of good optional, while at the same time acknowledging their great moral worth. It is something of a mystery what exactly this principled rationale is—or to put it another way, it is something of a mystery how the thesis of the overridingness of the morally ideal falls so easily to our realistic attitudes about persons while the thesis of the overridingness of the morally required stands so imperiously over moral life. It is hard to imagine that the distinction between the two sets of considerations is so clear that it can support such radically different statuses for the two theses.

Although this distinction between what is required and what is ideal is notoriously hard to draw (and although we do wonder about people who never do more than what is required) some form of the distinction seems necessary to block a conception of morality that is so demanding that it precludes the acquisition of goods, the development of traits and talents, and the undertaking of projects that are, from some reasonable perspective, deemed desirable.[16] The talented student of the sitar who spends several hours a day practicing is doing something admirable, as well as developing an admirable trait. Whereas he violates no moral requirements by diligently practicing, he does what is less than morally ideal. He could after all be spending his time doing what Mother Teresa does.

It seems to me irrefutable that there are many admirable traits, talents, and projects that are incompatible with a life of moral sainthood so conceived. Even Robert Merrihew Adams, a critic of Wolf's views on sainthood, is committed to this conclusion.[17] Adams argues that our actual criteria for calling someone a "saint" are not based on the moral worthiness of his every *act*, but rather on his overall worthiness as a person (the criteria for assessing this need to be spelled out more fully than Adams has yet done); and he insists that although a saint will "commonly have time for things that do not *have* to be done . . . [s]aintliness is not perfectionism."[18] In speaking of Albert Schweitzer, Adams reminds us that

> in the midst of his humanitarian activities in Africa, he kept a piano and spent some time playing it. . . . Very likely that time could have been employed in actions that would have been morally worthier, but that fact by itself surely has no tendency to disqualify Schweitzer from sainthood, in the sense in which people are actually counted as saints.[19]

Adams of course is right that our actual criteria for ascribing sainthood are realistic in just the way he suggests (indeed Kantians might plausibly argue that their moral saint, like the religious and virtue-theoretical saint and unlike the utilitarian moral saint, is realistic in the sense that he has no obligation to produce moral good in every act—only to be morally worthy over all). But the fact that our actual criteria are realistic helps support the important point: namely that the models of moral perfection Wolf describes are not all that attractive as ideals of persons. Although we understand the idea of moral sainthood, it does not grip us. Most of us feel neither regret nor disappointment, even upon reflection, for not achieving or even aspiring to a life in which each act is a moral contribution. Both the depth and universality of this reaction undermine the view that the morally ideal is overriding.[20]

Realism and Points of View

One wonders whether, once we've rejected the thesis of the overridingness of the morally ideal, we can't also reject the thesis of the overridingness of the morally required. My own view is that we can—not because the notion it expresses of more or less worthwhile goods is unimportant, but because qua philosophical thesis it lacks content and does little action-guiding or dispute-resolving work. This is not to deny that the most weighty reasons for action, all things considered, ought to be decisive; nor is it to deny that we learn to use the word "moral" to refer to very weighty considerations. What I question is the usefulness of a philosophical thesis that tells us that whatever is morally required is overriding, in a cultural context in which there is widespread disagreement about what morality is, and thus about what is morally required. There are two plausible and allied lines of attack here: one by way of (Nagelian) points of view, the other by a direct attack on moral realism. Wolf prefers the former strategy; I prefer the latter.

Wolf suggests that one way to read the incompatibility between the morally ideal and the personally ideal is as a conflict between two competing points of view. The moral point of view involves the recognition "that one is just one person among others equally real and deserving of the good things in life."[21] The point of view of individual perfection, on the other hand, presupposes the saliency of each person's particularity—the saliency of the kind of life it would be best for each of us qua individual to live. Whereas the moral point of view comes with pressure toward impartiality, the point of view of individual perfection comes with a built-in emphasis on each person's particularity.[22]

Our actual behavior, and our realistic attitudes (I wouldn't want to call them theories), indicate that we have gone some distance toward accommodating both points of view. We reject the thesis of the overridingness of the morally ideal because it fails to allow enough room for the development of nonmoral traits and talents. And we reject models of persons that do not make some accommodation to moral demands.

Once we have accepted the idea of competing and, at some level, incommensurable points of view, and have made this first accommodation, we have effectively rejected the thesis of the overridingness of the morally ideal. Furthermore, once we are motivated by the logic of points of view, it is not clear that we can avoid rejecting the thesis of the overridingness of the morally required as well. The move to points of view, after all, is predicated on the thesis that no perspective has sovereignty purely qua point of view. This is why Wolf says that when we take up the point of view of individual perfection "and ask how much it would be good for an individual to act from the moral point of view, we do not find an obvious answer. . . . [A]t any rate . . . the answer is not 'as much as possible.'"[23]

Thomas Nagel puts the same point this way:

Human beings are subject to moral and other motivational claims of very different kinds. This is because they are complex creatures who can view the world from many perspectives—individual, relational, impersonal, ideal, etc.—and each perspective presents a different set of claims. Conflict can exist within one of these sets, and it may be hard to resolve. But when conflict exists between them, the problem is still more difficult. Conflicts between personal and impersonal claims are ubiquitous. They cannot, in my view, be resolved by subsuming either of the points of view under the other, or both under a third.[24]

The problem with both versions of the overridingness thesis now emerges. It is the utter incommensurability of the demands of the morally ideal with the demands of personal perfection, which makes us reject the doctrine of the overridingness of the morally ideal. Whereas this initial incommensurability is systematic, it is entirely possible that we will continue to meet particular conflicts even after we've lowered our sights— conflicts between what is morally required and what is required from some other point of view. The problem is that, once both points of view have been put on the same level (this does not entail that all goods are at the same level), there is no longer any a priori answer—nor any answer based on the essential nature of persons or the social world—to the question of which set of requirements, which set of claims, is overriding.[25]

There is another strategy for undermining the overridingness thesis that is related to, but somewhat more direct than, the attack by way of competing points of view. This strategy involves a direct assault on moral realism. One attraction of this tactic is that it avoids one problem that the other tactic has. Although the motivation behind the whole idea of incommensurable, competing points of view with no a priori ordering among them is antifoundationalistic, the points of view themselves are often described as if they were fixed in metaphysical stone. There is the subjective point of view, the objective point of view, the moral point of view, the point of view of individual perfection, and so on.

An idea seriously worth entertaining is that the points of view themselves change (both structurally and substantively) over time. Indeed some may even appear and disappear. When a particular point of view has the sort of integrity and stability that allows it to be clearly characterized for a particular community, this tells us that there is consensus about a picture of the world and about how to use certain words; it does not necessarily tell us that we have uncovered some deep fact about the nature of subjectivity, or objectivity, or morality, or the ideals of individual perfection. One possibility is that things such as these have no nature.

Let me flesh out this idea. The belief in the sovereignty of the good, in the supremacy of moral considerations over all others, goes best overall with a certain kind of moral realism. If (1) the "moral" picks out a well-behaved kind—a clearly discernible set of considerations with a clearly discernible order among them, and (2) one prominent property of members of this kind is their sovereignty, their overriding importance relative to other kinds of consideration, then the idea that morality is supreme is plausible. There have been a wide variety of attempts to establish (1) and (2)—all unworkable.

The most implausible realist views are flagrantly essentialist and hold that the moral features of reality constitute a natural kind, or, alternatively, a nonnatural (platonic) kind. Adopting Hilary Putnam's terminology, I call such views *external realist*.[26] The trouble with "external realism" in ethics is this: even if it could be shown that "the moral" picked out a natural kind, it is hard to see how (given what we know about natural kinds) this kind would have associated with it the required property of supreme importance. This problem is easier for the platonist or intuitionist to handle. He will tell us that he who has seen "the good" also appreciates (or experiences) its overriding importance. But the intuitionist or platonist will fail utterly to convince the uninitiated that there is a nonnatural kind called "the good" with this property.

What Alasdair MacIntyre calls "the project of the Enlightenment," the project that gave rise to both utilitarianism and Kantianism, also proceeded on realist assumptions.[27] The project was to provide a theory which specified the domain of the moral and which ordered goods and obligations within that domain in a way that gave rise to a general procedure for resolving moral issues. Neither Kantianism nor utilitarianism, however, needs to be read as presupposing "external realism," although the progenitors of both theories might have conceived of their projects that way. Indeed, in retrospect, the best way to understand both these theories is as promoting alternative visions of morality, alternative conceptions of where moral weightiness attaches rather than as revealing the moral order as God or nature carved it.

This way of looking at the project of the Enlightenment does not necessarily undermine all kinds of moral realism. "The moral" might pick out a well-behaved kind, without picking out a natural or platonic kind. It is conceivable, after all, that "the moral" might name a recognizable part of the world, in the way, say, Cubism, sonnets, Balinese cock-fighting rituals, contemporary Catholic funeral practices, and the current IRS tax code do; and that there might be clear and determinate procedures for resolving moral issues in much the same way that there are procedures for producing cubist art, writing sonnets, declaring the winner in a cock fight, having a Catholic funeral, and computing one's income tax. "The moral" might, in effect, designate a theory-determined segment of reality, a homogeneous form of life and thought, without naming a natural or platonic kind.

Call this weaker view *internal realism*.[28] Internal realism in ethics would make both the domain of the moral and the question of whether (and how) morality was overriding relative to a particular moral theory, or more likely, a particular set of shared social practices. The sort of internal realism that could help a relativized version of the overridingness thesis is the type where "the moral" picks out a well-behaved *and* overriding kind—that is, where (1) and (2) are satisfied—from the point of view of the adherents of some particular moral theory or from the point of view of some particular set of shared social practices.

Does internal ethical realism, so understood, obtain today? The most honest answer is, I think, "not really," and this is bad for the view that "the moral good" is sovereign, because it suggests that there is widespread disagreement about the nature and order of moral goods. But without agreement as to what the most weighty considerations are, the thesis that the most weighty considerations should serve as decisive reasons for action lacks substance—at least any more substance than is carried by the slogan that individuals should act according to their consciences.

Reflection on either contemporary social practice or philosophical theorizing both yield this answer. Take Kantianism and utilitarianism (not because these are the only currently available moral theories but only because they are the most worked over and widely discussed). The trouble with both these theories, and it is worth emphasizing, is that they are vague. As we saw in the earlier discussion of admirable immorality, Kantians and utilitarians are able to go any number of incompatible ways in picking out the morally salient features of reality and in ordering goods and obligations.[29] There are, for example, Kantian and utilitarian arguments on both sides of the abortion controversy. The basic problem is one of giving action-guiding content to the abstract slogans that mark off the respective theories, of giving values to their respective theoretical variables—duty and happiness. To be sure, the utilitarian will tell us that we should seek to maximize the greatest good overall. But what utilitarians are eternally bickering about is what the goods are and how they are ordered. Kantians, meanwhile, will insist that we should meet our categorical obligations and that we must be willing to universalize the maxims that guide our actions. What Kantians have trouble doing is spelling out in a detailed and convincing way what our categorical obligations are (remember Kant's own implausible view regarding the obligation to tell the truth); and in placing non-question-begging limits on the degree to which the maxims we universalize can be fine-grained and contextually sensitive.

This last point is important. Either we keep the maxims that guide our actions at a very general, contextually insensitive level, in which case we may be led to such oddities as not being able to tell a small lie for a terribly important purpose; or we are allowed to universalize maxims that are as fine-grained and contextually sensitive as we want, in which case we can will whatever we please without any inconsistency whatsoever. But this problem of drawing the line on the level of grain of the maxims is just the problem of deciding what features of the world are morally relevant and in what ways. It is around just these issues that the deep disagreements characteristic of contemporary moral debate revolve.

But if there is widespread disagreement, of both an intertheoretical and an intratheoretical sort, about the nature of the moral domain and about the nature and order of goods and obligations, then there is good reason to think that the overridingness thesis, the belief in the sovereignty of the moral good, is itself a less contentful, interesting, and weighty thesis than we have been led to believe. Contemporary moral theories—be they utilitarian, Kantian, contractarian, or virtue-theoretical—radically underdetermine both the picking out of the morally salient features of reality and the solutions to particular moral problems. This is not to say that traditional moral theory has not made enormous contributions by giving voice to important aspects of moral life. It is just that each theory has elevated its favorite aspect to the status of the essence of morality.

The claim here is empirical.[30] The required kind of internal moral realism was no doubt operative in the past, especially within certain homogeneous religious communities. It is simply not very plausible to think that such consensus exists today, even intratheoretically. This means that neither the morally salient features of reality nor the order among them is fixed with precision by any contemporary moral theory.

Ironically, the view I am suggesting receives support from Lawrence Kohlberg's program in moral psychology, a program that sees itself as supporting Kantianism over utilitarianism, utilitarianism over contract theories, and contract theories over virtue theories. Kohlberg's program has serious and, to my mind, insurmountable problems, but he has made two observations of note.[31] First, our culture is populated by individuals with widely divergent moral conceptions. Second, a particular moral conception ("stage," in Kohlberg's theory) cannot be typed according to the content of moral decisions it gives rise to but only by certain structural, largely stylistic, features of moral discourse.

The point I want to press in conclusion is simply this. If my overall diagnosis is correct, then we have (at least recently) been addressing issues concerning the good life without any moral theory or principle (certainly any single one) doing much work. This suggests that we have been addressing such problems without the concept of "morality" itself being of much service, despite the ubiquity of the word "moral." What we have been doing, sometimes well and sometimes badly, is talking about the order of goods and obligations from a wide variety of perspectives—talking, that is, about actual and possible worlds and visions of human flourishing therein. This seems to me to be a good way, indeed the only way, to do things. Acknowledging this much may, if we are lucky, help break the grip of the view that when things go well it is because the actors involved understand the true nature of morality and its supreme importance; and that, conversely, when things go badly, it is because those involved lack such understanding. That view, I think, is based on the deeply mistaken view that morality has a nature that can be revealed by moral philosophy.

Notes

Acknowledgments—I have benefited from comments on earlier drafts by Marcia Baron, Larry Blum, Burt Louden, Ruth Anna Putnam, Amélie O. Rorty, Michael Slote, Michael Stocker, and especially Ken Winkler. This essay first appeared in a slightly different form in the *Journal of Philosophy* 83, no. 1 (January 1986): 41–60.

1. See Bernard Williams, "Moral Luck," in *Moral Luck* (New York: Cambridge, 1981); Susan Wolf, "Moral Saints," *Journal of Philosophy* 79, no. 8 (August 1982): 149–39; Michael Slote, "Admirable Immorality," in *Goods and Virtues* (New York: Oxford, 1983); Philippa Foot's work, especially "Morality and Art" (1970), reprinted in *Philosophy as It Is,* ed. Ted Honderich and Myles Burnyeat (New York: Penguin Books, 1979) and "Are Moral Considerations Overriding?" in *Virtues and Vices* (Berkeley: California University Press, 1978) is another serious challenge to the overridingness thesis.

2. Slote, "Admirable Immorality," 79.

3. Ibid.

4. Ibid., 84.

5. See Bernard Williams, "Moral Luck," and Thomas Nagel, "Moral Luck," in *Mortal Questions* (New York: Cambridge University Press, 1979), for illuminating discussions of the way in which the fortuitously good consequences of morally questionable acts may arouse feelings of retrospective justification.

6. Slote, "Admirable Immorality," 79 (my emphasis).

7. Ibid., 82 (my emphasis).

8. Ibid., 92 (my emphasis).

9. In correspondence Alasdair MacIntyre makes the following interesting point: "It is not vicious traits as such which connect interestingly with commendable actions as such. . . . The interesting contention is that certain *social roles* cannot be adequately filled unless they are filled by people with vicious or at least dubious traits and yet we require that these roles be filled and commend—even admire—some at least of the actions of those who fill them successfully. One example to which you allude is that of the spy. The relevant thesis is that in order to be successful in any outstanding way as a spy, one must develop traits of deviousness, cunning and deception which not only would be regarded as vicious if exhibited by others in everyday life, but which have to be developed by the successful spy to the point where he or she cannot escape exhibiting them in the rest of his or her life as well as in his or her spying. . . . [I]t is of course a contingent fact that spying of a certain kind requires the development of immoral traits; and it is equally a contingent fact that successful spying is required for the victory of certain just causes. But the connection between the vicious trait and the admirable action is a *systematic* one in the case of this kind of social role." MacIntyre's insight, it seems

to me, is fully compatible with my line of argument, since even systematic connections are not intrinsic in Slote's sense.

10. See Marcia Baron, "On Admirable Immorality," *Ethics* 96, no. 3 (1986): 557–66, for an interesting discussion of the excuse/justification issue. Harry Frankfurt, "What We Care About," *Synthese* 53, no. 2 (November 1982): 257–72, also advocates the view that we can sometimes be justified, not merely excused, in subordinating moral considerations to other considerations. See especially 257–59.

11. Wolf, "Moral Saints," 421.

12. Ibid.

13. Ibid.

14. See Andrew Oldenquist, "Loyalties," *Journal of Philosophy* 74, no. 4 (April 1982): 173–93; and Owen Flanagan and Jonathan Adler, "Impartiality and Particularity," *Social Research* 50, no. 3 (Autumn 1983): 576–96.

15. This relates to the cases mentioned earlier where some constellation of character traits makes immorality more probable. If one takes the ideal of moral sainthood seriously, then any one of a large number of nonmoral commitments will obstruct achieving moral sainthood, and any large constellation of them will effectively preclude being good. See Michael Stocker, "The Schizophrenia of Modern Ethical Theories," *Journal of Philosophy* 63, no. 14 (August 1976): 453–66, for more on overvaluing morality.

16. See Frances Myrna Kamm, "Supererogation and Obligation," *Journal of Philosophy* 82, no. 3 (March 1985): 118–38; and Thomas Nagel, "Living Right and Living Well," from his book *The View from Nowhere* (New York: Oxford University Press, 1986), for interesting discussions of supererogation and obligation.

17. Adams, "Saints," *Journal of Philosophy* 81, no. 7 (July 1984): 392–401.

18. Ibid., 396.

19. Ibid.

20. It might be argued that these points are irrelevant to the truth of the thesis of the overridingness of the morally ideal, since that thesis (like the thesis of the overridingness of the morally required) is simply a thesis about what is right and what ought to be done and carries no implications whatsoever about affective leftovers or about how high or low we have in fact set our moral sights. My reaction to this objection is that deep-seated and widespread feelings cannot be irrelevant to our considered judgments of morality—that a reasonable moral conception should not be deeply psychologically unrealizable.

21. Wolf, "Moral Saints," 436.

22. See Flanagan and Adler, "Impartiality and Particularity."

23. Wolf, "Moral Saints," 437.

24. Nagel, "The Fragmentation of Value," in *Mortal Questions*, 134.

25. Although no one point of view automatically overrides any other because it is the point of view it is, it will undoubtedly be the case that, for any particular agent, there will be a set of considerations that, *ceteris paribus*, are usually considered overriding for him. These may well, depending on how the particular agent is

socialized and how words are used in his community, fall under what is called "the moral point of view." But there is nothing necessary about this.

26. See Putnam, *Reason, Truth and History* (New York: Cambridge, 1981).

27. See MacIntyre, *After Virtue* (Notre Dame, Ind.: Notre Dame University Press, 1981).

28. See Putnam, *Reason, Truth and History*. It is commonly, and plausibly, argued that John Rawls's *A Theory of Justice* (Cambridge, Mass.: Harvard University Press, 1971) articulates the theory of distributive justice as seen from the liberal point of view, but certainly not from every defensible point of view. Indeed Rawls himself is willing to admit that this is the case. On such a reading, Rawls's book is an internal-realist treatise on justice. But Rawls himself is a skeptic about internal realism (of the required kind) for a "theory of good." See, e.g., 448. I sketch an internal realist conception of moral objectivity in "Quinean Ethics," *Ethics* 93, no. 1 (October 1982): 56–74.

29. Samuel Scheffler admits that this is true of consequentialist theories, in his defense of them: "Different consequentialist theories, of course, incorporate different principles for ranking overall states of affairs, and hence embody different conceptions of what it is best to have happen in the world" (*The Rejection of Consequentialism* [Berkeley: California University Press, 1982], 123).

30. My diagnosis of the current situation is like MacIntyre's in *After Virtue*. MacIntyre, however, unlike me—and unlike Stuart Hampshire, c.f. his *Morality and Conflict* (Cambridge, Mass.: Harvard University Press, 1983)—is very worried that lack of moral consensus fosters a kind of chaos that the social fabric cannot tolerate. MacIntyre can be read, therefore, not as asking us to return to the right external-realist moral theory but rather to create a communal internal-realist theory. Michael Sandel in *Liberalism and the Limits of Justice* (New York: Cambridge University Press, 1982) has similar concerns about our lack of "constitutive community," but from a more liberal perspective. The issue of how important consensus is, is itself important (although I don't think that there is any deep, atemporal answer to whether and where it is important). One thing is certain: the more a culture is in the grip of a naive external realism the less it will be able to understand and therefore tolerate lack of consensus. See also Charles Taylor's "The Diversity of Goods," in *Utilitarianism and Beyond*, ed. Amartya Sen and Bernard Williams (New York: Cambridge University Press, 1982), for another diagnosis which sees a wide array of incommensurable, but defensible, moral perspectives operative in our culture.

31. See my *Science of the Mind* (Cambridge: MIT Press/Bradford Books, second edition [1991]), chap. 5; "Virtue, Sex, and Gender: Some Philosophical Reflections on the Moral Psychology Debate" and "Reply to Lawrence Kohlberg," both in *Ethics* 92, no. 3 (April 1982): 499–512 and 529–32; and Flanagan and Adler, "Impartiality and Particularity." See also L. Kohlberg, "A Reply to Owen Flanagan and Some Comments on the Puka-Goodpaster Exchange," *Ethics* 3 (April 1982): 513–28.

12

Self-Confidences

Here Is Something to Think About

Most of us understand how a married person might come to recognize that she and her husband have grown apart, or not grown together, despite their good intentions and the seriousness with which they took their vows. And we understand how the situation might be experienced as sufficiently intolerable—for any variety of reasons—that the individual sees no choice but to inform her loyal and relatively contented spouse that she intends to leave him. Her future is unclear, and there are costs.

No standard moral theory will yield the right result—that she goes. But we understand why she does go, why perhaps she must go. She leaves, we might suppose, as an *unconfident confident.* Confident that the time has come to seek better things elsewhere, perhaps in a new relationship, perhaps not; unconfident because the costs are unclear and because she, like the rest of us, understands too little why comfort is neither enough nor even a great good for creatures like us. We have high expectations for meaning and worth, and we understand challenging ourselves to excel. Maybe we are—some of us at any rate—meaning-in-life overachievers. Prospects for greater worth and meaning trump morality, narrowly construed, and everything else. We are sometimes impatient and dissatisfied with things that are just OK. Perhaps we are silly in this regard. I think not.

How Can We Explain This?

My aim is to understand better why, despite involving costs, we so readily understand that such situations must be part of the fabric of human life;

that there are great goods worth taking great risks for. That when push comes to shove, some things matter enough to life's meaning to trump a host of other things that matter. The reasons I say these things are complex, and not well understood by me, so let me start at the start and see if I can get anywhere.

The Start

A firm and invigorating sense of one's self, a sense of one's agency, and respect for who one is and what one aims at are great goods. Self-esteem and self-respect have something to do with confidence—what exactly that is I am unsure. Self-knowledge is also a different thing. One can have it and lack esteem, respect, and confidence. And one can have these other goods and be a buffoon when it comes to self-knowing.

All these attitudes, confidence, esteem and respect, can be held with respect to things other than one's self, and they can come apart. But they are goods, so it matters that we understand them and the relations among them more clearly—hardly work just for the philosophers, but perhaps we can say some useful things.

Here Are Some of My Useful Things

There are several kinds of confidence. First, there is *self-confidence simpliciter,* or not so *simpliciter,* which is a state we ascribe to those who exude evidence of the state, as when we say of someone that he is extremely or even supremely self-confident. This can come as a general character trait ascription or it can be ascribed to the self in a domain. So we might say of the world's fastest sprinter that he is supremely confident whenever he races—but not say the same about his feelings or demeanor in interpersonal contexts. And, of course, the world's fastest sprinter may not be confident in the domain in which he most deserves to be—and it is not clear what this says about him or whether it matters.

When we say of some individual that she is supremely self-confident, domain be damned, it is not usually a compliment, despite the recognition that this may well be a useful trait for getting ahead in life.

Second, there is confidence *about* the choices one has or is in the process of making, confidence about one's projects, aims, commitments, relationships—about the direction of one's life. I'll call this *project confidence.* When confidence extends to traits that are central to one's character, to the way one is, the kind of personality one displays and character one has, I'll call it *character confidence*.

People can be confident about their projects without having even thought about whether they have the sort of character that might sensibly choose such a project and carry through on it. It seems to me especially important when one enters into projects whose costs are high and whose future shape is unclear that one think about the kind of person one is. If a certain project, a new open-ended project makes sense, it can only be because the person behind the project does. So self-confidence with respect to one's character and personal capacities is often what brings whatever confidence can be brought to choices the outcomes of which are obscure. Some risks are worth it. But when the future is very unclear, and the possibility exists that it may be worse than the present (this possibility always exists), it helps with self-respect and the confidence to go on, to trust, but not blindly, in one's self. Confidence, esteem, and respect are great goods but untempered by self-knowledge, a narcissistic void lies.

There is also confidence about matters unconnected to self, about who will win the race, the election, how talented a particular student is, and so on—*confidence about external states of affairs.* Making such judgments involves confidence in one's judgmental capacities and in that way presupposes self-confidence. But when we speak of confidence in such matters our interest is focused on the *content* of the confident judgment not on qualities of the agent. Furthermore, no interesting inferences—beyond the minimal one just mentioned—can be made on the bases of such judgments about self-confidence or project/or character confidence.

The first thing I'm inclined to say with conviction is that project confidence and character confidence are quite a bit more important to us than is self-confidence *simpliciter.* And I've already said that when it comes to major changes in projects that character confidence is important—if for no other reason than to assure oneself, but possibly no others, that one is not mad. These types of confidence often do not coexist in the same person, and all three can be unwarranted. Self-confidence is a good if warranted, but it is more of a characterological accessory, nice to have if one can, but quite a bit less important to the meaning of life than project confidence or real confidence that one's traits will serve one well in the daunting project of making a good life. Of course, a person who is confident about the projects she is pursuing has reason to respect herself. Whether she does, of course, is a different matter.

To keep things interesting, I'm going to focus my main examples on cases of character confidence involving, first, attitudes toward gender identity and then on project confidence in partnerships of love—like the example I opened with. I'll also say some things about the worth of being unconfident about matters of great importance and the problem of teaching the young to be unconfident in these ways. But first I want to say some things about two different styles of self-examination. The reason is this: The style of self-scrutiny one starts with will have a lot to do with how one emerges from the scrutiny.

Dueling Attitudes

I will talk about two general attitudes toward self: that of the *strong evaluator* and that of the *ironist,* not because these are the only options or even my favorite options—although I find both deeply attractive—but because both have much to be said in their favor, and I've always wondered about combining seemingly contradictory attitudes—playing "attitude tennis" with oneself. Integration may be overrated, at least if it demands a single method when we are engaged in self-reflection and self-scrutiny.

First, there is strong evaluation. Charles Taylor argues that the capacity for strong evaluation is a necessary feature of persons: "the capacity for strong evaluation is essential to our notion of the human subject. . . . Without it an agent would lack a kind of depth we consider essential to humanity."[1] I first want to say what strong evaluation is; then to think about how it has evolved in Taylor's own thinking through *Sources of the Self*[2]—it has taken him to a state of existential vertigo. This I claim shows a downside to moral seriousness.

Taylor employs Frankfurt's distinction between first-order and second-order desires[3] as a basis for drawing the distinction between strong and weak evaluation. For Frankfurt "someone has a desire of the second order either when he wants simply to have a certain desire or when he wants a certain desire to be his will."[4] Suppose I have a desire to go to drinking with my pals but wish that I didn't have this desire. The typical case is one in which if I have a desire to have a certain desire it is because I am trying to affect or adjust my motivational tendencies. I want not to want to go drinking with my pals because I want to have the strength of will to prevent me from going drinking with them. When we develop second-order desires of this kind we are in fact constructing second order volitions, and it is second-order volitions that Frankfurt sees as "essential to being a person."[5]

The aim of the game is to develop one's character in such a way that one's reflective second-order volitions win out when it comes to action. When second-order volitions are impotent in the face of first order volitions we think of ourselves as suffering weakness of will.

Taylor's idea of weak and strong evaluation develops the basic idea in the following way. A weak evaluator satisfies two conditions. First, the weak evaluator has a set, possibly an ever changing set, of first order desires. Second, the weak evaluator evaluates among its desires in terms of quantitative saliencies. The lion faced with two equally easy kills—an elk and a giraffe—will presumably calculate which is tastier. Lions also perhaps schedule desires in certain sequences: so now it is time to eat, now to drink, now to sleep.

The strong evaluator differs from the weak evaluator in the following main respect. She is concerned with the quality of her desires, her commitments, and her plans. Indeed, she is concerned with the quality of her character, her reason, and her will. It is distinctive of persons that they are, or, at least, can be strong evaluators. The lion, being a weak evaluator, takes her desires for granted. A person who is also a strong evaluator understands that desires can be evaluated in terms of their value, their worth. She does so with the aim of creating a character that is not merely self-governing but that self-governs with the highest standards.

What sort of qualities matter to the strong evaluator? The strong evaluator is concerned that her desires, commitments, plans, and character satisfy high ethical or spiritual standards. The strong evaluator is morally serious. She evaluates her desires, commitments, plans, and character in terms of such categories as "nobility" and "worth." What makes her evaluation strong is that she engages systematically in moral inspection. The qualities she is looking for in her desires, plans, projects, and character are moral ones. Furthermore, strong evaluation involves *depth*. The lion being a weak evaluator evaluates along a single vertical dimension. For the lion faced with the elk or giraffe choice, tastiest wins. The person who is a strong evaluator evaluates competing desires vertically and horizontally. Faced with the same sort of choice as the lion the hungry strong evaluator will see a third option: neither elk nor giraffe. The strong evaluator might consider, for example, the question of the moral status of nonhuman animals. Perhaps she will eat the mushrooms instead. In assessing situations this way, the strong evaluator moves to a level beneath or behind the field of play to considerations and principles that cast the field in ethical hues that were not initially visible.

My Suspicion

Now I said earlier that the greatest defender of strong evaluation, Charles Taylor, ends up in a funny place at the end of *Sources of the Self*. He writes that high moral standards need "strong sources," and he worries that none are available. Commitment to human rights, and the health of the environment, to justice and benevolence, to truth, to gay rights, opposition to racism and sexism, and so on, can pass strong evaluation if we stick to the requirement that credible judgments of worth can be made. What they cannot pass are skeptical challenges. Judgments of nobility and worth don't take one to self-evident foundations. Taylor ends *Sources* hoping that God, the God of Christianity, can do the rest. This is odd, and one could treat it as an aberration, for a strong evaluator need not be a foundationalist attitude. But then again, Taylor's own fall is telling, for it encourages a suspicion I have: Strong evaluation may well be a good attitude to adopt sometimes, but it doesn't, and I don't see how it could, contain, internal to itself, a principle about when reflection had gone deep enough. Is the strong evaluator allowed to satisfice? To stop self-scrutiny because she is getting mental cramps, having passed from things that can be said with some assurance to things that are mixed up and unclear? If not, the place Taylor ends up is inevitable. This follows trivially if I am right about the unfathomability of the self to itself, for self-scrutiny will take us to places we do not—indeed cannot, at least yet, understand.

The strong-evaluative attitude certainly seems like a good thing in many respects. It involves evaluative seriousness. But interpreted one way, the attitude is too demanding. It engenders moral self-indulgence and has no hope in ending one up in a state of reflective security, despite a pretense to do so.

I want to sketch out the second attitude I'm interested in, that of the "ironist." One virtue of "ironism," we will see is that it provides a rationale for quitting the Sisyphean job of requiring everything to pass strong-evaluator muster.

Ironism

Richard Rorty defines a "final vocabulary" as the "set of words" we use to "justify" our actions, beliefs, and lives. He then characterizes an "ironist" as someone who fulfills three conditions:

> (1) She has radical and continuing doubts about the final vocabulary she currently uses because she has been impressed by other vocabularies, vocabularies taken as final by people or books she has encountered; (2) she realizes that argument phrased in her current vocabulary can neither underwrite nor dissolve these doubts; (3) insofar as she philosophizes about her situation, she does not think that vocabulary is closer to reality than others, that it is in touch with a power not herself.[6]

The main point is that a "final vocabulary" is not the one that "puts all doubt to rest," although it may well be a conversation-stopper for a group of like-minded speakers.

The ironist relishes and is amused by contingency, including the contingency of her character, aspirations, projects, and so on. She is not confident that her final vocabulary has things right. Indeed she is confident that it doesn't. She's too much of a historicist to think otherwise. She's a confident unconfident. I like her. Why? Because she's a realist, and realism is a form of authenticity, and authenticity seems to turn out—on the strong-evaluator story as well as all others—to be good, better, at any rate, than the alternative.

Confidence and Reflection

Bernard Williams has, more than anyone else, pushed the idea that reflection can undermine confidence. If I'm right so far, we can see how a commitment to strong evaluation can do so, despite aspirations to the contrary. Ironism, however, is not so much a confidence-undermining attitude as it is an attitude adopted by individuals already convinced of their contingency—and convinced as well of the fact that the ways they think things through, distinguish the ethical from the rest of life and so on—is so much contrivance—possibly wise, useful, and well-motivated contrivance, but contrivance nonetheless, and something that may well be found laughable from another time and place.

Some doubt that an ironist could be serious and comic at the same time. I don't see why not. An ironist seems like a natural to stably occupy this space I admire—the space of *the confident unconfident.* But it is worth arguing about. Do so if you wish. The ironist is reflective, she is a virtuoso of playing mirrors off against herself, of saying "right . . . but then again." Or, "I'm going ahead in this way, there's more to be said, and some of that more will undermine my present confidence in going ahead in this way, but there is not world enough and time. So here I stand." Maybe she sees things the same way seven of ten times, and maybe, just maybe, that's good enough.

Kidding the Kids

Before I proceed further, I want to spend a moment on the problem of believing in the importance of teaching the young certain values and in having them acquire the destabilizing attitudes of reflection and ironism that I've been recommending. There are issues of hypocrisy and paternalism at stake, and there are issues about learning things on one's own—joining the secret society when and if one is ready—and about when it is, as the psychologists say, "developmentally appropriate" to learn certain things. Here are two passages that pose pretty clearly the problem I'm worried about.

Richard Rorty writes:

> Even if I am right in thinking that a liberal culture whose public rhetoric is nominalist and historicist is both possible and desirable, I cannot go on to claim that there could or ought to be a culture whose public rhetoric is ironist. I cannot imagine a culture which socialized its youth in such a way as to make them continually dubious about their own process of socialization. Irony seems inherently a private matter.[7]

In a similar vein Bernard Williams writes:

> To be confident in trying to make sure that future generations shared our values, we would need, it seems to me, not only to be confident in those values—which, if we can achieve it, is a good thing to be—but also convinced that they were objective, which is a misguided thing to be. If we do not have this conviction, then we have reason to stand back from affecting the future, as we have reason to stand back from judging the past. We should not try to seal determinate values into future society.
>
> We also have reason to take some positive steps. We should try to leave resources for an adequate life and, as means to that and as part of it, we shall try to transmit what we take to be our knowledge. We cannot consistently leave out the reflective consciousness itself and practices of free inquiry needed to sustain it and to make use of it.
>
> To our immediate successors, our children at least, we have reason to try to transmit more: it is a mark of our having ethical values that we aim to reproduce them. But this does not affect very determinately what remoter generations will hold. If new developments were to give us more influence on their outlooks, we would do better not to use it, beyond sending them, if we can, free inquiry and reflection, a legacy we can see as created by our knowledge. That will be enough of a legacy, and it will show a proper respect for the relativism of distance that we should not try to send them more.[8]

Teach Your Children Well

I think Williams has it more right than Rorty. The ironist who keeps his ironism private reminds me of Nietzsche's peacock, who hides his true colors and calls them his pride. I don't see why one cannot convey—quite publicly—and to the youth, that contingency, historicism, and the like properly yield reason for bewaring *overconfidence*. To be sure, there probably are developmental reasons not to teach relativistic, second-guessing, and ironic attidudes to the very young. But I see no reason not to want to make one's children reflective, historicist, antiessentialist, fallibalist, ironist, relativist, and morally serious all at once. There, my cards are on the table.

Pomposity

One reason I think this way, is that it seems to me that it is overconfidence in one's values, pompous self-righteousness, and moralistic posturing that promotes intolerance, disrespect, repetition of asinine moralizing on the part of the young as they age, as well as, most importantly, a resourcelessness in the face of the constant requirement to make a decent self and worthwhile life in the face of the unpredictable and multifarious contingencies that are bound to come one's way. It is a failure on the part of adults to convey to the youth, although perhaps not to the very young, that we, us grown-ups, have trouble finding our way. Knowing that, and then seeing that we go on, sometimes with assurance, sometimes in fear and trembling, willing to bear costs, but always in the hope of finding greater good and meaning, seems both honest and practically wise. There are things worth fighting and dying for, but the more one is an *unconfident confident* the less one is likely to see such things in most places where there is, in fact, fighting and dying.[9] Furthermore, since there will be times when things come apart for each of us, times when the center cannot hold, it will be harder to maintain self-respect, self-esteem, and not suffer unraveling identity if one thinks or has been deluded into thinking that in the right and normal course of life, especially if one has made the right choices, things go smoothly.

The Grand Inquisitor lies to his charges in the *Brothers Karamozov* to keep them happy and protect them from the horrible truth that there is no God. Dostoevsky, like Nietzsche, thought that most people can't bear the truth, can't bear to see how life goes, how dangerous it is, and how vulnerable one is as a creator of a meaningful life. But I see this as underestimating persons. Or better: if true, it is, like all else, historically conditioned. We could get used to the news.

Can a Strong Evaluator Relish Good Old Rock 'n' Roll?

Let me lighten things up before making them heavy one last time. I want to talk about the way adopting the two different attitudes—that of strong evaluation and that of ironism—might play out in a scenario where one was engaged in the project of thinking about one's gender identity.

In some respects at least, the maintenance of self-respect, self-esteem, and self-confidence favor conservatism. If things are going OK and one is not a creep, it seems sensible to continue to orient oneself toward the ways of being that are, as it were, the shortest distance from one's current self—possibly not to even worry about projects of self-adjustment, transformation, and the like.

But a problem arises because we rightly think that certain traits, in particular ones associated with our gendered identities, are problematic. Many feminists have emphasized the downside of some of the alleged "feminine" virtues, for example, care. Care is not an unequivocal virtue, any more than fairness is. Care comes in self-effacing, autonomy-undermining forms. The same is true of traits associated with males. Independence, autonomy, emotional strength have problematic histories and problematic forms. (To make things more complicated, it is not clear that their stereotypical bearers—males or females, as the case may be, standardly possess these traits, despite what gender hype would have us think.)

The short point is this: There is little reason to think that a general normative assessment of our life form will eventuate in the judgment that we are wisest to continue to orient our lives around traits that are most representative or, what is different, that are deemed most appropriate for persons of our gender (the same could be said about social role, race, occupation, nationality, and so on). Engaging in strong evaluation, subjecting one's traits to moral scrutiny can be identity-undermining. It can result in loss of self-, character, and project confidence if things don't measure up to the high standards strong evaluation sets, and if, in addition, one can't muster the ability to change. On the other hand, strong evaluation, assuming one finds a place to put on the evaluative brakes, can help secure self-respect if one's character can pass strong moral inspection.

Meanwhile the ironist understands that he would not be the way he is, and would not suffer certain benefits and costs associated with his gender identity had life not situated him in a certain way. For the ironist seeing that *who* he is is as much a matter of cosmic contingency as *that* he is at all—that he is something rather than nothing—undermines excessive seriousness in self-regard and self-righteousness. It might lead to a healthy acceptance that there are certain things about one's being that are absolutely quirky and contingent and that are best accepted with a wry smile acknowledging as much. The desire of a woman to be sexually appealing according to gender-specific criteria, to wear lace, to have her hands manicured and nails done, to show her neck and chest and back; or for a man to want to convey the look of a Calvin Klein model—handsome, strong, sexy, but in complete control of his emotions, except when enmeshed with the laced body of his true love, carressed by her painted fingers and her mouth moist with lipstick—might in the greater scheme of things—warrant little or nothing in the way of criticism. But the whole picture will drive certain impatient types—pompous moralists and *moral*-value over-achievers—up the wall.

The rock 'n' roll point is trivial. Listen to the lyrics of any classical rock 'n' roll song. If it says anything more than "Let's twist again like we did last summer" (and possibly especially if it says that), it says things that are problematic for a person attuned to issues of gender, to matters of political correctness. Ricky Nelson's "Travelin' Man," the Ronnettes' "My Boy-friend's Back," Elvis's "Love Me Tender," all fit this bill; as do Billy Joel's "Catholic Girls," Rod Stewart's "Maggie May," and virtually every song by the Rolling Stones, and most by the Beatles. How much should this bother us?

The downside to strong evaluation is that it can make us want to trans-form our selves in ways that are unnecessary or impossible or that involve a failure to appreciate the pleasures involved in quirky contingencies, such as the ways of rock 'n' roll. The downside to ironism is that it might lead to the complete surrender of moral seriousness in the face of the ridiculous arbitrariness of human life and living—the contingency of gender iden-tity, selfhood, and everything else. So both routes seem unsatisfactory. Perhaps the idea of an ironic strong evaluator is not as oxymoronic as it first sounds. If it is possible, there are things to be said in its favor. The project of serious self-criticism is a good and worthy one. And there are many aspects of our gender identities that we can reasonably try to adjust, modify, and change. But it is also good to be able to take a certain pleasure in the quirky identities we have, to enjoy our selves, and to see where the projects of self-transformation will not succeed, are not worth it, or origi-nate in taking ourselves too seriously.

Love and Marriage

We are valuers, not simple repositories of beliefs and desires at different levels. One danger with Frankfurt- and Taylor-like models has to do with the distinction of orders or levels. The idea is innocent enough when the second order is introduced to refer to a metastate, the state of taking an attitude toward or assessing a state of simple desire. It ceases to be useful, or so I will now suggest, when we are dealing with reflective agents whose lives are evaluative through and through. For such a person, a modern reflective person, having a desire for a daily nap and wanting to work as much as one can, are *not* fruitfully thought of as involving a simple first-order desire versus a thought-out second-order preference. Suppose that it is true that every day a desire to nap overtakes me. Even if this were true, I don't know what it means for me, an adult with lots of experience with nap desires and lots of thoughts about the importance of working and not napping, to have my desires and preferences neatly ordered so that once I see the order, I know what to do: higher-order wins. This is the wrong picture. What is a better one?

Let me return to a variation on the example with which I began, the example designed to discomfort, and to make us confused about confidence. Imagine again a married person with children who lives with a loyal and decent partner. They are good parents, they respect and admire each other. But they are out of sync in certain respects, respects they have on occasion discussed. Their interests differ. Passion was set aside for the sake of having and raising children. With work they could probably get closer again. But one partner to her surprise finds an attraction with another person grow to a depth that she can't get to with her partner under the best-case scenario. Passion, and hope, and prospects for a new relationship in which certain excellences are cultivated present themselves. What to do?

Now strong evaluation is in most respects a formal and not a contentful procedure, so I don't want to put words in the strong evaluator's mouth. But here is how I think it might go from the strong evaluator's perspective. People in fact say what I am about to say all the time. Regarding the first-order, second-order issues, there are two ways to stack the deck: one temporal, the other straightforwardly evaluative. The first way simply says what is true: that there are standing promises, fidelity and constancy are virtues, and these all came before the new true love. It might seem akin to this: I agree to rake your lawn for five dollars, your neighbor offers me ten dollars but wants me to do it now, just as you do. What to do? The answer is not obvious even in this case, since too much information is left out. But there is no doubt some additional weight be given to the first in the order of commitments, purely by virtue of its temporal priority.

The second approach says something Kierkegaardian, something like this: There is the ethical life, whose virtue is marriage, and there is the life of the aesthete, Mozart's Don Giovanni, whose aim is sex. Remember it's Either/Or—either one or the other. They are incommensurable. Furthermore, whereas there can be a teleological suspension of the ethical for God, there is no similar dispensation for sexual relations—new ones, ones that involve reneging on old agreements.

But there is something wrong here. First, sex does not figure in all lives the way it does for Don Juan, who wouldn't know what intimacy was were he to hold it in his hands. Second, we care—shy and confused as we are about being embodied—to weave sexuality into the fabric of intimate relations. It is important to reveal ourselves and be revealed in more than physical ways in love. But it is equally important to reveal our physical being and to intertwine it with our mental being. And sexual relations are the main location in which this can happen mutually.

The main point requires only a variation on the Gauguin case. Forget the choice between family and art, the standard situation in our culture involves changing partners or leaving relationships. I have nothing to say about why this happens so often, or the reasons why, or whether it is usually a good thing—I suspect it often isn't good. But surely there are cases where it is worth moving on, going for what the new relationship, or being alone, promises in terms of pleasure, growth, and having a better life. Sometimes I'm sure it's a waste—merely moving, but not, in the end moving on to something better, something more authentic or meaning-conferring. Sometimes we wise up in time, sometimes not. And often, once one path is taken, there is no knowing which would have been the better path. The unconfident confident must bear with this.

My financial well-being may turn on leaving you to rake your own leaves and taking the better offer, but the meaning of my life probably won't turn on the monetary difference. Love, perhaps, is different. The meaningfulness of one's life may well turn on making the right decisions about love, intimacy, and partnership; these goods are *that* great. There are costs and no guarantees that the whole thing doesn't end in an awful mess. The stakes are daunting, so it will be good to think things through carefully, recognizing full well that there may be no choice that preserves all things of worth, that doesn't produce harms.

If the strong evaluator thinks that one ought to have confidence *only* when there is a clear and unequivocal judgment that can be made about what is truly noble, worthwhile, and integrated—a judgment that dissolves all cognitive dissonance—then it just won't happen in these really significant cases.

Ironism might help. One might laugh that one is so lucky to have new chances to grow and to learn, and one might cry—happy and sad tears—that one has new chances. New chances are good after all. But working on what one has, even if it is not the best, is also good. Furthermore, it is honorable.

Where does all this leave us? Here's the lesson I am inclined to draw. Think hard about your character and your projects when faced with chances for change. This will make you as confident as you can be under important, meaning-constituting circumstances. But this may not be all *that* confident. Still, one has grounds for self-respect if one has done this much honest labor. That's the most one can ask for under the circumstances. Confidence in one's character, commitments, and projects are great goods. But it is not just reflection that jeopardizes confidence. Valuable things, meaning-conferring commitments, new and difficult challenges can make a set plan, a confidently worked-out plan loosen its grip. Most of the best things in life involve risks. Who I am is never done.

We may have to reorient ourselves, our lives, because novel options of seemingly great worth come our way or are just now noticed by us—it may be doing art in Tahiti, or switching careers, giving up one's work as a professor because working for Amnesty International calls, or it may be that a new relationship holds promises for going to places one has never been. We are social beings and what we do affects others. This is especially so when what we do involves striking out on new paths that seem worthwhile, but may involve disrupting, even rupturing certain ties, unilaterally changing, even damaging other lives. We are open, and should open ourselves, to charges of self-indulgence in such cases. But sometimes, at any rate, persons need to move on, admit to self-indulgence, or refuse to let the charge stick, or not know what to make of it. A lot will depend on how things turn out. In such cases we move ahead confident that there is or may be great good in store, but also unconfident about how things will go. This seems to me like a brave way to live, dangerous, and all that. But it places an excellent life, a rich and meaningful life, in the location it belongs—in the space of the "not easy."

Notes

Acknowledgments—This essay was prepared for a conference on "Confidence, Meaning, and Morality," at LaTrobe University, Melbourne, Australia, June 14–15, 1994. Many people, among them Michael Smith, Tim and Eve Oakley, Susan Wolf, and Graham Nerlich, provided immensely helpful responses.

1. Taylor, "What Is Human Agency?" *Philosophical Papers* 1 (Cambridge: Cambridge University Press, 1985), 28, first published in *The Self: Psychological and Philosophical Issues,* ed. T. Mischel (Oxford: Basil Blackwell, 1977).

2. Taylor, *Sources of the Self* (Cambridge: Harvard University Press, 1989).

3. H. Frankfurt, "Freedom of the Will and the Concept of the Person," first published in *Journal of Philosophy* 68, no. 1 (January 1971): 5–20, reprinted in H. Frankfurt, *Philosophical Essays: The Importance of What We Care About* (Cambridge: Cambridge University Press, 1988), page references are to the reprinted version.

4. Frankfurt, "Freedom of the Will," 16.

5. Ibid.

6. R. Rorty, *Contingency, Irony, and Solidarity* (Cambridge: Cambridge University Press, 1989), 73.

7. Ibid., 87.

8. Bernard Williams, *Ethics and the Limits of Philosophy* (Cambridge: Harvard University Press, 1985), 173.

9. I am thinking of the ethnic and nationalist killing that mar this time, as all times past.

13

Epilogue: Save the Last Dance for Me

When it is over, when the bell tolls, when time is out on this life, I want it to be just the two of us, you and me, face to face, one on one. Possibly there will be no time to think about it—this life, and its meaning, that is. Perhaps there will be time. But it will, if we are lucky, be just the two of us: me thinking about you—where "you" are the way this life has been, has gone, and where "I" am this thinking thing looking back at you over an instant, "jumping-jack-flash"—a moment, only a moment ahead of you. Perhaps we should do this sooner, this dance, maybe even on a regular basis, since there might be, as I've said, no chance in reality for that last dance with each other, not at least the way I am envisaging it.

In fact, this is surely the best strategy. I still have things to learn from you. Perhaps you feel this way too. So it will be good if we spin and change places in this dance. You, my self examined, should get a chance to lead, to teach me—the critical I—how to be less clumsy, when to lead, when to follow, when to just dance, and say or think nothing. I guess we've been doing this for a long time now. But I haven't always noticed, and we are both a bit stubborn. Perhaps this is why we are almost a unit, almost one, almost a unified self, but only almost. We disobey each other sometimes. I've even hid things from you. I suspect you've done the same: you are more verbally reticent than I am, after all. I've also tried to trick you into behaving better—perhaps you've done the same.

Have we failed because we are almost one, but not quite one? I think not. At least we have not failed in the way other selves have succeeded. Our kind of sapient animal, our way of being-in-the-world comes with fancy reflexive capacities: capacities to look backward and forward, to engage in self-scrutiny from every conceivable angle, and to second and

216

third guess ourselves. It is not easy to make a single person one. Our problem is typical.

So, we've been dancing together all along. Still the last dance seems especially important. Let's make believe it will happen, that it must happen. Then this is what I want to say.

"Darling self, it is inevitable, but it also my wish, that you save the last dance for me. Never mind the clumsiness, we know each other well by now. And let's hope—this seems both romantic and reasonable—that value is detected as we embrace and look into each other's eyes. Perhaps there will be time to articulate the value we detect. Perhaps there will be time for expression of feelings. It matters, even if there is neither mind nor time for these things, that we would have detected value, worth, and meaning, had there been mind and time. A glance, a kiss, the shadow of our smiles would do. But it should be more than mere infatuation. It should *really* matter. It, this life, that is, should *really* mean something. Respect, even self-referential respect, should be warranted. It will be good to feel peace of mind, to be comfortable, to sense integrity, and effort, and to recognize that we have had some fun. Remember, if anyone knows you—really remembers and knows you—especially how you dance, it is me. Me, myself and I. Cha, cha, cha."

Index

DUE DATE

DE